Cold War US Foreign Policy

Key Perspectives

STEVEN HURST

Edinburgh University Press

For Andrew and Jane

© Steven Hurst, 2005

Edinburgh University Press Ltd
22 George Square, Edinburgh

Typeset in Ehrhardt by
Hewer Text Ltd, Edinburgh, and
printed and bound in Great Britain by
The Cromwell Press, Trowbridge, Wilts

A CIP record for this book is available
from the British Library

ISBN 0 7486 2079 6 (hardback)

Contents

Acknowledgements

All books are collective endeavours, even if there is only one name on the cover. In this case I would particularly like to thank Jules Townsend for suggesting that I write this book, and providing constant encouragement throughout the, somewhat longer than planned, process. Jules also read the whole typescript, for which effort I am very grateful. In addition to Jules, Ian Jackson read everything, and his critical comments and suggestions were particularly helpful. I would also like to express my gratitude to John Dumbrell, Lloyd Gardner and Mel Leffler, who all generously agreed to read various chapters and provided much useful food for thought. My thanks also to Edinburgh University Press, and especially to Nicola Carr, for so enthusiastically and efficiently supporting the project, and to Janet Beer for suggesting them as a publisher in the first place. My greatest thanks, as always, go to Sam Faulds, who has better things to do than read my books. All books are also parasitic on other books, but none more so than a historiographical work such as this. To write such a book, and to engage with the finest minds in the discipline, is a humbling experience, but it is also a pleasure and a privilege. My final thanks therefore go to those historians whose work is discussed herein. John Ruskin said that the best way to learn about a subject was to write a book about it. I have learned a lot in writing this book because of the quality of the histories that I have read. Doubtless I have not learned enough, however, so for those errors that remain, I accept full responsibility.

This book is dedicated to my brother Andrew and his wife Jane. I thought it would make a nice wedding present. Good plan. Still, a year too late is not bad by academic standards.

Introduction

Explaining American foreign policy during the Cold War is a complicated business. The proliferation of books and articles on this most written about of episodes in the history of US foreign policy presents the reader with what can at times appear to be an overwhelming and irresolvable mass of contradictory arguments. The logical way to begin to get a grasp of the topic and its parameters is to examine the surveys of the literature that are available. When one does so, however, it soon becomes clear that there is a sizeable gap in the historiography. There are books that provide a very comprehensive overview of the literature on US foreign policy during the Cold War.[1] These, however, necessarily sacrifice depth in favour of breadth. They provide excellent bibliographies but only limited discussion of the content of the books therein. There are, alternatively, books that seek to demonstrate how different theories and concepts can be usefully applied to the history of American foreign relations in an attempt to explain US foreign policy.[2] While these can be the source of potentially fruitful insights, the discussion tends to be rather abstract, with little effort to demonstrate the practical applications of the ideas under discussion. Finally, there are books that engage in an in-depth analysis of the explanatory frameworks that have been used by historians of US Cold War foreign policy. The problem with this group of works is that they tend to get only as far as the school of thought known as revisionism.[3] If you want an analysis of post-revisionism, corporatism, world-systems theory or post-structuralism, then the pickings are much thinner.[4]

The objective of this book is to continue in the tradition of this third group of writers and to bring their analysis of the historiography of US Cold War foreign policy up to date. Rather than a superficial overview of everything that has been written on the subject, the objective here is to provide in-depth descriptions and analyses of the half-dozen key perspectives that have dominated the historiography of US Cold War foreign policy. Instead of discussing how different concepts and ideas might be applied to that policy, this book shows how they have been applied in concrete detail. In examining traditionalism, revisionism, post-revisionism, corporatism, world-systems theory and post-structuralism/culture, my aim is to illuminate for readers how the most influential diplomatic historians have sought to explain US Cold War foreign policy and what the key differences between their perspectives are.

While this book will, therefore, fill a significant gap in the literature, it is important to emphasise what it does not do. In the first place, as has already been stated, it is not a comprehensive overview of every important book or article about US foreign policy during the Cold War. My choice has been to focus on what I believe are the six most influential perspectives or schools of thought to have developed over the second half of the twentieth century. There are historians and histories that do not fit comfortably within any of the six perspectives examined and whose work is therefore not discussed.[5] There are also historians and histories that do fit within the perspectives under discussion that are nevertheless not examined in detail. This should not be understood by the reader to represent a judgement on the quality of the work in question. As with the decision to focus on just six key perspectives, this choice reflects a desire not to sacrifice depth of analysis to breadth. Within each of the key perspectives there are one or two historians whose work is central to its development. Concentration on the work of these individuals is the most effective way of explaining the perspectives under examination. In some cases (corporatism and world systems, for example) no dilemma results, because only a few historians have utilised the perspective. In other cases, however, the effect is that the work of a lot of important historians is reduced to an endnote.

This book also avoids engaging in a systematic empirical analysis of the perspectives discussed. While the occasional comment about how well various perspectives accord with the empirical data is ventured, there is no attempt herein to subject each perspective to a thorough test against the historical evidence. On a practical level, such an effort would simply be too time-consuming and too difficult within the space allotted. More importantly, however, it is simply not the purpose of this book to engage in such an exercise. The objective here is to clarify and analyse the various perspectives at a theoretical level, thus enabling the reader to reach his or her own judgement about how well the various explanatory frameworks explored fit the empirical data.

Of course it is not actually possible to discuss these perspectives without some discussion of the empirical evidence. One important feature of this book is that it seeks to provide readers with concrete descriptions of how the perspectives give different explanations of the same set of events. For that purpose the period of the early Cold War, from approximately 1945 to 1950, has been used. Each chapter shows how the perspective under discussion explains US foreign policy in that period. The early Cold War was chosen as the basis for comparison simply for reasons of utility. Most of the historians discussed have written specifically about the early Cold War and it has been the focus of most of the debate between them. This fact should emphatically not lead readers to the conclusion that this is the only period of US foreign policy to which these perspectives can be applied. They should focus on the explanatory framework, not the particular events that it has been used to explain thus far. All these perspectives have the potential to be used to explain a wide variety of US foreign policies, before, during and after the Cold War. To demonstrate this point, in most of the chapters a brief discussion of how the perspective addresses, or might address, the implications of the end of the Cold War is offered.

Finally, and on a related point, this is not a book about the origins of the Cold War. While much of the debate between the proponents of the various perspectives under discussion has tended to become polarised around the question of 'whose fault' it was, or 'who started' the Cold War, that question is irrelevant to this book's purpose, which is to examine explanations of US foreign policy, not to attribute responsibility for the Cold War. This also means that there is no significant discussion of, or attempt to explain, Soviet foreign policy. To explain US foreign policy we need at most to know how US policy-makers perceived the USSR and its actions; we do not need to explain those actions ourselves.

I have stated that this book examines the six most important perspectives used by diplomatic historians to explain US foreign policy during the Cold War. The word 'perspective', however, is ambiguous and requires some clarification. I could have said that what this book was about were the different 'theories' that historians had employed. This would probably have produced greater recognition on the part of the reader, but it would also have been somewhat misleading. 'Theory' can function at many levels of complexity, but if we understand by that word rigorous, thoroughly worked-out systems of thought that generate hypotheses that are capable of disproof by empirical testing (that is, the sort of theory used in the 'hard' sciences), then that is not what is under discussion here.

In fact, it is far from clear that such a version of theory actually has much utility for 'doing' history. It is almost certainly not possible to produce what we might call a 'strong' theory of US foreign policy – that is, a theory that provides an all-encompassing, fully satisfactory, account that explains US foreign policy in terms of a single set of causal factors. In practice, the roots of US foreign policy are too complex and contingent for the pursuit of such a theory to be anything other than a hopeless task. No historian discussed in this book believes that a single 'theory' can explain all the events they discuss. But that is not to say that theory is useless or that we must simply resort to barefoot empiricism. If a 'strong' theory of US foreign policy is not possible, a 'weak' theory may be. A 'weak' theory is a set of theoretical guidelines that can be used to inform and structure an analysis of US foreign policy without seeking to explain everything in a crudely reductionist or determinist fashion. It would seek to identify the most important factors shaping US foreign policy over the long term, but it would note that those factors evolved over time, as does the weighting between them, and that they could combine to produce different outcomes under different circumstances and that contingent, historically specific factors may also enter the equation. 'Weak' theory, in short, would seek to identify the primary factors shaping US foreign policy and their impact while retaining room for contingency and change and avoiding determinism.[6]

The term 'perspectives' is used here to describe the weak theories used by historians because it captures better than 'theory' the somewhat loose and informal nature of the approaches under discussion.[7] There is no attempt, as we shall see, at formal theory or hypothesis generation by these writers. However, while they may not generate formal hypotheses, these perspectives nevertheless perform important analytical functions. What they do primarily, as with all theory, is to simplify reality and to prioritise certain aspects of that reality rather than others. In order to explain how the particular perspectives discussed here do this, and how they differ, I have used the so-called levels-of-analysis problem.[8]

The levels-of-analysis problem originated in the field of international relations theory, and it has various dimensions. At its simplest it is merely an ontological problem – what levels of analysis exist as possible objects of study? Candidates range from the smallest possible unit – the individual – to the largest – the international system. More important, however, is the epistemological dimension of the problem. Above all, the levels-of-analysis problem should be understood as revolving around the question of how one best accounts for the actions of the unit of study, whether that unit be an individual, a state or the international system.

The naive or common-sense position attributes causal primacy to the individual. The traditionalist perspective examined in the first chapter, for example, treats US foreign policy simply as the product of the choices of American policy-makers. In some sense, of course, this assumption is always valid, since policy does indeed emanate from human decision-makers. Further reflection, however, leads to the recognition that those decision-makers do not live in a vacuum. They, and their decisions, are the subject of a wide range of factors and forces external to them that shape and constrain the decisions they make. Those factors, and the levels they operate at, are multiple. They might include, for example, the balance of power in the international system, the social background of the policy-maker and the nature of a state's economic system or aspects of a particular culture. The essence of the level-of-analysis problem, therefore, is whether, even if we accept that individual humans make the final policy choices, those choices are in fact better explained by factors operating at a higher level that constrain or even determine those choices?

If we examine the levels-of-analysis problem in more detail, we can see that there are actually two distinct elements to the argument about how best to explain the behaviour of whatever unit is under discussion.[9] First, there is the question of the level of the international system at which one locates the explanatory cause. Secondly, and more fundamentally, there is the issue of the particular factors or qualities operating at that level to which one attributes the explanation. For each possible level of analysis, that is to say, there are multiple possible explanatory factors. At the level of the international system, there are the qualities of both the state system, such as anarchy and polarity, and the global economic system, such as the nature of the production process, in which to root explanation. At the level of the state, a whole host of possible factors emerge, including domestic politics, socio-economic structure and culture and ideology.

Each perspective discussed in this book can be understood as a weak theory of US foreign policy which combines different levels and factors of analysis. What I have attempted to do here is to strip back the historical argument that surrounds the perspectives so that the reader can identify this explanatory skeleton. This, in turn, allows the reader to see what the key disagreements between the perspectives are. Once they are stripped back to the bare bones, it becomes possible to see that one perspective emphasises economics at the systemic level and another economics at a societal level; another politics at the level of the international system and yet another culture at a societal level. The argument about US foreign policy is an argument about which combination of actors, levels and fields provides us with the best explanation of that policy.

Another dimension of the argument about explaining US foreign policy during the Cold War has to do with the question of synthesis. 'In the social universe, events often have more than one cause, and causes can be found in more than one type of location.'[10] Recognising this, and seeking to build more complete explanations, diplomatic historians have sought to create synthetic perspectives that combine levels and factors. One of the central questions running throughout the book is whether synthesis is actually possible. Indeed, the question of how to combine different sources of explanation into a total understanding is one of the great unresolved problems of social theory.[11] David Singer, for example, argued that each possible level of explanation contained inherent biases. Systemic explanations exaggerated the uniformity of states while state-level explanations overemphasised their differences.[12] Simply adding two analyses using the different approaches together is not possible. It would be, to use an analogy borrowed from Singer, like trying to combine two different map projections that exaggerated the size of different continents.[13] Others have argued that the various levels of analysis are not ontologically separable but mutually constitutive.[14] In that case, it is not even clear that we can talk about explanatory factors being separate in the first place, let alone try to add them together. Even if one adheres to the view that such an additive process, in which various weights are attributed to different explanatory factors, is feasible, there remains the difficulty of whether such an approach is reconcilable with the retention of explanatory power. In simple terms, the more complex and multi-causal the theory generated, the more subject it will be to contingency and historical specificity and thus the less generalisable it will be.

In order best to grasp how the search for synthesis has progressed, the book's six chapters are organized into a rough chronological order. Such chronological organization allows the reader to understand how each perspective relates to those that go before it and how they both critique and build upon their predecessors. The individual chapters are not organised around a rigid structure but rather according to what seemed to me the most effective way of explaining each perspective. Nevertheless, each does contain three basic elements: a description of the work of key historians and their explanation of US foreign policy between 1945 and 1950; an elaboration of the 'theoretical' framework that underpins that explanation and the levels and factors that comprise it; and a critique of that explanatory framework, emphasising both its strengths and its weaknesses.

The first chapter examines the traditionalist perspective. This first cut of history, written in the late 1940s and 1950s, is characterised by a strong normative aspect in its determination to defend US foreign policy. In explanatory terms, however, it is notable primarily for its naivety and simplicity. It operates very much at the level of the surface narrative of events and the actions of individual policy-makers, making little effort to look beneath that surface for underlying explanatory factors. As such, its utility lies chiefly in its description of events and in its demonstration of the inadequacy of a historical method that treats those events as self-explanatory.

Revisionism, discussed in the second chapter, represents the first serious effort to illuminate the underlying sources of US foreign policy. A self-conscious attempt to refute traditionalism's celebratory narrative, revisionism is sharply critical of US foreign policy for its allegedly aggressive and expansionist nature. That expansionism, however, is explained in two different ways. One form of revisionism, associated primarily with the work of William Appleman Williams, roots US expansion in ideology and culture. The other, exemplified here by the writings of Gabriel Kolko, roots it firmly in the needs of American capitalism. Both versions of revisionism, however, emphasise the explanatory primacy of factors internal to the USA.

Post-revisionism is an attempt to go beyond traditionalism and revisionism to provide a more complex and multi-causal explanation than either. Partly influenced by the 'neorealist' thinking of international-relations theorists, post-revisionism downplays economic factors and ideology. Its central emphasis is on the explanatory significance of geopolitics, the structure of the international system and 'security' considerations. It thus places the key factors explaining US foreign policy outside the United States at the level of the international system.

With corporatism the focus returns to domestic factors. In the tradition of revisionism there is a central emphasis upon the socio-economic roots of foreign policy. Corporatists, however, provide a more nuanced account than revisionists like Kolko. Rather than explaining US foreign policy as the expression of the interests of a unified capitalist class, corporatists stress the importance of sectoral economic divisions and cross-class alliances in their explanation of US efforts to reshape the global economic and political order.

World-systems theory also has an affinity with revisionist accounts. However, while it shares their concern with economic factors, it transfers the focus from the domestic to the international. The crucial explanatory insight of this perspective is that the USA is part of a world capitalist system that constrains and even determines its foreign policy choices. The extent of that determination depends upon which version of world-systems theory one is using. Thomas McCormick's analysis, heavily informed by the ideas of Immanuel Wallerstein, is strongly deterministic. Bruce Cumings's version, in contrast, incorporates a much more nuanced and complex interplay between domestic and systemic factors.

The final chapter discusses post-structuralism and 'culture'. This form of analysis presents not merely an alternative explanation of US foreign policy but also an alternative approach to the possibility of explanation itself. With its emphasis upon how language serves to 'construct' reality, post-structuralism directs us to look much harder at the language of policy-makers to see how their use of metaphors and tropes serves to privilege certain views of the world and to exclude others. That linguistic emphasis also, however, raises the question of how we, the observer, perceiving the world through our own veil of language, can ever be sure that we grasp the 'reality' of the past as we seek to explain it.

On a final note, it must be observed that some readers will object to the process of categorising historians that I have engaged in in writing this book. Some of the historians discussed will doubtless dislike the label that I have attached to them. Such objections are not without justification. There are real dangers in the process of categorising or labelling.[15] Ideas can be distorted for the purpose of organisational clarity, and subtle differences and inflections can be ignored in the search for commonalities. Above all, perhaps, labels and categories can become lazy caricatures that substitute for actual engagement with the thought of those so labelled or categorised. At worst, normative judgements become attached to labels so that simply to include writers in certain categories is immediately to attach a negative interpretation to their work. Labelling, at worst, becomes a tactic of distortion and exclusion, designed not to illuminate but to obscure.

I hope and believe that I have not fallen into these traps. There are commonalities that justify the categories used in this book but there is no pretence that each perspective is a completely coherent whole. Differences have been emphasised as much as common elements. In any event, the purpose of the book is not to prove the utility of the categories so much as to illuminate the writings of the individual historians. The question that should be asked is not whether an individual really is a post-revisionist or a revisionist but whether I have treated his or her arguments fairly. Ultimately, the only way for the reader to make sure my labelling and arguments are accurate is to read the historians discussed themselves. That is as it should be, since this book is intended to be a critical companion to the works of history it discusses, and not a substitute for them.

NOTES

1. e.g. Hogan (ed.), *America in the World,* is the best.
2. e.g. Hogan and Paterson (eds), *Explaining the History of American Foreign Relations.*
3. Melanson, *Writing History*; Siracusa, *New Left Diplomatic Histories*; Thompson, *Cold War Theories*; Tucker, *The Radical Left.*
4. Here the reader must mainly rely on journal articles discussing individual perspectives. Most of the best have been published in the journal *Diplomatic History* and are included in the bibliography. The best short discussion of the perspectives (except post-structuralism) analysed in this book is Stephanson, 'The United States'.
5. Scholars whose work does not fit into any of the six perspectives discussed but whose work is no less important for that reason include Noam Chomsky, Ronald Steel and the various 'European revisionists' mentioned briefly in Chapter 3.
6. The idea of 'strong' and 'weak' theories is taken from Jessop, *State Theory,* p. 249.
7. On this subject and the application of theory to history in general, see Woods, 'The uses of theory in the study of international relations'.
8. Singer, 'The level of analysis problem', is the original source. Good contemporary summaries can be found in Buzan, 'The level of analysis problem', and Hollis and Smith, *Explaining and Understanding International Relations,* pp. 7–9, 99–101, 203–16.
9. Buzan, 'The level of analysis problem', pp. 201–2.
10. Ibid. p. 198.
11. Carlsnaes, 'The agency–structure problem'; Hollis and Smith, 'Beware of gurus'; Hollis and Smith, 'Structure and action: Further comment'; Wendt, 'Bridging the theory/meta-theory gap'; Wendt, 'Levels of analysis vs agents and structures'.
12. Singer, 'The level of analysis problem', pp. 80, 83.
13. Ibid. p. 79
14. Cohen, 'Structuration theory'; Giddens, *Central Problems in Social Theory,* pp. 69–73.
15. Cumings, ' "Revising post-revisionism" '.

ONE

Traditionalism

The first interpretation of US foreign policy that I am going to discuss was described by Anders Stephanson as of 'mostly archaeological interest now'.[1] By this he meant that the traditionalist perspective, dominant from the late 1940s until the 1960s, has been superseded by the interpretations I will be examining later in the book. While this is a broadly fair assessment, there remain a number of reasons that make a description and evaluation of this approach valuable.

In the first place, the various perspectives under discussion, while separate and competing, also comprise a meaningful whole. While I do not accept the idea that historical understanding of US foreign policy in the Cold War has advanced progressively, with each perspective building on and transcending those that came before it,[2] it is nevertheless the case that the various interpretations do not exist in isolation from each other. Rather, they are interconnected parts of an ongoing debate that has developed over more than half a century in which they have responded to, developed and critiqued each other's arguments. To leave out the first step in the debate would be to make the rest that bit more difficult to understand.

Secondly, Anders Stephanson is only partially correct in his implication that this interpretation is no longer a 'live' one. While it is true that one would be unlikely to find a contemporary historian of US foreign policy who subscribes to traditionalism in its entirety, revised versions of traditionalism are not uncommon[3] and important elements of this interpretation can be found in later ones, most notably in post-revisionism. This becomes clear only if one begins by examining the traditionalist perspective.

Finally, in outlining this perspective, I have taken the opportunity to provide a narrative of the main events of the early Cold War period, since one can hardly compare interpretations of US foreign policy without some knowledge of the events in question. By providing a detailed empirical account in this chapter I have avoided the need for repetition in later chapters, where the discussion assumes that the basic knowledge of events has already been gleaned. It is important to note that the empirical description in this chapter is not intended to be neutral or objective. As in the other chapters, what is presented is a particular interpretation of events. The only difference is that in this chapter my account of the interpretation is much lengthier in order to allow for the incorporation of the basic historical details.

A TRADITIONAL HISTORY OF US FOREIGN POLICY

Whereas the other perspectives discussed in this book are clearly products of the Cold War era itself, traditionalism is better understood as an extension of the prevailing pre-Second World War historiography of American diplomacy. That historiography was remarkably consensual, and at the heart of that consensus was a celebratory, even triumphalist, interpretation of American foreign policy to that point.[4] At the heart of that celebratory evaluation was the belief that, uniquely amongst nations, the United States had, since its inception, pursued a foreign policy based upon principle rather than power. While the states of Europe conducted their foreign policies 'according to the naked principles of Machiavelli', American diplomacy was 'idealistic in nature'.[5] What follows is a short summary of the traditionalist interpretation of the history of American diplomacy to 1941.

In the first place, as we have noted, American diplomacy was assumed to have been guided by ideals and principles that usually comprised of some or all of the following – isolationism, the Monroe Doctrine, freedom of the seas, the open-door policy and peaceful settlement of disputes. Isolationism and the Monroe Doctrine kept America out of European politics and Europeans out of the Americas respectively. Freedom of the seas and the open-door-policy were designed to protect the overseas trade that helped America prosper. Peaceful settlement of disputes reflected the desire to banish war as a means of resolving interstate conflicts. Collectively, these principles enabled the United States to remain isolated from international politics for the vast majority of the nineteenth century. In that time Americans expanded westwards to the Pacific, and the United States itself changed from a weak agrarian republic into the most powerful industrial nation in the world.

The twentieth century, however, would not allow the United States to continue to advance in peaceful and prosperous isolation. President Woodrow Wilson tried to keep the United States out of the First World War, but ended up taking it into that conflict in response to German violations of the American assertion of the neutral rights of American citizens and shipping. At the end of the war Wilson then sought to forge a peace based on the principles outlined in his famous 'Fourteen Points'. Self-determination, democracy, free trade and collective security would ensure the spread of the American example of peace and prosperity to the rest of the world. 'Wilsonianism' thus represented a modification of American foreign policy. It meant abandoning isolationism in order to exercise international leadership. But the purpose of that leadership was to change international politics for good. European power politics had dragged the United States into war; now Wilson was going to ensure that that did not happen again. By creating a world of prosperous free-trading democracies in America's image, he would remove the causes of war. As added security he would create a collective security organisation – the League of Nations – to settle disputes and punish international miscreants. By globalising the principles that had made America prosperous and peaceful, he would make the world the same. Americans' attachment to isolationism, however, proved too strong, and American membership of the League of Nations was rejected by the US Senate. It took the events of the 1930s to demonstrate that isolationism was no longer an option. The spread of fascist aggression plunged Europe into another massive conflagration, which became the first true world war with Japan's attack on Pearl Harbor and Hitler's subsequent declaration of war on the United States.

In sum, according to traditionalists the history of American foreign policy was a history of an attempt first to secure its own freedom and prosperity through the application of principle and then, when forced to engage more fully with the world in the twentieth century, to promote global peace, democracy and prosperity in a similar fashion. The principles had altered slightly – most obviously isolationism had to be abandoned – but international engagement did not alter the basic American view that democracy, the upholding of international law, free trade and peaceful settlement of disputes would bring the self-evident benefits of the American way of life to the rest of the world.

The record was not without its blemishes. The USA had accidentally acquired a colony in the Philippines as a result of a war with Spain in 1898. That was widely regarded, however, as an aberration and one that US policy-makers immediately sought to rectify by preparing the Philippines for independence at the earliest possible opportunity. More generally, it was accepted that not every initiative and policy conducted by American states-men met with triumphant success. American policy-makers were not infallible and did, on occasion, err. But those errors were almost always depicted as ones of excessive idealism rather than venality. In seeking to pursue a foreign policy of principle, Americans could, on occasion, be a touch naive in their hopes that others might be persuaded to do likewise. Overall, however, the record was deemed to speak for itself. Despite those occasional errors, American diplomacy was, overwhelming, a success. The transition from peripheral agricultural republic to the most powerful nation on earth and leader of the free world did not happen by accident. To most American diplomatic historians, American power and success were direct proof of the efficacy of American virtue.[6]

TRADITIONALISM AND THE COLD WAR

Traditionalist accounts of US foreign policy in the early Cold War posit an initial continuity with pre-war traditions. At the end of the Second World War the United States again sought to build a peace based on principle and prosperity for all. The United Nations would keep the peace, democracy would be established or re-established in victim and aggressor nations alike and US-designed international financial institutions would sustain the free trade that would expand global wealth. This time, however, American plans were thwarted not by the Senate but by the rise of a new menace in the shape of Soviet Communism. In the face of Stalin's refusal to abide by his agreements and his aggressive subordination of the states on his borders, the United States was compelled to take the lead in protecting freedom and democracy against the expansion of Communism. This section will provide a detailed summary of the traditionalist version of US foreign policy and the origins of the Cold War. It will, at the same time, describe the events that are going to serve as the basis for comparison of the competing interpretations throughout the rest of the book. The following description demonstrates the traditionalist view that the Cold War was a product of aggressive Russian expansionism, which forced the United States into a global defence of freedom.

The USSR and the United States were drawn into the Second World War within six months of each other as a result of surprise attacks by Germany and Japan respectively. There, however, according to the traditionalist account, the similarities end. Drawn once more against its will into a European power struggle, the United States, under the leadership of President Franklin Delano Roosevelt, was as determined as President Wilson had been that war would result in a lasting peace based upon principle. The principles in question were outlined in the Atlantic Charter, signed by Roosevelt and British Prime Minister Winston Churchill in August 1941. This document committed the leaders of the Western allies to seek a peace based upon self-determination, free trade, arms limitation and collective security. The Charter thus represented a combination of traditional American ideals and the principles introduced by Wilson earlier in the twentieth century.[7] In the meantime, until the war was won, American leaders refused to address post-war arrangements in any detail, approaching the war as a purely military exercise. Considerations of political gain or interest were not to be allowed to interfere with the requirements of military victory. Once that victory was secured, post-war arrangements could be put in place through a new collective security organisation designed to uphold the peace.[8]

For the Russians, however, 'war and politics were inseparably and necessarily connected, being but two aspects of the same struggle'.[9] This was clearly seen in the way that one of the first moves made by the Russians in their newfound alliance with Britain and the United States was to seek the latter's recognition of the legitimacy of the territorial gains Russia had secured in the Baltic and Eastern Europe as a result of the Nazi–Soviet pact.[10] Such an agreement would clearly have been in violation of the principles of the Atlantic Charter, and Roosevelt accordingly refused to countenance it.

The necessity of cooperation to ensure victory meant that such differences did not become major rifts between the allies. Nevertheless, the wartime relationship was marred by regular conflicts over issues such as the delayed second front in the West, the cancellation of convoys carrying Lend-Lease aid to Russia and the criticism and hostility directed towards Moscow by the London-based Polish government in exile. In all three cases, the Russians apparently suspected the latent hostility of capitalist states towards Communism and, in the case of the first two, a readiness to let Russia bear the overwhelming human costs of the war. Some traditionalist historians are prepared to concede that these fears were real and even, to a degree, understandable.[11] None, however, would consider them to be other than groundless. In their view, the reasons for delaying the second front and cancelling convoys were legitimate and had nothing to do with saving American and British lives at the expense of those of Russians. The fact that the Russians thought otherwise was seen by some as indicative of their characteristic ingratitude and the 'highly distrustful' nature of the 'communist mind'.[12]

Roosevelt agreed that the Russians were distrustful, but he felt that that distrustfulness was a product of insecurity and fear of encirclement by hostile powers rather than some innate quality of communist ideology. He believed that a cooperative and peaceful relationship was possible, both during the war and after, but that it would require the Western allies to recognise Russian concerns and interests and make a concerted effort to address them. 'By patience, proofs of good will and fair purpose, the mistrust of the Soviet authorities could be subdued.'[13] Thus, far from holding back Lend-Lease aid or the second front, no one was pushing for them harder than Roosevelt.

As the tide of war turned steadily in 1943–4, it became increasingly necessary to think seriously about organising the peace. The three allied leaders had met once at Tehran in November 1943, but the discussion there had been about military strategy, with only casual talk and no firm agreements about post-war arrangements.[14] In February 1945, however, with British and American forces on Germany's western borders and the Red Army sweeping through Eastern Europe, they met again at Yalta in the Crimea. A variety of issues were addressed here, including the questions of war reparations and the organisation of the post-war occupation of Germany.

The question that dominated, however, was the future of Poland. Britain had gone to war because of Germany's invasion of that country and the restoration of its sovereignty and freedom were matters of great importance both to it and the United States. For the Russians, however, Poland was a source of permanent insecurity and a corridor for invasion. More than anything else, they required a Poland that was friendly to their interests. Throughout the war, however, the relationship between the Polish govern-ment in exile and Moscow had been one of almost permanent conflict and distrust, primarily because of the Russian insistence on retention of the parts of eastern Poland that it had gained through the Nazi–Soviet pact. The Russians had responded to this conflict by forming their own cadre of Polish exiles whom they installed as the de facto government of Poland when the Red Army liberated that country from the Germans.

Roosevelt understood Soviet concerns, and at Yalta he and Churchill agreed that the Russians would keep their territorial gains and that the eastern border of Poland should be drawn along the so-called Curzon line. While he was prepared to accept the altering of borders, however, Roosevelt was committed to the creation of a world 'comprised of liberal, independent and democratic states'.[15] He therefore arrived at Yalta determined that the 'Lublin Committee' imposed by the Russians as a provisional Polish govern-ment be reorganised on a more democratic basis and that free elections should follow. After much haggling, he appeared to get his way when Stalin agreed to the inclusion of members of the Polish government in exile and other 'democratic elements' from inside Poland in a reorganised Polish provisional government and to the holding of elections. Moreover, this agreement on Poland was accompanied by a 'Declaration on a Liberated Europe', prepared by the United States State Department, in which the three powers called for free elections throughout the countries of Europe that had been, or were being, freed from the Nazi yoke.[16]

Roosevelt told the other two leaders at Yalta that he did not expect American troops to remain in Europe for more than two years after the German surrender. The US public would not support such a presence and US policy-makers had no desire to become embroiled in the future affairs of Europe.[17] 'Weary of war and eager for continued collaboration with the Soviets,'[18] the United States sought agreements that would secure peace and allow Americans to return to their own continent, leaving the soon to-be-established United Nations to watch over the peace.

However, 'Russia was soon displaying a callous disregard for her Yalta pledges'.[19] In March 1945 the Soviets effected a coup in Romania, overthrowing the existing Radescu government and installing a communist-dominated one.[20] Elsewhere in Eastern Europe, where the Red Army had advanced and occupied countries, the Soviet grip and the dominance of communist parties also appeared to be on the increase. Nowhere was this clearer, or the cause of more concern to the United States, than in Poland. The 'reorganisation' of the Lublin government turned out to be no more than the token addition of a couple of members of the government in exile. Polish resistance leaders allied to the government in exile were arrested after apparently having their personal safety guaranteed, and free elections were nowhere in sight. In the words of one traditionalist historian, 'no one [had] realized that the Russians would equate democracy with acceptance of communism and would enforce this view ruthlessly wherever the fortunes of war gave them power'.[21]

On 12 April 1945 President Roosevelt died and was replaced by Harry S Truman. Truman had no experience in foreign affairs but felt, like an increasing number of Americans, that the Russians were breaking their agreements. He told their foreign minister, Vyacheslav Molotov, so in no uncertain terms on 23 April 1945.[22] Despite this outburst, however, Truman had no intention of abandoning Roosevelt's policies or his goal of a cooperative relationship with the Russians. It might be necessary to be a bit tougher with them in negotiations, but the basic objective remained the same.[23]

Truman's goodwill and desire for cooperation manifested themselves in a number of ways. He sent Roosevelt's chief adviser, Harry Hopkins, to Moscow to patch up any differences that might have resulted from his brusque words to Molotov. As a result of these talks, and in return for a slight increase in the non-communist membership of the Polish provisional government and continued promises of elections, the Americans agreed to recognise the Polish regime.[24] Truman also rejected a proposal from the increasingly concerned Churchill that the Western allies should not withdraw their troops to the geographical lines agreed with the Russians before the end of the war but should leave them in their advanced positions in Central Europe to provide bargaining leverage. Truman and his administration viewed Churchill's plan as more likely to lead to conflict than to the cooperation that they sought.[25]

Truman arrived at the Potsdam conference in July 1945 still hoping to transform the wartime Grand Alliance into a 'lasting, working accord for peace'.[26] With the Americans having agreed to recognise the Polish government before the conference and the three allied leaders now finally agreeing a new western border for that country, the main focus of the conference was

Germany. To this point there had been no firm agreement reached as to what the future of that country should be. All the allies had organized were the occupation zones (with the French being given one along with the Americans, British and Russians). During the war there had been a vague consensus around the view that the main objective would be to ensure that Germany could never again pose a military threat to its neighbours. To that end the Americans had devised the Morgenthau Plan (after Treasury Secretary Henry Morgenthau), which would have handed over large parts of German territory to its neighbours, divided the rest into two states and dismantled its heavy industries.

As tempers cooled in the aftermath of conflict, both the Americans and the British began to row back from such a punitive peace. Recalling the disastrous effects of the Treaty of Versailles and fearful that if the German economy was not helped to recover they would be left with the costs of feeding the German people, they began to shift towards a more constructive position.[27] The Russians, however, had no such change of heart and were interested only in ensuring that Germany would never again threaten them and in extracting the maximum reparations possible to help rebuild their devastated country.

The conflict between Anglo-American concerns not to impoverish Germany and the Russian desire for reparations made the latter issue the most fraught at the conference. The Russians demanded that they get $10 billion in reparations, as agreed at Yalta. The Americans and British pointed out that that figure had been agreed as a basis for discussion only. Finally, in an effort to reach agreement and maintain a harmonious relationship with Moscow, the Americans proposed an arrangement that would allow each country to take reparations from its own zone. Otherwise, however, Germany was to be treated as a single economic unit with common policies across the zones. Finally, preparations for Germany's eventual return to democracy and sovereignty were to begin.[28]

Despite apparent agreement on the key issues of Poland and Germany, Russian behaviour continued to be a cause of concern to American policymakers. The second half of 1945 saw the continuation of moves towards communist control, rather than democracy, in the countries of Eastern Europe.[29] In early 1946, however, Russian behaviour became much more menacing. On 9 February Stalin gave a speech predicting that the instability of capitalism would inevitably produce further world wars. His rhetoric appeared to signal a return to the ideological hostility of the pre-war period and a shift away from the cooperative attitude of wartime.[30] Soviet actions, rather than words, however, were the principal cause for concern. In Iran, in clear violation of a wartime agreement to that effect, the Russians were refusing to withdraw their occupying troops. Worse, they were supporting an insurrection against government control in the north of the country. They appeared to be intent on reducing Iran 'to a Soviet satellite'.[31] Not only that, they seemed 'bent on trying, by subterfuge and subversion, to extend Soviet rule or influence, not only over northern Iran but down to the Persian Gulf and into the eastern Mediterranean'.[32] That suspicion was reinforced by the pressure the Russians were putting on Turkey to grant them base rights in the Dardanelles and make territorial concessions elsewhere – pressure that included the massing of Russian forces in Bulgaria.

In Germany the Russians were refusing to treat that country as a single economic unit 'in defiance of the Potsdam agreements'.[33] The Russian representative to the Allied Control Council consistently obstructed efforts to put economic reconstruction in train and the Russians blocked shipments of agricultural products from their zone to the western ones. They also continued to loot their zone of all available industrial plant, while the western allies poured aid into their zones in an effort to raise the standard of living. Politically, rather than laying the basis for democratisation, the Russians appeared, in their zone, to be working towards communisation.[34]

The American response was to begin to take a tougher line with the Russians. While not abandoning hopes for the creation of a peaceful working relationship, US policy-makers now believed that Moscow would have to be shown just what was, and what was not, acceptable if a modus vivendi was to be reached. The US government therefore encouraged the Iranians to confront the Russians and expose their behaviour in the UN Security Council. In the Turkish case Truman chose to repatriate the body of the deceased Turkish ambassador to the USA via the ostentatiously unnecessary means of America's largest battleship, the USS *Missouri*. In Germany, General Lucius Clay, the Deputy Military Governor of the American zone, halted shipments of reparations to the Russian zone in protest at the Russians' behaviour and in an effort to force them to cooperate in treating Germany as an economic unit.[35] At the same time, however, the Americans continued to offer the Soviets the hand of cooperation. In an effort to meet Russian concerns about a revived Germany, Secretary of State James Byrnes proposed a twenty-five-year four-power security treaty to keep Germany disarmed. Soviet rejection of this proposal offered further evidence of the Russians' paranoia and their apparent inability to trust the American government.[36]

Further evidence of American efforts to address Soviet fears is found in the Acheson–Lilienthal/Baruch Plan for the control and elimination of atomic weapons. In this the United States proposed voluntarily to surrender its atomic weapons once an international agency and inspection regime had been put in place to ensure that no one else would be able to develop them. The agency would operate by majority vote and no power would possess a veto. The Soviet refusal to countenance this plan and its counter-proposal for the immediate abolition of all atomic weapons without any regulatory regime other than the UN at best indicated the inherent Russian distrust of the West. At worst, it was a devious attempt to nullify America's current atomic advantage while the Russians sought to develop their own bomb.[37]

It was only in the early months of 1947 that the Truman administration finally abandoned its efforts to find a basis for continued post-war cooperation with the Russians. For two years they had tried to secure a mutually beneficial relationship that would ensure the development of a peaceful world order based upon the principles of self-determination, democracy and free trade. The Russians, in contrast, seemed bent only on self-aggrandisement and the spread of communism, violating the principles the USA sought to put in place and threatening the peace. The whole of Eastern Europe was being brought under communist rule; the Russian zone of Germany was being looted and communised and four-power cooperation was non-existent; Russian efforts to expand towards the Middle East and the eastern Mediterranean continued. It was increasingly clear to America's leaders that the men in the Kremlin 'had never really given up their aim of world revolution or their belief that Communism must destroy Capitalism or be destroyed by it'.[38] With such a regime there was no genuine possibility of cooperation, except on its own brutal terms, as the peoples of Eastern Europe were discovering to their cost. The Russians would have to be confronted and compelled to abandon their expansionist ways or pay the price.

The final event tipping the scales in favour of confrontation was the Greek–Turkish crisis in early 1947. In Greece the democratically elected government was engaged in a struggle against 'communist forces within aided by heavy infiltrations from Greece's three northern neighbours, all satellites of the Soviet Union'.[39] Throughout this conflict the Greek government had been supported by British troops and resources. In February 1947, however, the British government informed Washington that it could no longer afford to maintain this commitment and would be withdrawing its support in a matter of weeks.

American policy-makers now faced a crisis in which they had little choice but to act. If Britain withdrew, Greece would fall and Turkey and Iran would follow. Europe's flank in the eastern Mediterranean would collapse and communist domination of the Middle East would follow along with beach-heads into South Asia and North Africa. Western Europe, demoralized and impoverished as a result of the war, would implode, and communist parties would seize power in France, Italy and elsewhere. 'In short, what was at stake in Greece was America's survival itself.'[40] Accordingly, Truman decided to assume Britain's commitments and extend American support to the Greek government. Truman also took the opportunity to provide substantial aid to Turkey in the same package. In the speech in which he asked the US Congress to extend this aid, Truman declared that it was his administration's intention

to 'defend free people everywhere' against the expanding forces of 'totalitarianism'.[41] This was the 'Truman doctrine' and with it the United States
moved to begin implementing what became known as the policy of 'containment'.

What was to be contained was communist expansion directed and led by
Russia. But that would not be halted by strong rhetoric and aid to Greece and
Turkey alone. It was increasingly clear to the Truman administration that the
continued socio-economic dislocation of Western Europe, and the apparent
inability of capitalist democracy to revive itself there, made the region acutely
vulnerable to communism. In countries like France and Italy there were
strong Communist parties ready, with Russian backing, to seize power at the
first opportunity.[42] In response to this danger, America acted to develop a
massive programme of economic aid, mostly in the form of grants, which
could be used to overcome Western Europe's chronic lack of capital and allow
it to invest and begin the process of economic recovery. This Marshall Plan
(after Secretary of State George Marshall) aid began to arrive 'in the nick of
time'.[43]

American policy in Germany also altered course. 'It was the Russians who
sabotaged attempts at a common policy for the four zones by repudiating in
practice the Potsdam agreement that Germany should be treated as an
economic unit.'[44] Given that fact, American officials felt little compunction
about abandoning efforts to address Russian fears of German revanchism in
favour of concentrating on the communist threat. As elsewhere in Europe, the
sorry state of the German economy and standard of living seemed to American
officials to harbour the seeds of potential upheaval. Denazification now
seemed to many less important than economic growth and stability. German
economic recovery, moreover, was pivotal to the recovery of Western Europe
as a whole.

In the face of Russian refusal to allow a unitary policy for Germany to
operate effectively, the Western powers, while still hoping eventually to
secure an agreement for a unified democratic Germany, had increasingly
integrated the functioning of their zones since late 1946. In early 1948, in the
face of Russian non-cooperation and the evident fact that the only unified
Germany the Soviets would accept was a communist one, the Western powers
decided to allow the formation of a German government in their zones. While
they insisted that this in no way precluded an eventual four-power settlement,
in practice it was the first step towards a division of Germany that would last
for forty years, a step that Soviet actions had left them 'no alternative' but to
take.[45]

The American change of course signalled by the Truman Doctrine, the
Marshall Plan and the unification of the Western zones of Germany soon
began to have the desired effect. Western European morale began to recover,

along with its economy. The greatest proof of the wisdom of American actions, however, lay in the nature of the Soviet reaction. In February 1948 Stalin moved to secure his grip on Eastern Europe when the Czech communists staged a ruthless coup in Prague. He then tried to force the Western powers out of Berlin (which was actually inside the Soviet zone) by preventing supplies getting to the Western zones of that city (the Berlin Blockade). Stalin thus sought to prevent the formation of a separate West German state, to undermine the Marshall Plan and to destabilise Western Europe as a whole by undermining the credibility of American power.[46]

The Berlin Blockade was eventually overcome by round-the-clock flights of food and fuel into West Berlin. The brazen aggressiveness of Russian actions, however, 'suggested that economic recovery, if not backed by military capability, might still leave individual democracies at the mercy of the totalitarian colossus'.[47] The United States and its West European allies consequently signed the North Atlantic Treaty in 1949, providing for mutual defence in the face of Russian military aggression. Eventually this alliance would spawn the North Atlantic Treaty Organisation (NATO) and a permanent US military presence in Europe.[48]

With American actions stabilising the situation in Europe, Russia turned its attention to East Asia. Indeed, it had already begun expanding its influence there almost as soon as the Second World War had ended. In 1945 Stalin had agreed to recognise the right-wing regime of Chiang Kai Shek (then engaged in a civil war with the Communist forces of Mao Zedong) as the legitimate government of China. The Red Army was also withdrawn from Manchuria, whence it had advanced against the Japanese when Russia entered the Pacific war in August 1945. In withdrawing, however, the Russians engaged in their usual practice of looting whatever industrial goods they could carry and left Japanese arms to fall into the hands of Mao's forces. It was not long before the Chinese communists were 'receiving sub rosa assistance and cooperation from the Russians in direct contravention of recent Russian promises'.[49] Despite American intervention and efforts to find a resolution that accommodated both warring parties, by 1949 Mao's forces were in control of mainland China.[50]

Having captured China, the communist forces then turned their attention to its neighbour Korea. The Korean peninsula had been occupied by both American and Russian forces at the end of the war. While the Americans had wished to see the country reunited under the auspices of the UN, the Russians had 'lowered the iron curtain at the thirty-eighth parallel'[51] and installed a communist government in the northern half of the country. In response, the USA backed the creation of a democratically elected government in the south. In June 1950, having been heavily armed by the Russians, the North Korean army invaded democratic South Korea, an invasion that 'originated in

Moscow, not in Pyongyang [the capital of North Korea]'.[52] Having drawn a line in the sand in Europe, the Truman administration was now compelled to do so in East Asia as well, at the cost of thousands of American lives. With the advent of the Korean War, the United States was now engaged in a global struggle to contain communist expansion.

EXPLANATORY FRAMEWORK AND CRITIQUE

Normally in this book the explanatory framework of the perspective under discussion and the critique of it are divided into two separate sections. In this instance, because of the relative brevity of the discussion, they are combined. The brevity of the discussion is itself partly a reflection of the nature of the traditionalist perspective. Traditionalism is characterised primarily by a powerful normative commitment to the fundamentally virtuous nature of American policies, an underdeveloped explanation of the same, and an explanatory framework that treats government decision-makers as the sole focus of analysis. In contrast to later perspectives, there is a marked absence of overt theoretical commitments or methodological reflections. On one level, therefore, there is simply not that much to discuss. On the other hand, the absence of theory in traditionalist accounts is itself deserving of comment. It is not so much the weaknesses of the theory as the weakness of the lack of theory that is the focus of the critique that follows.

Before that critique, however, it is important to stress that traditionalism, like all the perspectives discussed herein, is not a simple unitary phenomenon. In particular, there is a group of scholars, sometimes termed Cold War 'realists', who can be grouped with the traditionalists although they differ from them in significant ways.[53] Those differences, and the consequent diversity of traditionalist analyses, can best be understood if one thinks of the analysis of US foreign policy as comprised of two key elements: first, the explanation of US actions; and, secondly, the evaluation of US actions. Thus divided, it can be seen that realist and traditionalist interpretations are largely in accord with regard to the first of these, but in some disagreement over the second.

Realists agreed with traditionalists that US foreign policy before, during and immediately after the Second World War was driven by legal and moral principles. But whereas traditionalists saw this fact as largely praiseworthy, realists saw it as the source of most of America's problems. In the realist view, US foreign policy was not idealistic or principled so much as simply naive. The idea that peace among nations was a normal state of affairs, or that it could be secured through treaties, international law and collective security organisations was deemed to be profoundly misguided. The reality was that power and the pursuit of self-interest were the norms of everyday international affairs. For the realists the American adoption of the policy of containment in 1947 was as welcome as it was to the traditionalists, but it represented a belated recognition of the realities of power rather than a triumphant expression of American ideals.[54]

The realists thus half agree and half disagree with the traditionalists. But even that is an oversimplification, for in practice the dividing lines between realists and traditionalists are often blurred. There are traditionalist accounts that incorporate a fair dose of realism in their critique of American policy.[55] The categories of realist and traditionalist thus blur into each other, with many scholars straddling the dividing line rather than falling unambiguously into one category or the other.

Nor is that fact particularly surprising when one considers the degree to which, despite their differences, the two groups agreed on the fundamentals. Russian actions posed a threat and they were the aggressors; the United States had to respond and did so wisely in the form of the policy of containment. Realists and traditionalists alike would happily agree with that sentence. Whether US policies up until 1947 were principled or naive is a relatively trivial difference in comparison. Traditionalism and realism are 'merely subtypes' of a common perspective that 'differ in normative judgements rather than in interpretation'.[56] That is why realism is not deserving of a chapter to itself. It is largely of interest, as we shall see, as a precursor of later perspectives such as post-revisionism, rather than as a perspective in its own right.

There was certainly little or no difference between traditionalists and realists on the question of responsibility for the Cold War – the Russians started it. At the end of the Second World War the United States, in accordance with its historical approach to foreign affairs, sought the establishment of a mutually beneficial peace based upon the principles of self-determination, democracy, free trade and collective security. Aware of Russian fears and insecurity, President Roosevelt had gone out of his way to offer reassurance and to meet the concerns, with the result that 'the Russians generally had their way'[57] in the agreements he made with them. President Truman had continued this policy of seeking cooperation and peace. Despite the best efforts of the United States, however, the Russians had shown no interest in cooperation on any terms except their own. They 'deprived the West of a voice in the realignment of Eastern Europe, ignored a promise of free elections in Poland, spurned a four-power alliance to keep Germany disarmed . . . and violated their Yalta pledges for Asia'.[58] In short, they broke virtually every agreement they had made and were bent on expanding their influence and that of communism wherever possible. In the face of this unilateral expansionism, American policy-makers were reluctantly and hesitantly drawn to the conclusion that only a robust policy of containment would serve to compel the Russians to alter their behaviour.

Traditionalist accounts depict a Manichaean world of good versus evil in which American policy is always honest, generous and for the good of all and Russian policy always devious, self-serving and a mortal threat to mankind. Simply on the basis of common sense and everyday knowledge of the world, most readers will instinctively doubt the veracity of a picture that is better suited to fairy stories than to the real world. Placed in context, however, this black-and-white view of events is more understandable. Two aspects of that context in particular stand out. In the first place, traditionalism represents the first cut of history. These scholars were the pioneers in this field, with all the inevitable difficulties that that entails, the most obvious of which is the very limited range of resources upon which most of them could draw in writing their histories. A lack of Russian documents would remain a handicap for all scholars until the end of the Cold War, but the traditionalists, for the most part, did not even have significant access to US documents bar the limited range of publicly available ones. In consequence, and as a glance at the bibliographies of traditionalist accounts will demonstrate, they were forced to rely heavily upon the published memoirs, diaries and other accounts provided by the American policy-makers involved. With the most sceptical will in the world, scholars with such a skewed range of sources will always find it difficult not to write accounts that reproduce the interpretation that is provided therein.

The second key aspect of the context in which traditionalist history was written is that these scholars were not sceptical. They were not sitting back and reflecting dispassionately on events in the dim and distant past, but were writing in the very heart of the conflict itself. For many, if not most of them, their task was not merely to explain events, but also to rally the American people for the struggle ahead. In his presidential address to the Organisation of American Historians in 1961, Samuel Flagg Bemis warned that a 'great and virile people' was in danger of 'losing sight of our national purpose' through an excess of 'self-study and self-indulgence'. Americans had to learn to sacrifice if they were to preserve the blessings of liberty for themselves and others.[59] Such exhortations were far from atypical. These historians were participants in the Cold War.[60]

The strong normative dimension of traditionalist history is not surprising in view of the circumstances in which most of it was written. Nevertheless, the one-sided nature of the traditionalist attribution of responsibility is a weakness with consequences. Given that its primary concern is explaining US foreign policy, the fundamental failing of traditionalism is that the account of American policy it provides is really very insubstantial indeed. A list of American principles, values and broad goals is provided, but beyond that there is very little. Few, if any, concrete interests are attributed to the United States, and American policy-makers apparently pursued nought but the broadest and vaguest of objectives. Nor is there any indication that they had any kind of detailed strategy or plan for achieving them. Having made no post-war plans during the Second World War, the USA apparently just assumed that Soviet cooperation in the UN and other multilateral institutions would continue and that, once there were set up, peace and prosperity would necessarily follow. Above all, American policy in the traditionalist account is characterised by passivity and reaction. The US never initiates events. Everything it does is a response to an action by Russia. In their obsession with attributing responsibility for the Cold War to Russia and Stalin, traditionalist historians reduce USA foreign policy to a reactive spasm; its interests, goals and actions are all dictated by the behaviour of the USSR.

In methodological terms traditionalist accounts are characterised by what would now be regarded as an old-fashioned, not to say naive, empiricism. These historians do not utilise overt theoretical frameworks. Rather they take the view expressed by Herbert Feis that 'slow travel along the whole stream of eventful detail' will reveal the truth.[61] The facts, in other words, will speak for themselves as long as the historian discards his or her prejudices and trawls through sufficient data. If that were true, however, there would be no need for this book. We have more data about the Cold War than ever before and we also have more interpretations of US foreign policy during that period than we had in the late 1940s. Clearly, the accumulation of facts has not produced a truth upon which all are agreed.

The reason for this is clear enough and can be demonstrated by a consideration of Feis's own accounts of the origins of the Cold War. In terms of the narrative of events – meetings, conferences, treaties and so on – these books remain useful and largely accurate. This is because what happened, at that basic factual level, is not what all the arguments are about. The reason that there is so much disagreement and dispute is because of those things traditionalists do not talk about – theory and interpretation – why these things happened, what they demonstrate about the purposes of the parties involved and what they reveal about the causes of the events in question. The individual facts may be the subject of consensus. Revisionists do not claim that Stalin did not impose communist control in Eastern Europe. What is disputed is how that development is to be explained and the larger pattern into which it fits.

It is at this point, of course, that theories or conceptual frameworks enter into the process. The different assumptions and preconceptions contained within these lead the scholar to focus on different actors, causes and events. Crucially, even those who claim simply to be looking at the facts do not do so. It is not at all difficult to identify any number of 'theoretical' assumptions that shape the traditionalist interpretation of US foreign policy. In the case of Russia, for example, a total lack of evidence of motives is compensated for by a normative framework that says that communism is a wicked system and that it therefore follows that communist states will have wicked intentions. Conversely, in the American case, assumptions about the virtuous nature of the American way of life clearly shape the traditionalist interpretation.

Traditionalist histories also have a clear political/institutional bias. These scholars seek their facts in certain specific places and not in others. US foreign policy is assumed to be the product of the executive branch of government with occasional inputs from Congress and public opinion. The social and economic context in which those institutions are embedded and of which they could be argued to be an expression is almost totally ignored. Nowhere in traditionalist accounts will readers find analyses that depict US foreign policy as an expression or reflection of the dominant economic interests in society, because the assumptions underpinning the perspective do not allow for that connection.

Embedded within the political/institutional bias of traditionalism is another implicit assumption. In traditionalist accounts events are driven by the decisions and choices of men (women do not feature) in senior positions in the policy-making apparatus of their respective states. Traditionalism, in other words, tends to assume more or less unfettered human agency in its explanations. Policies are the product of the decisions of autonomous individuals. This is a world in which the reasons men give for their actions are the explanation for those actions. In fact, however, policy-makers are surrounded by structures – political, social, economic and cultural – that shape and constrain their decisions. If politicians pursue policies that conflict with the dominant structural forces that surround them, those policies will fail. In focusing on the individual policy-maker, therefore, traditionalism can be argued to be drawing our attention away from the more fundamental causes of US foreign policy.[62]

CONCLUSIONS

This chapter has been, as was suggested at the beginning, archaeology with a purpose. In describing the traditionalist account of the early Cold War, it has served to acquaint the reader with the course of events that are the subject matter of the various perspectives under discussion. In so doing, it provides a basis for beginning to understand the nature of their disagreements. It also, in its brief survey of the nature of traditionalism's explanatory framework, highlighted some of the theoretical and methodological issues that will recur in the following chapters.

As an explanation of US foreign policy, traditionalism is characterised primarily by shallowness and one-dimensionality. The policy-making process is reduced to the actions of senior governmental officials, guided solely by a handful of key principles and acting in isolation from all external pressures except Russian wickedness and an occasional concern for public opinion. Traditionalism focuses, justifiably, on those individuals who actually made US foreign policy. What it fails to do, however, is to explain the actions of those individuals by any factors other than the allegedly guiding principles. While the significance of those principles in explaining US foreign policy is not to be dismissed out of hand, they represent an inadequate basis upon which to mount a complete account of US foreign policy. Too many important factors are simply not considered in traditionalist accounts. There is little or no attempt to link decisions and decision-makers to the domestic socio-economic or political context or to the structure of the international system. Traditionalism operates, in short, at the level of the surface of events. In the next five chapters we will discuss various efforts to dig beneath that surface to the underlying sources of US foreign policy.

NOTES

1. Stephanson, 'The United States', p. 29.
2. See, for a discussion of this idea, Kimball, 'The Cold War warmed over', 1119. The problem with this notion is that, while it accurately captures the extent to which the various perspectives interact, it also contains a tenuous assumption of progress in which the latest interpretation necessarily incorporates while superseding those that came before it.
3. See e.g. Woods and Jones, *Dawning of the Cold War*; Gaddis, *We Now Know*.
4. Neu, 'The changing interpretive structure'.
5. Bemis, *A Diplomatic History of the United States* (1936), pp. 15, 66.
6. Representative accounts include Bailey, *A Diplomatic History of the American People*; Bemis, *A Diplomatic History of the United States* (1936); Bemis, 'American foreign policy and the blessings of liberty'; Coolidge, *The United States as a World Power*; Fish, *An Introduction to the History of American Diplomacy*; Hart, *The American Nation*; Leopold, *The Growth of American Foreign Policy*; Moore, *American Diplomacy*; Perkins, *The American Approach to Foreign Policy*; Pratt, *A History of United States Foreign Policy*.
7. Feis, *Churchill, Roosevelt, Stalin*, pp. 20–2.
8. McNeill, *America, Britain and Russia*, p. 30; Pratt, *A History of United States Foreign Policy*, p. 665.
9. McNeill, *America, Britain and Russia*, p. 30.
10. Feis, *Churchill, Roosevelt, Stalin*, p. 23.
11. Bailey, *America Faces Russia*, pp. 298–300; Feis, *Churchill, Roosevelt, Stalin*, pp. 57–70.
12. Bailey, *America Faces Russia*, p. 297.

13. Feis, *Churchill, Roosevelt, Stalin*, p. 596.
14. Ibid. pp. 254–79 is the most detailed of the traditionalist accounts.
15. McNeill, *America, Britain and Russia*, p. 315.
16. Feis, *Churchill, Roosevelt, Stalin*, pp. 518–29; Leopold, *The Growth of American Foreign Policy*, pp. 612–13; Pratt, *A History of United States Foreign Policy*, pp. 688–9; Spanier, *American Foreign Policy*, p. 21.
17. Feis, *Churchill, Roosevelt, Stalin*, p. 451; McNeill, *America, Britain and Russia*, pp. 404, 583.
18. Leopold, *The Growth of American Foreign Policy*, p. 640.
19. Pratt, *A History of United States Foreign Policy*, p. 691. Not all traditional accounts see things in such stark terms. Some acknowledge that the agreements reached at Yalta (and at the later conference at Potsdam as well) were sufficiently ambiguously worded for it to be unclear that the Russians could be said to be breaking them. Feis, *Churchill, Roosevelt, Stalin*, pp. 527–37; McNeill, *America, Britain and Russia*, pp. 564–5. This did not, however, alter the authors' conclusions with regard to the essential venality of Russian actions.
20. Feis, *Churchill, Roosevelt, Stalin*, pp. 564–7; McNeill, *America, Britain and Russia*, p. 575.
21. Pratt, *A History of United States Foreign Policy*, p. 689.
22. Feis, *Churchill, Roosevelt, Stalin*, p. 578.
23. Feis, *From Trust to Terror*, pp. 15–18.
24. Ibid. p. 47; McNeill, *America, Britain and Russia*, pp. 586–8.
25. Feis, *From Trust to Terror*, p. 636; Pratt, *A History of United States Foreign Policy*, pp. 712–13.
26. Feis, *From Trust to Terror*, p. 43.
27. McNeill, *America, Britain and Russia*, pp. 549–50.
28. Bemis, *A Diplomatic History of the United States*, 5th edn, pp. 914–15; Feis, *From Trust to Terror*, pp. 37–9; McNeill, *America, Britain and Russia*, pp. 614–25.
29. Leopold, *The Growth of American Foreign Policy*, p. 636.
30. Feis, *From Trust to Terror*, p. 75.
31. Spanier, *American Foreign Policy*, p. 25.
32. Feis, *From Trust to Terror*, p. 86.
33. Leopold, *The Growth of American Foreign Policy*, p. 638.
34. Ibid. pp. 638–9; Feis, *From Trust to Terror*, pp. 117–19.
35. Feis, *From Trust to Terror*, pp. 86, 117–19; McNeill, *America, Britain and Russia*, p. 716.
36. Feis, *From Trust to Terror*, pp. 131–2.
37. Ibid. p. 140; Pratt, *A History of United States Foreign Policy*, p. 704.
38. Pratt, *A History of United States Foreign Policy*, p. 710.
39. Ibid. p. 719.
40. Spanier, *American Foreign Policy*, pp. 34–5.
41. US President, *Public Papers of the Presidents of the United States: Harry S Truman, 1947*, pp. 176–80.
42. Feis, *From Trust to Terror*, p. 235; Spanier, *American Foreign Policy*, pp. 42–3.
43. Feis, *From Trust to Terror*, p. 235.
44. Pratt, *A History of United States Foreign Policy*, p. 718.
45. Feis, *From Trust to Terror*, pp. 267–82; Leopold, *The Growth of American Foreign Policy*, p. 656.
46. Spanier, *American Foreign Policy*, p. 60.

47. Leopold, *The Growth of American Foreign Policy*, p. 656.
48. Ibid. p. 661; Spanier, *American Foreign Policy*, p. 49.
49. Pratt, *A History of United States Foreign Policy*, p. 734.
50. Leopold, *The Growth of US Foreign Policy*, pp. 666–9; Pratt, *A History of United States Foreign Policy*, pp. 733–7.
51. Pratt, *A History of United States Foreign Policy*, p. 738.
52. Leopold, *The Growth of American Foreign Policy*, pp. 681–2.
53. Cold War realist accounts include Graebner, *Cold War Diplomacy*; Halle, *The Cold War as History*; Kennan, *American Diplomacy*; Lippman, *The Cold War*; Morgenthau, *In Defense of the National Interest*. The Cold War realists were profoundly influenced by the contemporary development of a 'realist' school of international-relations theory, which rejected idealistic and legalistic approaches to international affairs in favour of a perspective that explained foreign policy as driven by the pursuit of power and the 'national interest'. The classic statement is Morgenthau, *Politics among Nations*.
54. To some it did not even represent that, for, while the Truman Doctrine clearly acknowledged the necessity of maintaining the European balance of power, it also appeared to commit the United States to the global defence of freedom, which was just another manifestation of naive idealism in realist eyes; Graebner, *Cold War Diplomacy*, pp. 39–40.
55. Bailey, *America Faces Russia*; Leopold, *The Growth of American Foreign Policy*; McNeill, *America, Britain and Russia*, for example.
56. McCormick, ' "Drift or mastery?" ', p. 329 n.4.
57. Pratt, *A History of United States Foreign Policy*, p. 671
58. Leopold, *The Growth of American Foreign Policy*, p. 641.
59. Bemis, 'American foreign policy', pp. 304–5.
60. Novick, *That Noble Dream*, pp. 306–9.
61. Feis, *Churchill, Roosevelt, Stalin*, p. v.
62. Kaldor, *The Imaginary War*, p. 77.

TWO

Revisionism

T he Cold War revisionists are so-called because their writings represent an attempt to revise the celebratory story of American Cold War foreign policy, which had been created by traditionalism. An alternative label that has also been attached to this group of scholars is that of 'New Left' historians.[1] That tag reflects their rise to popular prominence in the late 1960s and early 1970s and the adoption of their arguments by critics of the war in Vietnam. The term 'revisionism' is used throughout this book, however, for two principal reasons. First, the two leading revisionist historians of US foreign policy, William Appleman Williams and Gabriel Kolko, simply do not fit the New Left label very well. Williams's seminal works were published well before the emergence of the New Left, and his politics were quite different from those of the radicals of the 1960s.[2] Kolko, for his part, was certainly a man of the left, but his Marxist politics were more old than new. The New Left tag is also problematic because it is freighted with ideological baggage. Its use is often a tactic of exclusion, a means of placing those labelled with it outside the acceptable mainstream and thus of discrediting their work by innuendo rather than argument. Revisionism, while not without similar connotations in the minds of some, lacks the same polemical quality.[3]

The emergence of revisionism prompted the most vituperative debate in the history of the history of the Cold War, due in no small part to the tenor of the times. The turmoil of the late 1960s and early 1970s in the United States was less than conducive to cool debate, and the contents of revisionist arguments – questioning both the wisdom and the morality of US Cold War foreign policy – guaranteed a hostile reception from policy-makers and traditionalist historians alike. Even many years after the events, the topic of revisionism can still arouse fierce passions,[4] and readers need to be aware of this context as they explore the perspective and the many works of scholarship that it has stimulated.

The revisionist writings that instigated such angry debate are characterized by a variety of emphases, but four in particular stand out as common to most and, more importantly, as giving the perspective its original and distinctive flavour:

1. an insistence on the centrality of economic factors to US foreign policy, whether as objective material causes or in the beliefs/ ideology of decision-makers;
2. the placing of 'expansion', both territorial and economic, at the heart of US history and foreign policy;
3. a stress on the dynamic nature of US foreign policy in contrast to the traditionalist image of US actions as reactive and hesitant;
4. an implicitly or explicitly critical (in the negative sense) view of US foreign policy, whether because of its intentions or consequences, or both.

Despite these common elements, nevertheless, there is no single revisionist model, explanation or theory that is rigidly applied by everyone associated with this perspective. There are, however, two broad explanatory frameworks that dominate revisionist writings. One, deriving from the work of William Appleman Williams, focuses on the role of ideas, while the other, associated principally with the work of Gabriel Kolko, concentrates on the role of material economic factors. Accordingly, this chapter will concentrate upon the writings of these two men. In the case of Kolko, that focus is easily justified, since no other Marxist historian has produced a body of work on American Cold War foreign policy that is remotely comparable in scale. In the case of Williams, however, the narrow concentration on a single author is more contentious, as his ideas have been built upon and developed by a number of historians whose work is probably more widely read and influential today than Williams's own.[5] Williams, nevertheless, is a more appropriate focus, since he was the founder of the 'open-door' perspective developed by those other historians and because that perspective is found in its clearest and most fully developed form in his writings.

WILLIAM APPLEMAN WILLIAMS

William Appleman Williams may be regarded as the founder of the revisionist perspective. Between 1959 and 1980 he produced a body of work that spans the entire history of the United States from colony to empire, as the title of one of his books put it.[6] His critique of US foreign policy during the Cold War is a fragment of a much larger analysis that locates that episode within a holistic explanation of US history.

At the heart of that explanation lies an insistence upon the centrality to US history of expansion:

> The essence of American foreign relations is so obvious as to have been often ignored or evaded. It is the story of the evolution of one fragile settlement planted precariously on the extreme perimeter of a vast and unexplored continent into a global empire.[7]

In the first instance this expansion was territorial. The original thirteen states drove westwards in order to claim most of the rest of the North American continent, ruthlessly expropriating those, most notably the Native Americans, who stood in their way. By the end of the nineteenth century, when there was no more contiguous territory to grab, Americans began to look overseas. However, unlike that of the European states of the late nineteenth century, US overseas expansion did not (with notable exceptions) take the shape of the seizure of overseas colonies. Rather than seek direct territorial control, American leaders strove instead to ensure that the rest of the world remained open to American exports, investment and raw material exploitation. This policy of 'informal empire' was formalized in the 'open-door' notes of 1899–1900, and the 'open-door policy' subsequently became the basis for American foreign policy in the twentieth century.

The open-door policy was a 'classic strategy of non-colonial imperial expansion' designed to establish conditions under which America's preponderant economic power could expand around the world.[8] In the first half of the twentieth century the United States intervened in two world wars in order to prevent Germany and Japan from creating empires that would seal off large parts of the globe from American commerce,[9] and in the mid-1940s it began to see the Soviet Union as a third such threat. Williams's explanation of US foreign policy during the Cold War treats it as an extension of the open-door policy and as a manifestation of a particularly twentieth-century tendency to use military power to preserve the open door. Where the traditionalists saw a marked break in US foreign policy and a reaction to external threat, Williams saw continuity and the pursuit of long-term internally created objectives.

Williams argued, contra the traditionalists, that the Soviet Union was a weak and cautious power after 1945, seeking only to protect its security by maintaining a sphere of influence around its borders. While he viewed the question of who was to blame for the Cold War as unimportant, Williams argued that it was the Americans' refusal to recognise the Soviet need for security and consequent demand for the extension of the open-door policy to Eastern Europe that threatened the USSR and led it to impose total control in that region, 'crystallising' the Cold War as a result.[10] The American refusal to accommodate Soviet interests in Eastern Europe stemmed from the basic premisses of the open-door policy compounded by a strong sense of American power. US policy-makers believed that an open door must be maintained to all parts of the globe and that the USA had the power to realise that objective, come what may. Because they saw the USSR as wicked but weak and the USA as good and strong, they believed the USA both could and should organise the post-war world along open-door lines. The USA was ultimately responsible for the development of the Cold War, because it never even considered meeting the Soviets halfway. Instead it simply expected them to accept the American goal of an open-door world, and when they resisted Washington moved to contain them.[11]

It is fundamental to Williams's argument, therefore, that US foreign policy after the Second World War was purposeful and self-confident rather than reactive and hesitant. US policy-makers knew what kind of global order they sought and were not about to brook any opposition to that purpose. The fact that US actions were driven by the needs of the open door rather than the Soviet 'threat' was confirmed by American actions towards the United Kingdom. For the USA the British Empire and its closed trading bloc were as great an obstacle to the open-door policy as Soviet control of Eastern Europe. Washington consequently used Britain's economic weakness and need for a post-war loan as levers to compel the break-up of the sterling bloc and the opening of the British Empire to American business.[12] US policy was driven not by fear of communism but by the perceived need to ensure an open door. The USSR just happened to be the greatest obstacle to that objective.

The articulation of the policy of containment in the late 1940s and its focus on Western Europe reflected the primacy of open-door concerns. The inability of Western Europeans to rebuild functioning economies, plus the danger of leftist success in Greece and elsewhere, threatened the maintenance of an open-door world. Without a thriving capitalism in Western Europe the USA could not sustain its own economic growth. The American response to this dilemma was twofold. The Truman Doctrine represented the ideological side of the open-door policy and the need to stop revolutions that threatened US economic access. The Marshall Plan was the economic side of the coin and reflected the need to bolster European economic revival.[13]

Explanatory Framework

To explain the persistent expansionist drive in American history, Williams utilised the concept of *Weltanschauung* (literally translated as 'world view'). According to Williams, a *Weltanschauung* is a 'conception of the world and how it works and a strategy for acting upon that outlook on a routine basis as well as in times of crisis'.[14] Expressed thus, *Weltanschauung* is more or less synonymous with the more familiar concept of ideology, which has been defined by Michael Hunt as 'an interrelated set of convictions or assumptions that resolves the complexities of a particular slice of reality to easily comprehensible terms and suggests appropriate ways of dealing with that reality'.[15] The attempt to define and explain the development of the American *Weltanschauung* or ideology of expansion was the central intellectual project of Williams's life. Each of his major works is a contribution to that core task. His thinking on this question changed and evolved over the years and remained a work-in-progress right up until his last writings, but the closest thing to a definitive version is to be found in *Empire as a Way of Life*.

At the heart of Williams's argument is the idea of an inextricable link between a particular form of economic organisation and the unique benefits of the American way of life. Williams argued that Americans came to believe, more or less as an article of faith, that everything that was good about their way of life, from material prosperity to democracy and political and social freedom, depended upon the existence of a free market economic system. Deriving originally from the writings of John Locke and Adam Smith, this was the key assumption of the American *Weltanschauung* from which everything else followed. Accompanying this belief was a persistent fear that, should America's free market economic system come to grief, so would the whole American way of life. US elites believed that the primary threat to the free market was conflict over access to material goods if the system produced insufficient to satisfy everybody (that is, class conflict). The way to avert that possibility was to ensure ever-expanding economic growth and thus absolute, if not relative, material gain for all. Economic growth, in turn, was believed to depend upon overseas expansion. In the first instance, growth had been ensured by the incorporation of new land and resources from the North American continent. Later it would be based on creating an open door to the rest of the world for American business. Over time, 'the idea that new and expanding frontiers provided the solution to America's difficulties became one of the nation's basic and pervasive assumptions'.[16]

'Given this expansionist theory of prosperity and history, the activities of foreign nations were interpreted almost wholly as events which denied the United States the opportunity for its vital expansion.'[17] For Williams, the 'tragedy' of American foreign policy was that a nation born with a burning commitment to revolutionary self-determination gradually became quite unable to countenance other states exercising the same right to determine their own destiny if that meant choosing ways of life that denied America economic access.[18] As the *Weltanschauung* became embedded, the USA adopted a foreign policy, the open-door policy, designed to shape the world in America's own image. Any attempt to pursue an alternative way of life, or to resist the American attempt to impose it, had to be repressed. Ultimately, 'the only way to preserve the American [way of life] was to organize the world according to American principles'.[19]

Critique

Williams has probably been the subject of more criticism than the rest of the revisionists put together, much of it having little or nothing to do with his scholarship.[20] Leaving aside the politically and personally inspired, however, we still find a substantial body of work with which to engage.[21] In keeping with the overall focus of the book, the following discussion will concern itself primarily with the adequacy of Williams's explanatory framework, and above all his conceptualisation of the *Weltanschauung* of expansion.

David McClellan has argued that 'ideology is the most elusive concept in the whole of social science'.[22] It is hardly surprising, therefore, that much of the critical analysis of Williams's work has focused on the adequacy of his conceptualisation and utilisation of the *Weltanschauung*/ideology of expansion. For the purpose of discussion, we can divide the critical concerns into three areas. First, Williams's explanation of the roots or causes of the *Weltanschauung*; secondly, the nature of the *Weltanschauung* and the beliefs that comprise it; and, thirdly, its utility in explaining US foreign policy.

The first of these issues is unquestionably the most complex. In essence it is an argument about how a *Weltanschauung*/ideology is caused and/or how we are to explain it. Specifically, the debate has focused upon the extent to which the beliefs contained within an ideology can be explained simply as the product of economic interests; whether Williams explains the *Weltanschauung* of expansion in that way and, if he does not, whether he provides a coherent alternative explanation of the *Weltanschauung*'s roots.

Some of Williams's critics assert that he is an economic determinist. That is to say, they claim that his account of the roots of the *Weltanschauung* of expansion is a variant of the Marxist theory of ideology where ideology is derived from an individual's or class's relationship to the means of production. Michael Hunt, for example, has claimed that Williams's is an 'interest-oriented approach. Ideology was functional; a tool used by the grandees of American capitalism to maintain their economic power and with it their socio-political control.'[23] James Kurth likewise groups Williams with scholars such as Gabriel Kolko and Harry Magdoff, who depicted the US ideological superstructure as determined by its capitalist base,[24] and Robert W. Tucker, after a lengthy and nuanced analysis, nevertheless ultimately concludes that Williams's *Weltanschauung* must be a reflection of economic interests.[25] According to these critics, in sum, Williams explains the *Weltanschauung* of expansion as a product of the needs of US capitalism and of the interests of the US capitalist elite.

On a surface reading of his work, the assertion that Williams is an economic determinist is understandable. The *Weltanschauung* he describes is, fundamentally, 'an economic definition of the world'[26] comprised of beliefs about economic necessity – the 'argument of economic necessity won wide acceptance'; American policy-makers were driven by the 'idea that economic expansion provided the *sine qua non* of domestic prosperity and social peace';[27] by the middle of the twentieth century 'American leaders had internalized, and had come to believe, the theory, the necessity and the morality of open door expansion'. It is also possible to find in Williams's writings many instances where he seeks to demonstrate that American capitalism did need to expand into foreign markets to sustain itself.[28]

The reason that Williams's critics raise this issue is that the straightforward attribution of ideological beliefs to material economic causes is easily disproved. While the Marxist theory is powerful, in as much as most people can be shown to hold ideological beliefs that reflect their economic status (poor people tend to believe in the redistribution of wealth while the rich are less keen, for example), there are also poor conservatives and rich socialists who disprove the existence of any necessary determining role, or even primacy, for economic interests. Protestant fundamentalists in the United States are one of the most economically conservative groups in that society despite having an income below the American average, which indicates that factors other than economic interest are decisive in shaping their beliefs.[29] If Williams was a crude economic determinist, therefore, his argument could easily be dismissed.

But Williams was not an economic determinist. At least, he did not believe overseas economic expansion was, in any strict sense, determined by economic need. It is no accident that, in the various quotes cited above, the words 'idea', 'believed' and 'thought' repeatedly appear. Williams's essential claim is that 'Americans thought their domestic welfare depended upon overseas economic activity . . . and their actions followed from that supposition'.[30] That belief, in turn, was generated not directly by the needs of the US economy but by 'practical experience, received wisdom and continuing analysis'; by the application of '[Frederick Jackson Turner's] . . . frontier-expansionist thesis to the problems of late nineteenth and twentieth century American diplomacy'; and by '[Adam] Smith's logic [that] . . . market expansion was the necessary condition for the realization of individual freedom and liberty'.[31] Williams, in short, gives greater emphasis to ideas than to economic interests in his explanation of the *Weltanschauung* of expansion.

Most of Williams's more acute critics do in fact recognise that fact, but this only leads to the tendering of alternative accusations. Michael Hunt argues that if Williams was not an economic determinist then he was a victim of a 'conceptual confusion', since he typically explained US foreign policy by reference to objective economic interests but sometimes acknowledged the autonomy of ideas, thus undermining his central, economic determinist, argument.[32] Anders Stephanson, for his part, thinks that Williams was unclear as to whether American capitalism needs to expand, merely tends to expand or whether expansion is due to an ideological belief in the need to expand.[33] Richard Melanson and Robert W. Tucker similarly accuse Williams of shifting between one argument asserting economic necessity and another implying that US policy-makers were the victims of a mistaken belief in such a necessity.[34]

All these arguments rest upon the same assumption – namely, that the two positions Williams takes up are at best contradictory and at worst mutually exclusive. That is to say, if the *Weltanschauung* of expansion reflects real economic interests then it is not a mistaken belief, and if the belief in the necessity of expansion is mistaken then it does not reflect real economic interests. It is not possible, therefore, for Williams to include both arguments in his explanation if that explanation is to be coherent and logical. He must choose one argument or the other. But the economic determinist argument, as we have seen, is easily refuted. Reliance on the argument of mistaken belief, however, reduces the whole of US foreign policy to an intellectual error, which is equally difficult to believe.

It is far from clear, however, that the either/or dilemma posited by Williams's critics is a valid one. There is a strong case for arguing that Williams's incorporation of both economic interests and ideas represents a better solution than the either/or choice that his critics insist upon. The closest Williams came to spelling out his position on this question was in the introduction to *The Contours of American History*. There he explained that his goal was to provide three things:

(1) a fundamental description of the structure and circumstances – the reality – of American society at various periods; (2) a characterization of the definition and explanation of the world entertained by Americans at different stages of their development; and (3) various explanations of the way such views of the world arose out of the immediate and remembered reality and in turn changed that reality.[35]

What Williams was arguing is that the *Weltanschauung* of expansion is to be understood as the product of a dynamic relationship between ideas and 'reality' in which reality shapes ideas and ideas shape reality and neither can be reduced to the other. It is 'through the interaction of existing ideas and continuing experience' that the *Weltanschauung* emerges.[36] Williams's application of this method can be seen later in *Contours*. There he describes how, in the 1890s, American policy-makers, faced with certain socio-economic realities – primarily economic depression and consequent social unrest – responded by 'intensifying their efforts to formulate ideas that would account for the crisis and provide practical solutions'. Influenced by a long-standing idea that the success and health of American society were interdependent with an expanding frontier, they concluded that overseas economic expansion was a crucial part of the solution to domestic problems.[37]

It cannot be claimed, therefore, that Williams did not think about this problem or produce a coherent solution to it. He did refuse to make a choice between material economic causes and ideas in explaining the *Weltanschauung* of expansion. But his insistence upon incorporating both elements is defensible on the grounds that it approximates better to our present understanding of the nature of ideology than the critics' insistence that it must either be determined wholly by economic interests or entirely undetermined by them. As was noted above, few would deny that most political ideologies are powerfully shaped by economic interests, and equally few would insist that the latter were the sole sources of ideology. Williams's ambiguous compromise is more faithful to the historical reality than the either/or choice his critics demand.[38]

Williams's critics' objection to his explanation of the *Weltanschauung* of expansion is generally invalid. But on one level it still holds good. If Williams's explanatory framework is as I have suggested, then it is fundamentally empirical and historical rather than theoretical. Without the assumption of the determining power of economics, the *Weltanschauung* of expansion is a contingent phenomenon, not a necessary or inevitable one. Williams does not provide a theory so much as a heuristic framework made up of general categories – ideas/'views of the world' and material factors/'reality'. The content of those categories and the exact nature of their interaction is a question for empirical investigation rather than theoretical assumption. The relationship between material and ideal factors in shaping the *Weltanschauung* of expansion is not, and indeed cannot be, specified a priori. To the extent that they were arguing that Williams did not provide a satisfactory theory of US expansion, his critics are correct.

This fact is not necessarily problematic in and of itself, but it poses serious problems for Williams when we come to the second criticism relating to the *Weltanschauung* of expansion – namely, the nature of its content. Many of Williams's critics have observed that US policy-makers over the years have cited a multitude of reasons, other than the need for an open door for US business, to explain their foreign policies. Yet in Williams's various accounts those other reasons are either ignored, treated as a smokescreen for real goals, or, typically, integrated into the argument in such a fashion that they are reduced to secondary factors that either reinforce or result from the primary expansionist drive.[39] National-security objectives and arguments are explained in terms of protecting the open door, while the purpose of spreading democracy is to create a world in America's image that will be open to US business and ensure the maintenance of the US way of life. Even in later works such as *Empire as a Way of Life*, where Williams places greater emphasis on non-economic ideas about race and missionary Christianity, they are still incorporated in such a way as to emphasise how they supported and rationalised the economic expansionist impulse.

The problem with this, as has been argued by J. A. Thompson,[40] is that, if Williams's argument is essentially an empirical one, without the assumption that ideology is economically determined, there is no logical reason to assume the primacy of economic ideas and objectives over all others, as Williams does. If economic interest does not wholly determine the ideology that drives US foreign policy, then why are economic ideas always central and primary and other ideas always peripheral and/or secondary? The only possible response for Williams to give would be that he had demonstrated empirically, through all the evidence that he had gathered, that they are. But, while Williams did produce a wealth of evidence to indicate the importance of economic goals to US policy-makers, he never engaged in a systematic consideration of alternative explanations or gave equal consideration to non-economic beliefs.[41] Without a persuasive theoretical rationale, Williams has no justification – other than his own assumptions – for the subordination of the other reasons cited by US policy-makers to the overarching purpose of economic expansion.

Similarly, if it is the case, as is argued here, that Williams's argument is not determinist, then there is an implausible discrepancy between the contingent, undetermined nature of both the *Weltanschauung* and US foreign policy and the continuity that Williams identifies in that policy. If the *Weltanschauung* of expansion is not determined by underlying economic needs, then why does it persist for so long? And how can Williams adequately account for the degree of continuity and persistence in US foreign policy without an explanation that is in fact rooted in some determining factor?[42]

Finally, we have the problem of the explanatory utility of the *Weltanschauung* of expansion. On one level this is a simple empirical question of looking at the facts and determining whether this belief actually did determine US foreign policy or not.[43] But there is also an important methodological problem with Williams's argument, a problem that also relates to Williams's insistence upon the continuity and persistence of the *Weltanschauung* of expansion, but in a slightly different way. The latter argument addresses Williams's failure adequately to explain such persistence; this one relates to its function as an explanation of American foreign policy. Put simply, the problem is Williams's insistence upon the role of the *Wel-*

tanschauung as a total explanation of US foreign policy from the founding of the United States onwards.

This attempt to accommodate every US foreign-policy impulse and action within a single perspective leads to a serious methodological problem, best demonstrated by an examination of Williams's explanation of US policy-makers' response to Soviet expansion into Eastern Europe at the end of the Second World War. He was quite clear that their opposition to this development was a product of their desire to maintain open-door access to that region.[44] The obvious weakness of that argument, however, was the lack of significant existing US economic interests in Eastern Europe. Williams himself, while citing considerable evidence that suggests a general concern within the US elite about the open door, provided no argument about specific interests in Eastern Europe. Instead, he dealt with the problem by arguing that, by this time, 'American leaders had internalized, and had come to believe, the theory, the necessity and the morality of open-door expansion'.[45] In the grip of such a belief, rational economic calculations were an irrelevance. Williams accounts for the clearly economically irrational intervention in Vietnam in much the same way. By then, the open-door *Weltanschauung*

> had become so distorted and hardened that it not only overvalued the importance of Vietnam even to a capitalist economy . . . but its principal advocates had become almost completely incapable of recognizing and acting to correct the causes of its distortions and failures.[46]

Whether direct economic interests exist or not, therefore, the *Weltanschauung* of expansion explains US foreign policy. Whether or not there is specific evidence that US policy-makers reasoned in open-door terms about a region such as Eastern Europe, the *Weltanschauung* of expansion explains policy. But, in that case, what policy could not be explained as a product of the *Weltanschauung* of expansion? It is important to note in this regard that the objection is not that US policy towards Eastern Europe cannot be explained as a result of the *Weltanschauung* of expansion because there are no significant US economic interests there, since that would be a resort to economic determinism. If Williams cited evidence showing that US policy-makers believed Eastern Europe had to be kept open to US business, that would be perfectly satisfactory. The problem is that Williams asserts that the *Weltanschauung* of expansion explains US policy without providing any evidence and by resorting to an untestable 'internalised' belief.

A similar example can be found in the way that, when there were apparently grave disagreements over the pursuit of expansion among US policy-makers, as in the late 1890s or early 1920s, Williams dealt with the problems this posed for the *Weltanschauung* of expansion as a complete explanation of US foreign policy by arguing that these were merely tactical disagreements over the best means to achieve the same expansionist objective.[47] Likewise, open-door expansion is defined by Williams to cover every action from military intervention to normal trading relationships. In other words, all sorts of policies and actions, even apparently contradictory ones, and regardless of the absence of concrete evidence in some cases, are explained by the same mechanism. But the only way Williams can do this is to define the *Weltanschauung* of expansion so broadly and vaguely that it can be manipulated to accommodate any action. Ultimately 'it is difficult to conceive of any American policy, or any evidence about the reasons for its adoption, which could not be incorporated into Williams' interpretation'.[48] In short, Williams is guilty of the methodological error of irrefutability. His argument cannot, even in principle, be disproved. And a theory that explains everything actually explains nothing, since a theory that tries to explain intervention and non-intervention by the same logic cannot explain why it occurred in one case and not in the other except by the introduction of random factors from outside the theoretical framework.

Taken as an attempt at a complete explanation of US foreign policy, not only during the Cold War but throughout American history, Williams's *Weltanschauung* of expansion must be considered unsatisfactory. His argument is a victim of its own ambition. In insisting upon the persistence, continuity and total explanatory role of the *Weltanschauung*, Williams overreaches. On the one hand, he fails to provide a satisfactory explanation for the persistence of the open-door mindset, without some underlying determining cause. On the other, his insistence on trying to squeeze every possible reason and policy into the framework of the open door renders the concept so capacious as to be irrefutable and thus of little use as an explanation.

Or, rather, that capaciousness renders his argument invalid, assuming one applies to it the kind of social-scientific criteria of validity utilised thus far. It is not certain, however, that these are the only criteria that should be applied. Williams himself once noted that 'any book, however excellent, can be ostensibly destroyed' by finding 'a fulcrum outside the author's conceptual system and applying the lever of routine intelligence'.[49] In deference to that comment, it must be noted that Williams did not simply, or even primarily, write conventional diplomatic history. Rather, he attempted a kind of unique hybrid between diplomatic history and cultural/intellectual history. Once we understand that, a more sympathetic analysis of his argument can be produced.

As we have seen, what undermines Williams's arguments as diplomatic history is their totalising aspect – the insistence on pattern, continuity and persistence. But it is precisely those qualities that are central to the practice of intellectual and cultural history: 'For the cultural historian, the decisive criterion in the evaluation of his sources must be whether certain attitudes and expressions can be found in great frequency and serve as a means of communication over a long period.'[50] It is not a question, in other words, of looking for exceptions to the rule, or events or policies that seem to contradict it; quite the opposite, in fact. In Williams's own words, the historian who seeks to study an entire culture 'is engaged in ignoring, overriding or subsuming some facts in order to define, describe and characterize and explain a larger unity . . . The facts so scuttled remain true. They also remain incidental, if not irrelevant.'[51]

One key purpose of cultural history, at least in the nineteenth-century conceptualisation from which Williams borrowed, was 'recognizing and defining the particular character of a nation'.[52] That this was Williams's goal is implicit in his adoption of the concept of *Weltanschauung*, for, while that concept does, as we have seen, equate closely to the concept of ideology, that function does not exhaust its potential. The concept was originally articulated by the nineteenth-century German philosopher and historian Wilhelm Dilthey,[53] and in his formulation the concept of *Weltanschauung* represents 'the response of the whole mind to our experience as a whole'.[54] A world view is a combination of the mind and its ideas and emotions plus the total external reality to which it responds. It is the whole that connects the parts and represents the total meaning of existence.

Dilthey believed, as did Williams, that *Weltanschauungen* could belong not simply to individuals but also to cultures or nations. What Williams sought to do, therefore, was to identify not merely an ideology that guided foreign policy but rather the essence of the American world view.[55] For Williams 'the *Weltanschauung* of expansion is the American *geist* [spirit], the unifying principle that expresses itself in different ways in different times, as the social totality unfolds in history.'[56] It is, if you like, the very essence of Americanness, and as such it necessarily remained a continuous and dominant factor shaping American life and foreign policy. Because that 'single dominant principle pervades every part of the social totality', once you have grasped it there is no need to examine every detail or aspect of policy, since any single aspect, such as the ideology of policy-makers, will express the meaning of the whole.[57]

Once Williams's purpose is more clearly understood, then the insistence on totality, the identification of the *Weltanschauung* of expansion as evolving throughout American history and the subordination of other explanatory factors to that idea become explicable. The things that make Williams's argument problematic as conventional diplomatic history are typically a result of his attempt to write good cultural/intellectual history. What is often characterised as unacceptable in the former – ignoring facts that do not fit, focusing upon continuities and patterns while neglecting contingencies and randomness, intuitively grasping the American *Geist* rather than demonstrating cause and effect – is simply the norm in the other. In judging Williams by the criteria we have applied, therefore, it could be argued that we have taken a fulcrum outside his conceptual framework and simply applied the lever of 'routine intelligence'.

That would certainly be true if Williams had restricted himself to writing cultural history. In practice, however, Williams sought to combine diplomatic and cultural history, and it is that attempt, and the subsequent incorporation of practices better suited to the latter into the former, that produces the principal weaknesses in his work. It is the tension between the broad generalisations of cultural history, and the particularities of diplomatic history and the resolution of that tension in favour of the former, that lead to the strained attempt to incorporate all reasons and explain all actions by recourse to the single explanatory principle of the *Weltanschauung* of expansion. Which is not to say, of course, that the *Weltanschauung* explains nothing, that there are no continuities or patterns in diplomatic history or that Williams was wrong to focus upon them. Quite the opposite, this is the great strength of his work. But the identification of such does not require that every policy must be explained and accounted for as a direct result of those continuities and patterns. What is absent in Williams's work is a sense of the limitations of his perspective and of the need to relate it to other explanatory factors rather than simply subsume them within it.

GABRIEL KOLKO

Alongside Williams in the vanguard of Cold War revisionism was Gabriel Kolko. While the two are typically bracketed together (as, of course, they are here), in practice their differences are as important as their similarities. What they share is an emphasis upon American economic expansion, a belief in America's primary responsibility for the Cold War and opposition to its imposition of its way of life upon the rest of the world against the latter's will. However, while they share a focus when it comes to the manifestations and consequences of US foreign policy, their analyses of the causes of that policy are distinct. Williams's explanatory framework is deeply personal and effectively unique. It draws upon nineteenth-century cultural history and interpretative approaches to understanding for its inspiration and it places a central emphasis upon ideas. Kolko's perspective draws much more overtly and straightforwardly on Marxism than does Williams's and places material economic interests at the heart of its explanation.[58]

There are two distinct phases in Kolko's work on the United States and the Cold War. His first two books, the second of which was co-authored with his wife, form what is, in effect, a two-volume study of the early Cold War.[59] Two other works, written much later, concentrate on US policy towards the Third World.[60] As well as focusing on different aspects of US foreign policy during the Cold War, the two phases also demonstrate a significant shift in the form of explanation utilised.

In *The Politics of War* and *The Limits of Power*, Kolko(s) provided a far more lengthy and detailed account of US policies in the early Cold War than Williams did in *The Tragedy of American Diplomacy*, but one that is very similar on its surface. At the core of Kolko's argument is the idea that the emerging conflict between the US and the USSR was, to a great extent, peripheral to the real story of the Cold War. In fact, 'the so-called Cold War . . . was far less the confrontation of the United States with Russia than America's expansion into the entire world'.[61] Implicit in Williams's argument, this theme is much more central in Kolko's. The United States was pushing outwards to secure its global vision and pursuing a policy that would have developed regardless of Soviet actions. The imperative that underpinned this expansion was rooted in 'the problems and needs of American economic interests'[62] and its objective was to integrate 'the capitalist world into a cohesive cooperative system under US leadership'.[63] That ambition, however, faced three principal obstacles:

1. the USSR and its desire for a security sphere in Eastern Europe;
2. the United Kingdom's sterling bloc;
3. the rise of the left and the forces of nationalism in both the developed and underdeveloped world as a consequence of the political, social and economic upheavals generated by the Second World War.[64]

Those obstacles had to be eliminated if the USA was to create the post-war international order it sought. It was America's utilisation of its power to that end that was the defining feature of the Cold War.

In the case of the first obstacle, Kolko, like Williams, saw the USSR of 1945 as a weak and cautious state whose primary goals were to ensure its security and maintain a cooperative relationship with the USA. However, 'while the United States was moderately flexible on the future of Eastern European politics, it hoped to create the traditional economic relationship between Eastern Europe and Western Europe and the world, which meant restoring the pre-war economic *status quo*'.[65] America's insistence on Soviet acceptance of the open-door policy was incompatible with the Soviet need for friendly regimes in Eastern Europe and pushed Moscow into asserting total control in that region.

The second obstacle was the UK sterling bloc and its potential to exclude

US business from large portions of the globe. But the United Kingdom's economic weakness at the end of the Second World War made this the least problematic of America's difficulties. The US government managed the wartime Lend-Lease programme and its curtailment in such a way as to ensure the UK need for a large post-war loan – A need that was then utilised by Washington as leverage to secure access to the sterling bloc for American business as the price of economic assistance. The USA also used its economic muscle and the UK's weakness to end the latter's control of Middle Eastern oil.[66]

The third obstacle, the rise of nationalism and the 'left', is the most important in Kolko's argument. He regards the Cold War as a struggle between America's governing elites and the left throughout the world. Initially, American policy-makers had believed that the pre-war international order would re-emerge relatively unscathed after 1945 and that the private sector would soon restore the sinews of the international economy. However, by 1946–7 it was becoming clear that the damage wrought by the Second World War was far more severe than they had thought. The vital economies of Western Europe and Japan were failing to recover, the left was growing in power in those countries and nationalism was on the march in the Third World. Washington became increasingly aware that it would have to intervene far more forcefully and extensively than it had hoped to have to in order to revitalise international capitalism. Without large-scale infusions of credit the economies of Western Europe would continue to languish, and without the restoration of a healthy transatlantic trading relationship America's entire global vision was endangered.

The policy of containment evolved in this context, reflecting a genuine fear on the part of US policy-makers of the threat posed to their objectives by the USSR and the left in general. Nevertheless, Kolko argued, the anti-communism of US foreign policy in the early Cold War must also be understood in terms of domestic politics. The Truman administration faced a Congress, dominated by the Republican Party, that was generally hostile to foreign aid, that was holding up the proposed post-war loan to Britain, and that refused to ratify the new International Trade Organisation (ITO). In the face of this intransigence, the Truman administration chose to exploit the powerful politics of anti-communism to clothe economic policies in the guise of national-security imperatives.[67] 'Merging American global economic ambitions with anti-communism . . . became the key to political mobilization of a hesitant Congress.'[68]

The two principal manifestations of this merger were the Marshall Plan and NATO. In the case of the former, Kolko insisted that 'the ERP [European Recovery Programme] policy would have been the same had the USSR not existed'. Its purpose was the reconstruction of liberal capitalism in Western

Europe; the communist threat simply made this objective more urgent. Moreover, he argued, the USA designed the programme to ensure that the Europeans adopted the correct kind of liberal capitalism and abandoned their more dubious statist economic practices.[69] NATO also emerged out of economic rather than military need. In the face of recession at home, the continued stuttering of the West European economy and Congressional hostility to economic aid, the Truman administration simply altered the form of its European subsidy.[70] What was sold to the public and Congress as necessary to the containment of Soviet expansion was in reality a response to the failure of international capitalism to restore itself without massive infusions of US public funds.

Kolko's two later works on US foreign policy focus more or less exclusively upon his third obstacle to American global ambitions – namely the rise of the left and nationalism in the Third World after 1945. In these books the USSR hardly appears as an actor at all, as Kolko pursues his earlier argument that the Cold War was really about American expansion into the world, particularly the Third World. Again, the two books can be thought of as companion pieces. In *Confronting the Third World* Kolko conducts a panoramic sweep of US foreign policy towards the Third World from the 1940s through to the 1970s. He does, though, omit to discuss the most obvious manifestation of that policy – namely, the Vietnam War. That episode receives a book to itself.

The basic goal of US policy as articulated in both works is the same as in the earlier two – 'to create an integrated, essentially capitalist world format out of the chaos of World War Two'.[71] More specifically, American actions were guided by the need to retain open access to raw materials, markets and opportunities for investment not only for the USA itself but also for its allies in the industrialized nations. In order to emphasise the essentially peripheral role of the USSR in American policy, Kolko focused on US intervention in areas where the Soviet/communist threat was non-existent (Latin America in the 1950s, for example) and stressed that the USA took action against nationalist regimes of both left and right that threatened its economic interests.

In the long run, however, Kolko, like Williams, saw US policy as essentially self-defeating. America was committed to opposing nationalism and revolution in the Third World in a period in which the latter were an inevitable result of social, economic and political change. US interventions succeeded only in staving off the inevitable by installing and propping up unpopular authoritarian regimes whose actions merely reinforced the demand for change. The defeat of American efforts was thus inevitable and Vietnam only the bloodiest example of that failure.

Explanatory Framework

Like Williams, Kolko places a preoccupation with economic objectives at the heart of US Cold War foreign policy. But, where Williams explained that concern through a *Weltanschauung* or ideology of expansion that was only partially shaped by material economic interests, Kolko posits a much more straightforward connection between US foreign policy and the objective needs of the US economy. However, while Kolko's explanatory framework is much clearer and simpler than Williams's in its general assumptions, it remains somewhat elusive in detail. His insistence upon the centrality of economics leads readily to the assumption that his analytical framework is essentially a Marxist one. That assumption is reasonable, but it does not take us very far as it stands. Marxism is such a diverse phenomenon that the fact that Kolko's analysis obviously has its roots in the Marxist tradition tells us very little. What we really need to know is what kind of Marxist Kolko is and what kind of Marxist analysis underpins his argument. Perhaps, above all, we need to establish whether Kolko's analysis is underpinned by a fundamental assumption of economic or productive force determinism.

All Marxist analysis insists upon the centrality of the mode of production (the manner in which things are produced and how people produce their means of subsistence) to historical explanation. There is, however, great variation in the degree to which the mode of production is seen as determining rather than merely shaping history and therefore also in the degree of significance attributed to human agency, culture and other factors of historical explanation. Productive force determinism is a form of Marxism that insists on the fundamentally determining role of the mode of economic production. This determination can be conceived of as a three-tiered process. At the bottom are the productive forces that determine the nature of a society's relations of production (social or class structure), and together these two elements make up the 'base' of a society. These, in turn, determine the 'superstructure' of society, which is composed of elements such as ideology, politics (including foreign policy) and the legal structure. To put it in more concrete terms: in a capitalist society production for profit in the market (productive forces) determines the creation of a class society (social relations of production) dominated by the bourgeois or capitalist class, who own the means of production. The capitalist class necessarily adopts a legal, political and ideological superstructure that protects its interests in the continuation of this arrangement.[72] The foreign policy of the USA, therefore, in a productive-force determinist argument, necessarily serves the interests of the dominant capitalist class and seeks to preserve and expand the US capitalist system as its primary function.

There are good reasons to believe that some form of this framework does underpin Kolko's analysis. In the first place, even in his later works when he modifies his argument, Kolko always insists upon economic interests as the first and fundamental source of US foreign policy. Secondly, we have Kolko's clear and unmistakable insistence that the USA is a capitalist class society in which the ruling class determines the nature and objects of foreign policy.[73] Finally, despite the absence of any explicit declaration of allegiance, Kolko's arguments and language often imply the assumption of productive-force determinism. Thus, he declares that 'it is the expansive interests of American capitalism as an economy with specific structural needs that guide the definition of foreign economic policy and the United States' larger global role'.[74] Elsewhere he refers to the 'functionally defined needs' of American society and asserts that, 'given the society and its needs, American foreign policy could hardly have been any different'.[75] In each case there is an emphasis upon the inevitable course of US foreign policy, an implicit or explicit rejection of the idea that policy-makers had any real choice over that course, and an assertion that the necessity sprang from the requirements of American capitalism.

Alongside a rather abstract implication of productive-force determinism, Kolko also employs some rather more specific arguments based upon economic interests to explain US foreign policy. Of these, the most prominent is that the source of the US confrontation with the Third World after 1945 was the American need to have ready access to vital raw materials. Increasing US requirements for industrial raw materials, and the fact that 'whole industries and, indirectly, entire economic sectors of which they were a part, were dependent upon them',[76] created a 'structural imperative' in US foreign policy and a 'need for the integration of the Third World into a United States-led capitalist hegemony'.[77] In addition, Kolko at different times and to a lesser degree also argued:

1. that US foreign policy was designed to 'provide needed outlets for a vast industrial capacity at home'[78] because a lack of domestic demand for those goods threatened economic crisis (the surplus-production argument);
2. as a variant on the above, that the massive post-war military build-up was a form of 'military Keynesianism' utilised to generate the demand required to soak up surplus production and that the 'political logic of an army economy encouraged impulses to act [overseas] to accompany its economic utility' (the military–Keynesianism argument);[79]
3. that US foreign policy had to protect American businesses' overseas investments, which were producing an increasingly vital share of their profits (the foreign-direct-investment (FDI) argument).[80]

In his later works Kolko modified his argument significantly. In addition to the core economic forces shaping policy, he now introduced the 'essentially non-material and symbolic elusive considerations that increasingly entered into United States decisions'.[81] The key factor influencing this shift in his thinking appears to have been the Vietnam war. While Kolko would still insist that the first and foremost reason for American involvement in Vietnam was the need to protect US and Japanese access to raw materials in South-East Asia,[82] it was obvious that the price paid by the USA in the war was hardly explicable by any objective calculation of economic interest. Kolko therefore supplemented his economic focus with the concept of 'credibility'. If the USA was to preserve its global hegemony, then it had to demonstrate the capacity to do so in order to deter those who might want to oppose it. US military interventions in places like Korea and Vietnam were thus a form of 'political–military overhead charges' that had to be paid 'to prove that America's imperialist aspirations had the will as well as the material capacity to stop revolutionary advances and retain the world for itself'.[83]

Critique

The basic logic of Kolko's early works can be summarised thus: the structural needs of US capitalism required continued expansion and access to the rest of the world to survive and prosper, and US foreign policy was determined by that need. Taken as an argument for the strict necessity of economic expansion and US Cold War foreign policy, this argument is unsustainable either at the level of theory or in terms of the specific economic interests and arguments Kolko cites in his works. To make the argument stick it would be necessary to do two things: first, to demonstrate (rather than assume) that US capitalism needed to expand into the world economy and, secondly, to show that US foreign policy had been determined by that fact.

The productive-force determinism that underlies Kolko's analysis works through two stages.[84] First, the productive forces determine the social relations of production, and these in turn determine the form and content of the political, legal and ideological 'superstructure' (including foreign policy). Neither determination, however, can be sustained. In the first place, it is not possible to claim that the productive forces determine the social relations of production. Historically, it is not the case that class relationships have changed as a result of changes in the forces of production. The Industrial Revolution, for example, one of the most profound transitions in the forces of production ever seen, did not result in a change in the social relations of production, which instead remained essentially as they had been before the change in productive forces occurred. Nor is it possible to deduce the nature of social relations of production from the forces of production.

You can, for example, have factory production in both capitalist and socialist societies.

The first step in the argument thus fails. The form of the productive forces of a society do not determine its relationships of production. The fact that this is so, however, does not mean that the whole explanatory framework underpinning Kolko's argument must be thrown out. We still have the second stage of the argument – the determination of the superstructure of a society by its social relations of production. Kolko's argument could be reformulated simply to say that it is the nature of capitalist class relationships in America, and the dominance of the capitalist ruling class, that determines US foreign policy.

The first problem with this second claim is that, if class relationships are not determined by the productive forces, then they must also be shaped by other factors, and the only place those factors can originate is the superstructure. If that is the case, then the relationship between social relations of production and superstructure is not one of cause and effect but one of cause running both ways. So politics, for example, is not merely determined by the nature of the class system but also shapes it in turn. This means politics is an autonomous factor explaining foreign policy. The only way out of this dilemma for those who wish to retain the primacy of the social relations of production is to rethink the nature of those relations. It is possible to retain the separation of these from the superstructure only if we accept that elements commonly thought of as part of the superstructure – ideology or religion for example – can actually function as part of the social relations of production. For example, if an individual's position in a religious order secured them certain economic privileges, religion would form part of the class relations of that society. Social relations of production and superstructure are thus separated on a functional basis. Those elements of ideology, religion, law and politics that function as relations of production are part of that determining 'base' and those that do not are part of the superstructure. This apparent rescue comes at a very high cost, however, for anyone who believes in the primacy of the economic, for what it clearly demonstrates is that the economic sphere is not autonomous, nor is it determinant of the other elements in society. Rather, it is the case that those elements exist in a complex web of mutual determination.

It follows from this argument that it is not possible to derive a society's superstructure from the mere fact that it has a capitalist mode of production. That mode of production has the same basic form in each country in which it is the dominant economic practice, but in each case it is also historically specific; qualified and shaped by the particular cultural, political and ideological forms of the country in question. The United States, France and Sweden all have capitalist economies, but they have quite different political and ideological 'superstructures'. Moreover, the types of capitalism they practise are significantly different, indicating that those different histories, political systems, ideologies and cultures actually shape the mode of production. They also, of course, have quite different foreign policies, and it follows from the above argument that one cannot deduce a country's foreign policy simply from the fact that it is capitalist. That foreign policy may be shaped by economic interests, indeed it is highly likely to be so, but that influence needs to be empirically demonstrated rather than simply assumed.

Kolko's argument fares little better at the level of the specific needs he attributed to the US economy after 1945. In regard to the notion of surplus production or a lack of demand in the US economy, it can certainly be said that this is a recurring problem of capitalist economies. However, the argument that US foreign policy can be explained by a need to secure markets for surplus goods or capital is implausible at best. With regard to exports of capital, the argument runs into the rather problematic fact that such foreign investment has produced an inflow of income into the USA that typically exceeds the outflow (that is, it creates more capital).[85] In the case of exports, from 1945 to 1974 US net exports rarely exceeded 1 per cent of Gross National Product (GNP)[86] and thus hardly constituted a sufficiently vital economic interest to necessitate global interventionism. The argument that defence spending was used as a tool of demand management (military Keynesianism) is much more plausible given its size (7–13 per cent of GNP) and the correlation between high military spending and high demand. It is stretching credulity, nevertheless, to argue that US intervention in Vietnam was a product of the need to maintain defence spending.[87]

Finally, there is the argument that US foreign policy was driven by a need to protect overseas US investments, which produced an increasing share of corporate profits. Apart from the fact that this argument contradicts the surplus capital argument, it is also unsustainable on the evidence. Whilst US FDI certainly grew in importance as a source of US corporate profits after 1945, in the period from 1945 to 1970 it never amounted to more than 5 per cent of total US investment. Most FDI, moreover, was in the industrialized nations rather than the Third World. And, if investment in oil is excluded, then only 16.7 per cent of US FDI or less than 1 per cent of all American investment was in the Third World.[88] With the possible exception of the Middle East, therefore, US FDI created no necessity for an interventionist foreign policy.

Unless, that is, that necessity was created by American dependence on vital raw materials. This is the argument Kolko employs most often and it is the one that carries greatest plausibility. The problem with evaluating it lies in the nature of the subject itself, since it is not susceptible to the kind of crude statistical analysis employed above. Raw material dependence is a qualitative as well as a quantitative matter, since a vital material might constitute a tiny proportion of overall inputs into a production process yet be completely irreplaceable. What can be said with some confidence is that the USA was dependent upon foreign sources of raw materials and that that dependence was growing. On the other hand, as Kolko's critics observe, many of those raw materials came from America's allies in the industrialised nations rather than the Third World; there was no compelling reason to believe Third World nations would want to stop selling raw materials to the USA; and, even if they did, substitutes or alternatives could usually be found.[89] At the very least, it is difficult to see access to raw materials as creating an overwhelming necessity for intervention.

Kolko's work in the 1980s moved away from his earlier economic determinism by introducing other explanatory factors into the equation. It can be argued, however, that this shift was more apparent than real, for, while Kolko may have invoked 'credibility' and 'geopolitical analogies' like the domino theory that on first glance are separate from material economic considerations, it is not clear on reflection that they actually are. Let us take credibility as an example: Kolko invokes this to explain an American investment of blood and resources in Vietnam that is not explicable in terms of mere economic interests. If one follows that argument back, though, what it amounts to is a claim that US policy-makers felt that they had to preserve the credibility of American power if they were to preserve their ability to shape the open international economic order they desired. What appears at first glance to be an autonomous explanatory factor is, ultimately, reducible to material economic needs. Moreover, by adding credibility to his argument, Kolko reproduces the problem of irrefutability that we found in Williams. Credibility can be invoked to explain any intervention where direct US economic interests do not appear to be at stake. It thus creates a total explanation for any and every intervention that occurs

Kolko's argument that US foreign policy during the Cold War was determined by the needs of American capitalism is unsustainable as it stands. The theoretical assumptions he makes about the roots of that policy are invalid. It is important, nevertheless, that the baby is not thrown out with the bath water at this point. First, we should note that to demonstrate that a particular foreign policy was not absolutely necessary or functional for US capitalism in no way implies that the interests of US capitalism were not an important, or even the primary, cause of that foreign policy. Indeed, the rejection of crude determinism cuts both ways, since it also undermines arguments that simply invert Kolko's logic to insist that US overseas economic interests were too insignificant to explain US foreign policy. If that foreign policy was undetermined, then the question of whether certain policies were taken in pursuit of economic interests cannot be resolved a priori but must remain open to empirical investigation.

While it must, therefore, be an empirical question, the circumstantial case for the explanatory primacy of US capitalism remains strong. In fact, once we eliminate the impossible hurdle of demonstrating a necessary connection between US capitalism and US foreign policy, the revisionist case looks much stronger. This is so because of a few unavoidable facts. First, the US economy has become much more integrated with the global economy since 1945. FDI has flowed out of the USA to both the industrialized nations and the less-developed countries (LDCs). To argue that the US economy could, if necessary, have survived without all this and that it therefore follows that the US economy did not need to expand may or may not be strictly true, but it also misses the point. Unless one is prepared to argue that businesses operating in a capitalist system are not driven by the need for profit and/ or that American business leaders are largely incapable of making economically rational decisions, it is impossible to argue that US economic expansion was not driven by 'need'. American business became more integrated with the rest of the world economy because that course of action was 'necessary' to increase profits, which is not an optional extra for a business operating in a capitalist economy. Secondly, the United States is a capitalist state. Without exception, those who hold the reins of political and economic power seek to maintain and reproduce American capitalism. That is no more than a statement of the obvious and the empirically demonstrable. Nevertheless, since foreign policy is ultimately about maintaining the health of the state and society from which it issues, it follows that US foreign policy is also shaped by the goal of reproducing American capitalism. If US businesses needed to expand globally, and the US state seeks to secure the reproduction of US capitalism, then very probably the securing of a favourable international environment for US business was a principal factor shaping US foreign policy.

Given our rejection of any necessary relationship between the 'needs' of US capitalism and US foreign policy, nevertheless, it could, in theory, be the case that US foreign policy was conducted without any regard for the interests of American capitalism. Such an assumption, however, carries little if any plausibility for two related reasons. In the first place, it is not simply the case that the US government acts on the basis of some abstract calculation of the general interest of US capitalism or US society. The largest US corporations have important interests in overseas economic activity and in a foreign policy that nurtures and protects those interests. And they are uniquely well placed to ensure that those interests are heard by government, because their economic importance gives them unparalleled access to policy-makers. The fact is that one does not need to be a Marxist or a conspiracy theorist to recognise that big business is the most powerful interest group in the USA.[90] Nor is this to say that government responds only to business, merely that the latter carries more weight in government than any other section of society.

Moreover, even when business groups are not demanding specific government action, it does not therefore follow that policy-makers can ignore the needs of American capitalism. On the contrary, they are always subject to

> the simple fact of the massive constraint imposed on the state's actions by the capitalist class's control of the economy, of investment, production, finance and trade, its power to make decisions which determine what, where and how commodities are produced, decisions which influence wages, prices, profits and the balance of trade.[91]

The simple fact of the matter, in other words, is that, in a democratic capitalist state such as the United States, politicians can remain in power only by maintaining the health of the political system, social order and prosperity. These objectives depend in large part on the success of the economy. It is therefore imperative for the state to retain the support and confidence of the capitalist class, which controls that economy. Even if it is the case, therefore, that the state is autonomous and policy-makers are independent agents, the interests of the capitalist class do represent an objective constraint on the state inasmuch as policies that threaten those interests are likely to undermine the economic growth on which the state depends. For that reason such policies are unlikely either to succeed or to be pursued in the first place.[92]

The interests of American capitalism are best conceived of as a real objective structure that constrains, but does not determine, the foreign policy pursued by the American state. As a consequence, US foreign policy was, and normally will be, functional for the interests of the American capitalist class. How important those interests are in shaping US foreign policy depends upon what other factors may be challenging them for influence over the state at any given time, as well as the strength of the state itself. Thus, in an instance where the very survival of the state is threatened by an external danger, the capitalist class's desire for profit will become a rather secondary concern. Equally, narrow and specific policies may not be strongly influenced by the needs of the capitalist class. Nevertheless, any broad explanation of US foreign policy during the Cold War that ignores those needs is likely to be inadequate. What the exact mixture of forces acting upon the state at any given time was remains, however, an open historical question.

The goal of those who wish to develop economically oriented analyses along revisionist lines, therefore, should be a non-deterministic explanation of US foreign policy that retains a central role for material economic causes but does not deny the causal role of other factors. After all, if it is true that the US state cannot survive without maintaining its capitalist economic base, it is equally true that it cannot survive without adequate arrangements for self-defence, legal and political systems and so on.[93] The necessity for the US state to try and maintain the health of the US capitalist economy does not, therefore, demonstrate its primacy as a factor shaping US foreign policy. Kolko underpinned his argument with an implausible strong theory; future 'revisionists' should aim for a less ambitious weak theory. Probably the best source of ideas about how this effort might be pursued can be found in the work done by 'neo'-Marxists since the 1970s. Their ongoing debate about the 'relative autonomy' of the state addresses precisely this question of how to develop a non-deterministic theory that retains a central role for the capitalist mode of production.[94]

CONCLUSIONS

We have emphasised the limitations of both Williams's and Kolko's revisionist perspectives, but it is important to conclude by reiterating their strengths and continued utility for students of US foreign policy. Empirically, they made a number of significant contributions to our understanding of US foreign policy during the Cold War, of which three in particular stand out. In the first place there is their insistence upon the fact that US foreign policy after 1945 was not simply, or even primarily, a response to the actions of the USSR. The argument that US foreign policy was driven first and foremost by an ambitious vision of a reconstructed liberal capitalist world order is one that has largely stood the test of time and subsequent scholarship.

This aspect of the revisionists' work is of particular importance in considering the relevance of their analyses in the context of the end of the Cold War and the post-Cold War world. Put simply, the logic of the argument of both writers is that the collapse of communism, while dramatic, is essentially insignificant in terms of its implications for our understanding of US foreign policy. Since the primary motive forces of US foreign policy are perceived to be internal to the USA itself, changes external to the USA are secondary to explaining that policy. While Williams died in 1990, one can readily guess what he would have had to say about US foreign policy after the Cold War. A central point of his argument, after all, was that the Cold War was merely one episode in the ongoing history of US expansion. That expansion began well before the emergence of the USSR and, without some change to the USA's own *Weltanschauung*, would continue after its demise. America's recent military adventures, in short, would have been regarded by Williams as merely a continuation of the effort to maintain the open door.

Kolko, as has been noted, was even more explicit than Williams in arguing that the Soviet Union was essentially peripheral to a historical episode (the Cold War) that was defined primarily by the expansion of the United States, into the Third World in particular. In his most recent work he has even gone so far as to suggest that the collapse of communism has actually made life more difficult for the USA. From 1949 onwards, he argues, the European face-off between the superpowers was fundamentally stable, allowing the USA to divert its attention and resources to pacifying the Third World. The USSR's stabilising role 'had been vital to [US] interests',[95] a point belatedly acknowledged by the administration of George H. W. Bush as it sought to minimize the destabilizing impact of the break-up of the USSR in the early 1990s. For Kolko the goals of US foreign policy have not changed significantly and

> the prospect for confrontations and crises in the future therefore remains virtually as great as ever after Leninism's demise, because the opposition to the political and social regimes the US seeks to sustain in so many countries has become increasingly diverse, ranging from conservative nationalists and Islamic movements to the indigenous left.[96]

The second key revisionist contribution is their recognition of the centrality of economic interests and purposes to US foreign policy. Williams and Kolko were among the first historians to emphasise this crucial point. The world order US policy-makers sought to build was a capitalist one and this was a reflection of US economic interests and beliefs. That fact is of critical importance in understanding key aspects of US policy such as the insistence on the reconstruction of Germany because of its role as the engine of the West European economy, or the role of the Marshall Plan in rebuilding the transatlantic trade relationship.

At the conceptual level, the perspectives developed by Williams and Kolko also made some telling contributions. Williams's emphasis upon continuity – on understanding US foreign policy during the Cold War not as a break with the past but as an extension of it – is of fundamental importance. Even if he overstated that continuity, he directed us to look beyond the obvious novelty of US–Soviet confrontation to the longer-run trends and aspects of US foreign policy. In so doing both he and Kolko direct our attention to the importance of long-term structural elements in understanding US foreign policy. Rather than depicting that policy merely as a series of ad hoc decisions taken by individual policy-makers in response to events, they ask us to understand that it also, or even largely, results from forces that transcend individuals and that profoundly shape and constrain the choices those individuals make.

Of course, Williams and Kolko differ in terms of the structural forces they emphasised. For Williams, capitalism was unquestionably a key element in explaining the pattern and continuity in US foreign policy. But his principal contribution lies in his emphasis upon the importance of ideology and culture. This is true both in terms of the general usefulness of these concepts as explanatory tools (though only recently have other diplomatic historians begun to follow Williams in this regard) and in terms of the specific insights into American ideology and culture found in his work. We have seen that his *Weltanschauung* of expansion is unsatisfactory as a complete explanation of US foreign policy and that the attempt to conflate the methods of cultural and diplomatic history has problematic results. We should not allow this to blind us, however, to the potential insights to be gleaned from the kind of cultural approach pursued by Williams nor to the perceptiveness of his ideas about the nature of American ideology. In the case of Kolko, we have likewise seen the implausibility of any argument that tries to explain US foreign policy as a structural necessity of its capitalist economy. The basic insight that the needs of the US economy do impose a structural constraint that US foreign policy-makers must take into account remains, however.

Finally, we must note that, in the case of both writers, the structural forces that they perceive to be central to explaining US foreign policy are indigenous to American society. Ideology, culture and economic interests are all products of processes that are fundamentally internal. US foreign policy, therefore, is depicted as an expression of the nature of American society. This is in contrast to the traditionalist emphasis upon the external stimulus of the Soviet threat as the primary explanatory factor. This question of whether the primary causes of US foreign policy are external or internal to the American state is a vital one, as we shall see in the next chapter.

NOTES

1. Maddox, *New Left Historians*; Siracusa, *New Left Diplomatic Histories*.
2. Williams, *Contours*; Williams, *Tragedy*. Williams's politics were complex and idiosyncratic. He was a radical, but of a distinctly conservative hue, and he had little sympathy with the politics of 1960s leftists. In a recent internet search I found an article in praise of Williams by a fellow of the libertarian Ludwig von Mises institute. For an extended discussion of Williams's politics, see Buhle and Rice-Maximin, *William Appleman Williams*.
3. For a critique of the attempt to label and exclude revisionists, see Cumings, '"Revising postrevisionism"'. The extent of the politically motivated attacks on Williams's work is indicated in Buhle and Rice-Maximin, *William Appleman Williams*, pp. 186–96.

4. Bruce Cumings's vigorous response (Cumings, '"Revising postrevisionism"') to an article by John Gaddis (Gaddis, 'The tragedy of Cold War history') that contained explicit and implicit criticisms of Williams led Gaddis to refuse to allow his article to be reprinted alongside Cumings's in an edited volume: Hogan (ed.), *America in the World*.

5. The three key figures in question are Lloyd C. Gardner, Walter LaFeber and Thomas McCormick; Gardner, *Economic Aspects of New Deal Diplomacy*; Gardner, *Architects of Illusion*; Gardner, *Imperial America*; Gardner, *Spheres of Influence*; LaFeber, *The New Empire*; LaFeber, *America, Russia and the Cold War*; McCormick, *China Market*; McCormick, *America's Half Century*.

6. The key works are Williams, *Contours*; Williams, *Roots of the Modern American Empire*; Williams, *Tragedy*; Williams, *America Confronts a Revolutionary World*; Williams, *Empire as a Way of Life*. For a complete list of Williams's writings, readers should consult the bibliography in Buhle and Rice-Maximin, *William Appleman Williams*.

7. Williams (ed.), *From Colony to Empire*, p. 476.

8. Williams, *Tragedy*, p. 50.

9. Ibid. chapters 3 and 6.

10. Ibid. pp. 206–8.

11. Ibid. chapter 6.

12. Ibid. pp. 233–4.

13. Ibid. pp. 269–72.

14. Williams, *Empire as a Way of Life*, pp. 4–5.

15. Hunt, 'Ideology', p. 194.

16. Williams, *Contours*, p. 365.

17. Ibid. p. 365.

18. Williams, *America Confronts a Revolutionary World*, pp. 132–5.

19. Ibid. p. 148.

20. Buhle and Rice-Maximin, *William Appleman Williams*, pp. 186–96.

21. The best discussions of Williams's work can be found in the following: Becker, 'Foreign markets for iron and steel'; Crapol, 'Coming to terms with empire'; Eckes Jr, 'Open door expansionism'; Maier, 'Revisionism'; Melanson, 'Social and political thought'; Ninkovich, 'Ideology, the open door and foreign policy'; Perkins, 'The tragedy of American diplomacy'; Richardson, 'Cold War revisionism: A critique'; Stephanson, 'The United States'; Thompson, 'William Appleman Williams'; Tucker, *The Radical Left*.

22. McClellan, *Ideology*, p. 1.

23. Hunt, *Ideology and US Foreign Policy*, p. 9.

24. Kurth, 'Testing theories of economic imperialism', p. 12.

25. Tucker, *The Radical Left*, p. 71.

26. Williams, *Tragedy*, p. 229.

27. Williams, *Contours*, pp. 270, 355.

28. Williams, *Tragedy*, pp. 232–3; Williams, 'The large corporation', pp. 71–104.

29. For a rather more sophisticated critique of the Marxist theory of ideology, see Rigby, *Marxism and History*, pp. 276–95.

30. Williams, *Tragedy*, pp. 186–7.

31. Williams, *The Roots of the Modern American Empire*, pp. xiv, 61.

32. Hunt, *Ideology and US Foreign Policy*, p. 11.

33. Stephanson, 'The United States', p. 31.

34. Melanson, 'Social and political thought', pp. 402–3; Tucker, *The Radical Left*, 55–6.
35. Williams, *Contours*, p. 20.
36. Williams, *The Roots of the Modern American Empire*, p. 450.
37. Williams, *Contours*, pp. 354–6.
38. For some discussions that demonstrate the difficulties involved in this problem and the failure, or even non-attempt, to resolve them, see Geertz, 'Ideology as a cultural system'; Hunt, *Ideology and US Foreign Policy*, pp. 12–13; Larrain, *The Concept of Ideology*; McClellan, *Ideology*; Mullins, 'On the concept of ideology'; Rigby, *Marxism and History*, pp. 277–95.
39. For example, Melanson, 'Social and political thought', p. 404; Pletcher, *The Diplomacy of Trade and Investment*, pp. 2–3; Thompson, 'William Appleman Williams', p. 97; Tucker, *The Radical Left*, pp. 59–62.
40. Thompson, 'William Appleman Williams', pp. 97–100.
41. Melanson, 'Social and political thought', p. 404.
42. Thompson, 'William Appleman Williams', pp. 98–9; Melanson, 'Social and political thought, p. 403.
43. e.g. Becker, 'Foreign markets for iron and steel'; Eckes, 'Open door expansionism'; Maier, 'Revisionism'; Richardson, 'Cold War revisionism'.
44. Williams, *Tragedy*, p. 231.
45. Ibid. p. 206.
46. Williams, 'The large corporation', p. 105.
47. Williams, *Tragedy*, pp. 29, 110–11.
48. Thompson, 'William Appleman Williams', p. 104.
49. Williams, *Contours*, p. 2.
50. Gilbert, *History: Politics or Culture?*, p. 89.
51. Williams, 'Thoughts on rereading Henry Adams', pp. 12–13.
52. Ibid. p. 83.
53. Williams cites Dilthey in Williams, 'The frontier thesis,' p. 380, n.2. The concept of *Weltanschauung* is also discussed by Charles Beard in Beard and Beard, *The American Spirit*, Chapter 1. Beard was a key influence on Williams', thinking, and there are strong parallels between their respective bodies of work. Both were socially conservative radicals who opposed an expansionist US foreign policy in preference for a focus on rebuilding American society. They both placed economic motives at the heart of their arguments and pursued grand and totalizing explanations of US history. One can gain an important insight into Williams's ideas by reading Beard; Beard, *An Economic Interpretation of the Constitution*; Beard, *Economic Origins of Jeffersonian Democracy*; Beard, *The Idea of the National Interest*; Beard, *President Roosevelt and the Coming of War*; and see Borning, *The Political and Social Thought of Charles A. Beard*; Kennedy, *Charles A. Beard*; Williams, 'A note on Charles Austin Beard'.
54. Hodges, *Wilhelm Dilthey*, p. 85
55. Kucklick, 'Commentary', p. 121; Stephanson, 'Commentary: Considerations on culture and theory', p. 109.
56. Stephanson, 'Commentary: Considerations on culture and theory', p. 109.
57. Ibid.
58. In that regard, while Kolko did not have as much influence on the next generation of American diplomatic historians as Williams, his critique of US foreign policy is more characteristic of the general tenor of leftist critiques than Williams's idiosyncratic analysis. For analyses similar to Kolko's see Julien, *The American Empire*, and Magdoff, *The Age of Imperialism*.

59. Kolko, *The Politics of War*; Kolko and Kolko, *The Limits of Power*.
60. Kolko, *Confronting the Third World*; Kolko, *Vietnam*.
61. Kolko, *The Limits of Power*, p. 31.
62. Kolko, *The Politics of War*, p. 266.
63. Kolko, *Main Currents*, p. 350.
64. Kolko, *The Politics of War*, pp. 5–8.
65. Ibid. p. 423.
66. Ibid. chapter 3.
67. Kolko, *The Limits of Power*, pp. 329–39.
68. Kolko, *Main Currents*, p. 353.
69. Kolko, *The Limits of Power*, pp. 379, 429–52.
70. Ibid. pp. 453–73.
71. Kolko, *Vietnam*, pp. 72–3.
72. For more detailed explanations, see Rigby, *Marxism and History*, pp. 31–50, and Perry, *Marxism and History*, chapter 2.
73. Kolko, *Roots*, pp. 5–10.
74. Kolko, *The Limits of Power*, p. 8.
75. Kolko, *The Politics of War*, pp. 8, 625.
76. Kolko, *The Limits of Power*, p. 625.
77. Kolko, *Main Currents*, pp. 381–7; Kolko, *The Politics of War*, p. 254; Kolko, *Roots*, pp. 51–4.
78 Kolko, *The Politics of War*, p. 347.
79. Kolko, *The Limits of Power*, pp. 453–73; Kolko, *Main Currents*, pp. 318, 322.
80. Kolko, *Main Currents*, pp. 381–7; Kolko, *Roots*, pp. 73–8.
81. Kolko, *Confronting the Third World*, p. 5.
82. Kolko, *Main Currents*, pp. 365–6.
83. Ibid. pp. 364, 369.
84. The brief critique of productive-force determinism that follows is based primarily on Rigby, *Marxism and History*, and Jessop, *State Theory*, chapters 1–3.
85. Barratt Brown, 'A critique of marxist theories', p. 57.
86. Tucker, *The Radical Left*, pp. 133–8; Weisskopf, 'Theories of American imperialism', p. 47.
87. Weisskopf, 'Theories of American Imperialism', p. 47.
88. Miller, Bennett and Alapatt, 'Does the US economy require imperialism?', p. 15; Slater, 'Is United States foreign policy imperialist?', p. 226; Tucker, *The Radical Left*, pp. 126–32; Weisskopf, 'Theories of American imperialism', pp. 47–8.
89. Miller, Bennett and Alapatt, 'Does the US economy require imperialism?', p. 17; Slater, 'Is the United States foreign policy imperialist?', p. 227; Tucker, *The Radical Left*, pp. 122–6.
90. Berry, *The Interest Group Society*; Dye, *Who's Running America?*; Lindblom, *Politics and Markets*; Schattshneider, *The Semisovereign People*; Schlozman and Tierney, *Organized Interests*; Stern, *The Best Congress Money Can Buy*; Weisskopf, 'Theories of American imperialism', pp. 50–1.
91. Rigby, *Marxism and History*, p. 261; see also Miliband, *The State in Capitalist Society*.
92. Kaldor, *The Imaginary War*, pp. 34–5.
93. Jessop, *State Theory*, p. 84.
94. The literature is enormous; for useful general overviews, see Barrow, *Critical Theories of the State*; Chandhoke, *State and Civil Society*, Thomas, *Alien Politics*. Jessop, *State*

Theory, chapters 1–3 offers a rigorous critique, while the rest of the book provides a demanding but rewarding approach towards the basis of a weak theory of the capitalist state.

95. Kolko, *Century of War*, p. 450.
96. Ibid. p. 442.

THREE

Post-revisionism

According to John Lewis Gaddis, the initial hope of post-revisionist scholars was that 'if only we could take the strongest elements of these two previous approaches [orthodoxy and revisionism], discard the weaker ones, and ground the whole thing as much as possible in whatever archives were available, then truth would emerge'.[1] In this comment Gaddis captures certain characteristic elements of post-revisionism, and above all its desire for synthesis. Writing initially in the less febrile atmosphere of the 1970s, many post-revisionists saw themselves as consciously avoiding the ideological perspectives and one-sided judgements of traditionalists and revisionists in favour of an 'objective' approach that would dispassionately identify all the relevant causal factors and integrate them into an overarching explanation of events. In contrast to the simplistic and reductionist arguments of the historians of the 1950s and 1960s, post-revisionists would stress complexity and multi-causality in their explanations of American foreign policy. And, with new archival material appearing all the time, they would have the opportunity finally to ground their arguments in solid empirical evidence and thus to put an end to the arguments over who started the Cold War.

That, at least, was how many post-revisionists saw it. Others would argue, with some justification, that, rather than an attempt to build a synthesis from the best elements of both previous interpretations, post-revisionist accounts were often an attempt to justify the broad conclusions of traditionalism while neutralizing those of revisionism. Certainly, the characteristic method of post-revisionism in dealing with revisionist arguments is a 'yes, but' formula that consists of accepting the broad contention of the revisionists but reinterpreting its meaning and implications in such a way as to neutralise their conclusions. In contrast, the specific arguments of the traditionalists might be rejected, but their judgement that American policy-makers did the right thing is typically vindicated. It is perhaps not surprising, therefore, that post-revisionism is currently the dominant interpretation of American foreign policy within the academy.

Another reason for this might be post-revisionism's use of the dominant theory from the discipline of international relations in its interpretation. Although it always had something of a realist bent, in the 1980s the two leading post-revisionist scholars, John Lewis Gaddis and Melvyn P. Leffler, began to borrow from contemporary neorealist theory in a more systematic fashion. Their consequent emphasis upon the systemic sources of US foreign policy and the importance of placing the USA within an international geopolitical system is the most important theoretical contribution of post-revisionism to our understanding of US foreign policy. However, while it undoubtedly makes a major contribution to that understanding, post-revisionism does not achieve the transcendent synthesis that it had initially hoped for. In its efforts towards that goal it clearly overreaches itself, and in so doing demonstrates clearly the difficulty of reconciling theoretical incisiveness and synthesis as discussed in the introduction.

EARLY POST-REVISIONISM

The term 'post-revisionist' implies, in itself, no common core of theory or argument,[2] being merely a chronological designation. Nevertheless, while the usual arguments about the appropriateness of the title and the inclusion or exclusion of this or that scholar inevitably arise, it is not too difficult to recognise common features that justify the grouping of certain scholars in this category. These can be subdivided into purposes, argument, and theory and methodology.

With regard to purposes, as already indicated, these authors are united in responding self-consciously to the revisionist attack on US foreign policy. It could hardly have been otherwise, for, just as revisionism had to come to terms with traditionalism as the dominant interpretation of US foreign policy, so the post-revisionists had to respond to revisionism. In so doing they have tended to defend, explicitly or implicitly, the actions of US policy-makers, to the extent that, in the view of one critic, post-revisionism is simply 'orthodoxy plus archives'.[3] In practice, the post-revisionists are perhaps best understood as being spread along a continuum between the two poles of orthodoxy and revisionism. Some clearly come to revisionism in order to bury it. Others make a genuine attempt to build upon and incorporate revisionist arguments within a broader synthesis.[4] These differences, however, are more apparent in principle than in practice, as even scholars like Leffler, who demonstrates considerable sympathy towards revisionism, ultimately undermine its arguments by incorporating them within a conceptual framework that reduces the explanatory factors they prioritise to a secondary or residual status. As a result, whether consciously, or merely as a side effect of their theoretical commitments, post-revisionists have been engaged in an effort to 'contain' revisionism.[5]

This becomes clearer if we examine some of the substantive arguments of post-revisionism. One defining characteristic of the post-revisionist argument, for example, is some degree of acceptance of the revisionist argument that Soviet behaviour was driven by a conservative interest in national security rather than an ideologically motivated grand design for global domination: 'Stalin probably had no precise blueprint for the kind of settlement he wanted.'[6] However, rather than taking this to imply American responsibility for instigating the Cold War, post-revisionists argue that, even if Soviet actions were driven by security needs, this did not mean that they posed no threat, or were perceived to pose no threat, by US policy-makers: 'given Western convictions that only the diffusion of democratic institutions could guarantee peace . . . Moscow's imposition of influence in Eastern Europe seemed ominous, whatever its motives.'[7]

Some post-revisionists nevertheless take a line similar to that of the revisionists, finding the Soviet threat negligible, and some kind of outcome short of Cold War possible, if only US policy-makers had perceived Soviet actions more accurately.[8] Others see the Soviet drive for security as little different from a drive for world domination, inasmuch as it knew no boundaries and could only be halted by the application of decisive counter-measures.[9] At best, therefore, Soviet security needs had the same effect on US interests as a drive for global domination, and containment was entirely justified. At worst, Soviet actions could be seen by reasonable men and women as threatening, and, while US policy-makers may have exaggerated the threat, the US move to a policy of containment was a prudent worst-case response to a complicated and uncertain global situation.[10]

Post-revisionism has also incorporated the revisionist argument that US policy-makers were not naive, innocent or isolationist. Rather than being stirred from their insularity by Soviet aggression, the post-revisionists agree, US policy-makers were hard-headed practical men with an understanding of American interests and the kind of world that would serve them best. Just how clear that conception was, and how purposeful the American pursuit of it, is a source of disagreement. Closest to the revisionist position is Leffler, who sees US policy-makers as having developed a strategy to ensure a 'preponderance of power' before the Second World War had even ended. At the other end of the spectrum is Bruce Kuniholm, who sees American strategy as evolving largely in response to Soviet provocations.[11]

If the USA had interests and goals, however, the post-revisionists agree that the revisionists exaggerated the purposeful and confident way that it pursued them. US actions, they argue, were often uncertain and hesitant, driven by fear as much as ambition. This argument is seen very clearly in the typical post-revisionist account of US policy towards Eastern Europe. Senior US policy-makers are depicted as recognising and accepting the Soviet need for a sphere of influence in that region, but hoping that it could be implemented in ways compatible with US interests and principles. In the face of unilateral Soviet moves to impose direct control, and rejection of US calls for self-determination, the USA moved slowly and hesitantly towards a confrontational stance. That shift, however, took two years and was accompanied by much confusion, a reversal of course and general puzzlement about Soviet behaviour. Moreover, it was driven as much or more by fear and uncertainty about the consequences of Soviet actions – did they presage further efforts to control Germany or Western Europe? – as it was by a consciousness of American power and a determination to impose an American-designed world order. At no point, it is argued, did the USA really make any serious effort to halt the Soviet effort to dominate Eastern Europe.[12]

One of the most obvious ways in which post-revisionism seeks to contain revisionism is the manner in which it addresses the question of economic interests and motivations. These are dealt with by the post-revisionists in a number of ways. First, they made use of their access to new archival materials opened in the 1970s to compile empirical evidence that indicated that policy-makers were not preoccupied with economic issues.[13] This claim is reinforced by the citation of statistics to demonstrate that the USA was not dependent on foreign trade or investments for its prosperity.[14] More significant, however, is the way in which the post-revisionists accommodate economics within their typical 'yes, but' structure. Thus, there is usually an acknowledgement that the USA did indeed have economic interests and sought to pursue them, but the significance of this fact is deemed to have been greatly exaggerated by the revisionists. Economics was a concern of policy-makers, but merely one among many and not necessarily the most important.

Most importantly, post-revisionism contains economics as a cause of US foreign policy by inverting the logic of Gabriel Kolko, in which politics is determined by economics. The epitome of this technique is Robert Pollard's *Economic Security and the Origins of the Cold War*.[15] In this book Pollard accepts the revisionists' argument that US foreign policy after 1945 was designed to restore global capitalism while inverting their interpretation of that fact. US policy-makers were thinking in terms of the lessons of the 1930s, which taught that economic autarky produced war and free trade produced peace and prosperity. The US commitment to free trade was, therefore, essentially a political one, aimed at securing peace and stability. To the extent that economic self-interest played a part, it was a secondary one, and, since US policy-makers sincerely believed that free trade was good for all, it went hand in hand with American benevolence.[16] In later post-revisionism, which is increasingly influenced by neorealist theory, the driving causes of policy shift from the slightly woolly notions of peace and stability to a more clear-cut geopolitical preoccupation with power and security. The basic point, however, is the same: politics determines economics, not vice versa.[17]

At the theoretical and methodological level as well, we find post-revisionism defining itself, to a great extent, in terms of its differences with revisionism. Post-revisionists criticize revisionism for reductionism/mono-causality, economic determinism, and allowing normative judgement to get in the way of explanation. Thus, opined one, while there had been many analyses of the origins of the Cold War, 'since so many of them have been shots in the Cold War rather than disinterested explanations, the answer remains elusive'.[18] The post-revisionists, in contrast, were going to avoid the 'value-laden' judgements of their revisionist (and orthodox) predecessors and simply 'seek an understanding of what happened and why'.[19] Where the orthodox and revisionist scholars had been taking sides in the Cold War and had allowed this to affect their scholarly judgement, post-revisionist scholars were going to weigh the evidence dispassionately.

As well as being objective, post-revisionists intended to avoid what they saw as the reductionist and mono-causal nature of revisionism. That is, they not only attack the specific economic arguments of revisionism but they also denounce it for its alleged economic determinism. In contrast, post-revisionists tend to insist on the impossibility of reducing complex historical matters to single causes and to assert a preference for a more complex, multi-causal analysis.[20] Foreign policies emerged out of a tangle of interacting factors, not from one overarching cause.

In particular, and especially in the early stages of their evolution, post-revisionists emphasised the role of the domestic political process and public opinion in shaping US actions. US policy towards Eastern Europe and its apparent incoherence was often partially explained in this way; policy-makers' realistic recognition of the Soviet desire for a sphere of influence in that region was in conflict with domestic political pressure for self-determination and democracy there. The two objectives, unfortunately, were mutually exclusive, since democratically elected regimes in the region were almost bound to be hostile towards the USSR. Unwilling or unable to explain this reality to the US public, American policy-makers found it easier to shift towards confrontation with the USSR than to pursue a pragmatic accommodation at the expense of the peoples of Eastern Europe and risk a domestic outcry.[21]

The other element of the domestic political process that was also initially popular with post-revisionists was bureaucratic politics. That is, a form of explanation that attributes policy to the manœuvrings and conflicts within and between government departments.[22] America's German policy in 1944–5, for example, was often explained in terms of a conflict between the War, Treasury and State departments.[23] Lynn E. Davis similarly depicted America's East European policy as being determined almost exclusively by a handful of State Department bureaucrats.[24]

Related to the post-revisionist emphasis on multi-causality is a characteristic desire for synthesis. In part, this can be seen as a conscious effort to dominate the struggle to explain US foreign policy in the early Cold War by positioning post-revisionism as the end point of a process in which traditionalism is the thesis, revisionism the antithesis and post-revisionism the synthesis (as Gaddis implied in the quote at the very start of this chapter). It also, however, reflects an awareness that, if one is going to pursue an analysis that emphasises the influence of multiple explanatory factors, one needs to make some effort to integrate them into a coherent whole. Synthesis, however, is easier said than done. John Lewis Gaddis claimed a 'postrevisionist synthesis' in 1983[25] but, as the critics observed, it was not a synthesis at all. Rather, it was simply a list of arguments without any real effort to integrate them.[26] This was quite typical of early post-revisionist work, perhaps nowhere more strikingly than in the work of Thomas Paterson. Explicitly committing himself to a 'multi-faceted' synthesis, he explained the emergence of the Cold War as a result of pressures from the international system, ideology, economic and strategic needs, 'lessons of the past', power and diplomatic tactics. Having carefully itemised each of these elements and built them up, layer on layer, he reached the conclusion that the Cold War was a result of a combination of factors and that 'to attempt to rank these factors, to argue that one was more important than another, would be a futile intellectual exercise. They were intertwined, they fed one another, they were inseparable.'[27]

The impolite might suggest that not to make some attempt to establish more clearly the relationship between these factors is to take no intellectual exercise at all. More pertinently, we can see that we have moved from one extreme to another, from reductionist mono-causality to incoherent multi-causality. Piling up facts or factors and concluding that policies were a result of some combination of these, though it is impossible to disentangle them, or to say exactly which are the most important or caused what precisely, is less a step forward than sideways. Whatever has been gained in terms of the empirical richness of the explanation is lost in conceptual and theoretical incoherence. Indeed, in simply aggregating a series of causes without demonstrating how they interact with each other to bring about the events in question, the post-revisionists were not really offering an explanation at all.[28]

Whether stimulated by this critique or not, key post-revisionists did come to demonstrate an increased preoccupation with the conceptual framework within which they conducted their analysis and attempted to develop a more theoretically coherent synthesis. The core around which they sought to build this synthesis was neorealism. Ideas associated with the 'realist' tradition had always been a presence in post-revisionist writings, albeit in a rather unsystematic fashion. There had always been an emphasis on US policies having been guided by the defence of strategic interests and security and maintenance of the balance of power as the post-revisionists sought to refute the revisionist emphasis on economic considerations. These ideas were not systematically developed, however, nor were they used to provide the basis of an overarching theoretical framework. They were just part of the eclectic multi-causal mix.

From the mid-1980s onwards, however, there was a more systematic attempt to give post-revisionism a viable theoretical underpinning. This effort developed along two related lines, both deriving their framework from the neorealist theory of Kenneth Waltz.[29] In the first version, causal power is vested in the structure of the international system rather than within the state itself. The Cold War thus becomes the product of a bipolar international system and the post-war power vacuum, which leads, more or less inevitably, to conflict as the two superpowers seek to protect their national interests and power. The second approach also places the key causal stimuli of US foreign policy outside the state, in the form of the actions and events that occur in the international system. But it emphasises that the US reaction to those stimuli is governed by how they impinge upon its 'core values'.

The two individuals primarily responsible for developing these two attempts at a more coherent synthesis are Gaddis and Leffler. In terms of the scope and influence of their writings, they are undoubtedly the two most important post-revisionist scholars. Moreover, if post-revisionism is conceived as a continuum, rather than a unitary position, then Leffler and Gaddis represent, at least in some dimensions of that continuum, its two poles. For all these reasons, a more detailed examination of their arguments will more clearly illuminate the post-revisionist argument.

EXPLANATORY FRAMEWORK

John Lewis Gaddis

John Lewis Gaddis may have changed the framework within which he explains the origins of the Cold War, but the empirical core of his argument has remained strikingly consistent over the years. In both his first and latest studies, the USA, seeking peace and security in a world order based on self-determination, free trade and collective security, collides with a USSR unilaterally pursuing its own security through control of the countries on its periphery. The incompatibility of these two approaches to achieving security leads to the Cold War as American policy-makers feel compelled, in the face of what they see as Soviet expansionism, to adopt the policy of containment.[30]

In *The United States and the Origins of the Cold War*, Gaddis argued that 'both Washington and Moscow wanted peace, but strong internal influences caused each to conceive of it in different ways'.[31] At the heart of the emergence of the Cold War was Eastern Europe. While US policy-makers recognised and accepted the Soviet desire for a sphere of influence there, they were also committed to the principle of self-determination and, moreover, compelled to uphold it by the demands of domestic public opinion. The Soviet need for a sphere of influence in Eastern Europe and self-determination for the countries of the region were incompatible. No democratic regime in the region would be friendly to Moscow. The USSR therefore imposed its control unilaterally and by force. American policy-makers, frustrated by their inability to shape Soviet behaviour and under increasing domestic political pressure, mistakenly interpreted these moves as aggressive expansionism and moved to the policy of containment.

In the 1980s, without much altering this basic core narrative, Gaddis added elements, reinterpreted the significance and implications of elements already within it and altered the explanatory process involved by placing the events within a neorealist framework. The last of these elements was the most distinctive and significant change in Gaddis's work. Neorealism is so-called because it represents an adaptation of the much older realist tradition in international-relations theory. While it shares with realism a preoccupation with power and security as the fundamental concerns of the state, neorealism's innovation is to place the explanation of state behaviour not within the state itself but within the international system.

Kenneth Waltz's fundamental argument, from which Gaddis's interpretation borrows, is that the outcomes of the interactions between states are not explicable in terms of the intentions, goals or interests of policy-makers within those states. Rather, there are certain characteristics of the international system within which those states exist that explain the dominant characteristics of the relations between states. The characteristics of the international system in question are twofold. In the first place there is anarchy, or the absence of any authority higher than the individual state. This makes international politics a 'self-help' system where each state must look to its own resources to ensure its survival. The second characteristic is the distribution of capabilities (power) between the states within the system, changes in which alter the structure of the system and its polarity (bipolar or multipolar).

Waltz's point is that, while foreign policies are of course the result of processes internal to the state, which policies are eventually chosen, and the effects of those policies, are powerfully shaped by the structure of the international system, which deters certain courses of action, encourages others and affects the outcome of all of them. For example, the anarchical nature of the system encourages the building-up of armaments for self-defence and discourages disarmament, regardless of the instincts of policy-makers. The polarity of the system, in turn, shapes patterns of alliances and the stability of the system. In sum, anarchy and polarity together create a system structure within which all states must exist and to which they must tailor their behaviour if they are to survive.[32]

This idea of policy determination by the system enters Gaddis's work in 'The emerging post-revisionist synthesis' in 1983 and is consistently present in his work between then and the early 1990s. In 'post-revisionist synthesis' he refers to US policy as being driven by a 'national-security' imperative; the sense of vulnerability created by the Second World War leading US policy-makers to focus on the global balance of power and possible threats to it.[33] This depiction of US policy-makers thinking in explicitly geopolitical terms is also central to *The Long Peace, Russia, the Soviet Union and the United States* and *The United States and the End of the Cold War*. In all these books the course of action pursued by the USA after 1945 is explained by Gaddis as determined primarily by the need to preserve the balance of power.

The key point underpinning this analysis is that 'the United States is, and always has been, part of an international system, the characteristics of which add up to something more than just the sum of its parts'.[34] To understand US foreign policy it is therefore necessary to look outside the USA itself to the effects of the system. The new version of Gaddis' explanation thus ran as follows. Sensitized to the vulnerability of their nation by the impact of the Second World War, American policy-makers came to recognise that the security of the USA depended upon the maintenance of a favourable balance of power in the international system (a distribution of capabilities favouring the USA). They therefore set out to achieve that goal through the policies of free trade, self-determination and collective security. The Second World War had also, however, resulted in the creation of a bipolar international system and a power vacuum between the two remaining great powers. Under such circumstances, conflict is always likely as the powers move to fill the vacuum. In this case, the USSR set out to achieve its own security and a favourable balance of power by unilaterally expanding into Eastern Europe and else-where. Perceiving Soviet actions as a threat to the balance of power and its national security, the USA moved towards the policy of containment in order to prevent further Soviet expansion.

This neorealist logic can also be seen in Gaddis's explanation of the growth of an American 'empire' and its policy towards the Third World. Rejecting revisionist claims that ideology or economic interests drove US policy, Gaddis argues that US expansion was a result of insecurity. Driven by a fear of a shift in the balance of power if Soviet influence spread, the USA was drawn into global commitments and interventions. In the process it made errors and overextended itself, but it did so for defensive reasons.[35] US actions, in short, were determined primarily by anarchy (the need for self-help) and polarity (the US and USSR emerged from the Second World War as superpowers and the only potential threats to each other's security).

We thus have the same basic elements that were there in Gaddis's earlier argument, but placed in a more overtly theoretical context. America's policy goals of self-determination, collective security and free trade remain, but they are now depicted as part of a strategy of preserving a favourable balance of power that is driven by the structure of the international system. What fades, as a consequence, is the earlier emphasis upon domestic political factors. Whereas Gaddis had previously made domestic political pressures a cornerstone of his argument, they now played a much reduced, if never entirely non-existent, role. Rather than serving as the primary explanatory factor, they became a secondary element whose role was largely to explain deviations in US policy from the course of behaviour dictated by the logic of pressures from the international system.[36]

Two other elements that have become central to Gaddis's argument also first appear in 'The emerging post-revisionist synthesis'. Both draw heavily on the work of other scholars. In *Russia's Road to the Cold War*, Vojtech Mastny argues that Soviet actions after 1945 were driven by a desire for security but adds a new twist. That drive, he argues, was rooted in Stalin's personal sense of insecurity, even paranoia, which resulted in a 'craving for security [that] was limitless' and that no amount of territorial expansion short of complete global domination would appease. While Stalin did not want confrontation or a Cold War, the nature of his insecurity rendered him incapable of trust or cooperation and compelled him to seek domination of more and more territory. Therefore, while Soviet actions were not driven by a desire for world domination (*pace* the Traditionalists), they would nevertheless lead to that end. Moreover, given the nature of Stalin's mindset, there was no option other than drawing a clear line in the sand and mobilising the power to prevent the Soviets crossing it, if Soviet expansion was to be contained. To the extent that Mastny was critical of US policy, it was for not moving to such a confrontational stance early enough.[37]

The second argument that Gaddis has built upon in recent years is Geir Lundestad's 'Empire by invitation' thesis. In the article of that title, Lundestad argued that the revisionists had been correct to claim that it was American expansionism, rather than that of the USSR, that was most striking in the years after 1945. However, he added, while Soviet expansion was unilateral and coercive in most cases, that of the USA was typically the product of initiatives and invitations from those who were on the receiving end. The Western Europeans, in particular, asked for American aid and protection and willingly fell into line with American plans.[38]

Both of these arguments have the classic post-revisionist characteristic of apparently accepting a revisionist claim (Soviet behaviour was driven by a desire for security; the USA was the expansionist power) but then reinterpreting it in such a way as to undercut the conclusions the revisionists had drawn from it. Recently, however, Gaddis has moved beyond merely qualifying revisionist arguments to rejecting them outright in favour of a revived traditionalism. Originally, Gaddis had concluded that neither side was solely responsible for the Cold War, though the Soviet search for security was principally to blame.[39] By the late 1990s Gaddis has evolved towards a position that is scarcely distinguishable from traditionalism in laying the blame for the Cold War squarely upon the shoulders of Stalin: 'the "new" history is bringing us back to an old answer: that as long as Stalin was running the Soviet Union, a Cold War was unavoidable.'[40] In 1974 Gaddis had been mildly critical of US policy-makers for mistaking the Soviet desire for security for a plan for world domination. If he is at all critical today, it is because the same policy-makers did not see quickly enough that the Soviet desire for security had the same consequences as a drive for world domination and had to be contained accordingly.

Implicit in Gaddis's recent traditionalist position on the question of responsibility for the Cold War is a shift towards a traditionalist position on theory as well. In depicting Stalin as uniquely responsible for the Cold War, Gaddis aligns himself with a traditionalist focus on individual human agents as the primary source of explanation in history. In so doing he appears to be reverting to nothing so much as the good old-fashioned, 'great-man' approach to history. This shift is confirmed by a number of Gaddis's works of the 1990s, in which he apparently repudiated neorealism and the attempt to produce 'scientific' social science more generally.[41] The failure of neorealism to predict, or account for, the end of the Cold War was clearly a key factor in this shift in his thinking. If the end of the Cold War was a product of changes within the USSR, he asked, what use was system structure as an explanatory factor?[42] Along with contemporary changes in the sciences themselves, which, he argued, undermined the old-fashioned models of science that social scientists were trying to emulate, this led him to suggest that a return to traditional narrative history was in order.[43]

The final aspect of Gaddis's shift towards traditionalism is his growing moralism. Gaddis now defends US policy not only on the basis that it was the only course available to protect American interests, but as a positive moral good. This is most obvious in his exploitation of Lundestad's 'Empire by invitation' thesis. While Lundestad's argument is obviously of empirical and explanatory value, Gaddis has utilised it in a primarily normative fashion. The difference between America's cooperative and consensual 'empire' and the coercive Soviet bloc has become a key theme in his recent work. America, of course, sought to protect its security and power, he argues, but it did so in ways that were compatible with the interests and security of others, in clear contrast to the Soviets. The US 'empire' was thus clearly morally superior to that of the USSR.[44]

Gaddis has also become more generally concerned with issues of ethics and morality in Cold War history.[45] The basic theme of several recent pieces of work has been that historians of the Cold War have wrongly neglected to incorporate a moral dimension into their analyses. Borrowing from the perspectives of international-relations theory, they have mistakenly adopted a stance of 'moral equivalency', which judges states solely in terms of their foreign policies while neglecting the nature of their domestic regimes. In fact, says Gaddis, we should not ignore the fact that Stalin killed more people than Hitler, though he is unclear how this should affect our judgements. Except in one regard, that is: 'if departures from ideals existed in American policy, they were nothing compared with what the Kremlin had managed to achieve.'[46] There is no question in Gaddis's work of the 1990s but that the Cold War was a struggle between the good guys and the bad guys and that the good guys won.

In sum, as the traditionalists argued, the USA was forced into a policy of containment by Soviet expansionism (albeit expansion driven by a search for security) and the USA was fundamentally on the side of the right and acting for the good of the world in taking this course (even if it was preserving the balance of power and protecting its security as well). Neorealism thus combines with moralism in Gaddis's most recent work. While American actions may have been dictated, to some degree, by imperatives arising from the international system, this does not detract from the fact that they were ethically sound and certainly morally superior to those of the USSR.

Melvyn P. Leffler

Leffler has not written as much as Gaddis or over so long a period and his interpretation of events has not shifted as much as the latter's. In 1992, after years of research, he produced the summation of his thoughts on US foreign policy and the origins of the Cold War in a huge doorstep of a book entitled *A Preponderance of Power*. Leffler's argument in this book is that during the Second World War US policy-makers, prompted by the experiences of the 1930s and the war itself, began to formulate plans as to what would be required to preserve American national security in the aftermath of the war. The primary threat to that security, they concluded – and as had been shown by the war – was the possibility of a hostile power dominating the Eurasian continent. Such a development would isolate the USA, force it massively to increase defence spending, cut off trade and investment opportunities and ultimately compel it to become a 'garrison state'.

In order to render such an outcome impossible, it was necessary to ensure that the key industrial areas of Eurasia – Europe and Japan – were secured within the US sphere of influence and that the USA had the 'preponderance of power' necessary to guarantee that situation. While the most plausible threat to this outcome and US security was Soviet domination of Eurasia, US policy-makers did not expect or desire conflict with the USSR. Rather, they hoped that the USSR would acquiesce in the capitalist, democratic world order they planned to create. The USSR, however, driven by its own need for security, pursued its objectives unilaterally, most obviously in Eastern Europe. This refusal to cooperate, combined with the instability and chaos of the post-war world, generated real fears in Washington that the Soviets were seeking domination of Eurasia and that they might be able to achieve it. The USA therefore acted to put in place the policy of containment to ensure that did not happen.[47]

Leffler thus shares a number of important features of his analysis with Gaddis. Above all, both use the concepts of 'power' and 'national security' as the dominant frame within which US actions are interpreted. American policy-makers are depicted as geopoliticians, thinking in terms of 'correlations of power' and threats to security and how to address them. The USSR became a threat because its actions were seen to endanger the balance of power US policy-makers had decided was required to protect American interests. Neither Leffler nor Gaddis believes that either superpower sought or expected a Cold War, but that outcome is depicted as more or less inevitable given the incompatibility of the security interests and goals of the two superpowers. Finally, both believe that American policy-makers had little choice but to take the course of action they did in the face of Soviet actions and that the shift to the policy of containment was justified.

As has been noted, another element common to Gaddis and Leffler – and to post-revisionist writing more generally – is the subordination of economics to geopolitics. Leffler provides perhaps the most sophisticated example of how post-revisionists utilise theoretical elements drawn from the realist tradition to systematically invert the premiss underlying revisionist arguments. Whereas many revisionists regard capitalism as the fundamental dynamic underpinning state behaviour and geopolitics as a secondary manifestation of that dynamic (politics is determined by economics), post-revisionists reverse the order. Security and the balance of power are what drive states' actions; capitalism and economics figure to the extent that they are sources of power and tools used in the service of security (economics determined by politics).

Leffler pays much more attention to economic issues than does Gaddis. Indeed, they form a central part of his argument, according to which US policy-makers believed that the power and security of the USA would be threatened if its enemies could undermine its economy, attack it directly or develop superior military power. All three dangers would be averted, however, if the USA could integrate the key industrial regions and the primary producers of the Third World into a stable global capitalist order.[48] The clearest example of this policy in practice was the Marshall Plan. In his analysis of that policy Leffler seeks to demonstrate how the programme of aid to both Western Europe and the latter's colonies was designed to prevent economic nationalism in Western Europe and reintegrate the West European core economies with their Third World periphery. This, in turn, would maintain a liberal international economy that would sustain US preponderance in the global balance of power.[49]

Economic considerations thus play a central role in Leffler's version of the post-revisionist synthesis. He accepts the revisionist claim that the reconstruction of global capitalism was a primary goal of US foreign policy. Moreover, in his emphasis on the importance of the economic relationship between Western Europe and its colonies, he adopts a modified version of world systems theory and its stress on the economic importance of core–periphery relations.[50] Nevertheless, there remains a fundamental difference between Leffler's analysis and that of the revisionists and the world–systems theorists. According to Leffler, US economic interests were a 'not unimportant' but essentially 'secondary' consideration in the shaping of the Marshall Plan. The USA did not need the Marshall Plan economically; the USA needed the Marshall Plan because of 'vital security considerations'.[51] The Marshall Plan was about maintaining a favourable balance of power. Economic objectives were not an end in themselves, as in revisionism or world–systems theory, but merely a means to an end. The effect of this logic is to incorporate economics into the argument, but to strip it of any independent causal power. Economics, in post-revisionism, does not explain anything; it is a dependent variable to be explained by political calculations and considerations.

Leffler's attempt to incorporate economic factors into his argument reflects a final important common element in his and Gaddis's work, the goal of synthesis. How they go about achieving this goal, however, highlights significant, if subtle, differences in their respective theoretical frameworks. Gaddis, as has been discussed, came to use the systemic imperatives of neorealism as the framework within which other elements might be incorporated. Leffler has also been called a neorealist, and there is some validity in this, but his approach is nevertheless different from Gaddis's. He terms his model 'national security' and argues that it allows for a synthesis of all key explanatory factors by 'relating foreign threats to core values'.[52] The focus of this analysis is on how policy-makers react to external threats, a reaction that is shaped by the core values that they are seeking to protect and that emerge from within the state. Leffler argues that his approach therefore overcomes the division between approaches that root foreign-policy behaviour in domestic socio-economic factors (such as revisionism) and a post-revisionism like Gaddis's that places the explanatory factors outside the state in the international system. National security provides the basis for a synthesis because it incorporates both. The difference between Leffler and Gaddis in this regard is thus one of emphasis rather than substance. Both, in practice, include both systemic imperatives and internal causes in their explanations, but, whereas Gaddis places more emphasis on the former, Leffler does the reverse.

The most prominent disagreement between Leffler and Gaddis lies in their interpretation of Soviet behaviour. In contrast to Gaddis, who has shifted over the years from a position that approximated to that of the revisionists to something that is scarcely distinguishable from traditionalism, Leffler's position remains essentially revisionist. He does not accept Mastny's argument about Stalin's paranoia or the inability of the Soviet Union to halt its expansion unless confronted with force. He depicts Soviet behaviour as defensive, conservative and cautious, bent on seeking security but also on continued cooperation with the West. US fears of the USSR were thus exaggerated and often mistaken.[53]

Leffler also tends to avoid overt moral judgements of the kind apparent in Gaddis's recent works. Indeed, he is at pains to emphasise the amorality of US foreign policy. US policy-makers were 'anything but idealists'.[54] They were realists who cared little for the fates of those trapped inside the Soviet sphere. If they opposed Soviet control of other countries, it was not for the sake of democracy or human rights but because it affected the global balance of power and American national security. Equally, in the conduct of America's own foreign policy, principles like self-determination were pursued where they sustained American interests (Eastern Europe) and ignored where they did not (the colonies of America's West European allies).

Finally, Gaddis and Leffler disagree about who started the Cold War. For Gaddis, Stalin's insatiable search for security forced a USA that was searching for a modus vivendi with the USSR finally to adopt the policy of containment. For Leffler the USA was the dynamic actor. Powerful and confident, seeking to shape the world to its own ends, the USA encountered a potential threat to that plan in the shape of the USSR and acted to deal with it.[55]

We should not, however, make too much of these differences, and they should certainly not be allowed to obscure the common core of the post-revisionist argument – namely, the effort to create a multi-causal synthesis that transcends and incorporates previous arguments using a realist – neorealist framework. Gaddis may place more emphasis on systemic causes and Leffler may focus more on core values, but both seek a synthesis that incorporates both and see external/systemic threats as crucial to the explanation. In addition, both use the concept of national security as the unifying and primary element within their explanatory framework. This necessarily leads them to subordinate economic considerations and capitalism to an essentially secondary and minor explanatory role.

Their differences, in contrast, are relatively trivial, though they have generated a certain amount of polemic.[56] They are trivial above all because they do not relate to the fundamental issue of explaining American foreign policy. On that issue, as already indicated, they are in broad agreement. Rather, what these factors relate to is the evaluation of that policy. The later Gaddis finds little to criticise because he sees the Soviet threat as real and US actions as necessary for security. He also sees the actions of the USA as morally laudable, particularly when compared to its opponent's. Leffler is much more circumspect in his judgement because he doubts the extent of the Soviet threat and sees US actions as largely amoral. Ultimately, however, they agree even on the fundamental question involved here as well. Gaddis simply thinks US policy-makers got it right, Leffler thinks they exaggerated the danger but that such a response was understandable given the uncertainties they faced. Both agree that US actions were reasonable and justified under the circumstances.[57]

CRITIQUE

There can be no question that there is much in the post-revisionist argument that adds considerably to our understanding of US foreign policy and the Cold War. This wave of historians was the first to have extensive access to archival material and as such produced the first detailed reconstructions of the thought processes, arguments and decision making of the US policy-makers involved in the early Cold War. That access, in turn, produced new and important arguments, such as the claim that US policy, while active and guided by a vision of an appropriate world order, was less confident and coherent than the revisionists depicted. The post-revisionist depiction of policy-makers, seeking certain objectives but unsure of how to reach them, wanting both to avert Soviet domination and yet to maintain cooperation, driven by fear as well as by a sense of power, has a greater degree of plausibility than the naivety and innocence of traditionalist accounts or the relentless drive for global control portrayed by some revisionists.

Access to the archives also seemed to confirm to post-revisionists what their instinct and reasoning had already told them – namely, that US foreign policy could not be reduced to an expression of economic interests. Economics was part of the explanation, but no more than that. And Geir Lundestad's argument about the American 'Empire by invitation' was particularly important, not only because of its specific argument but because of the way it reframed the Cold War. Instead of simply perceiving events through a bipolar perspective, this approach acknowledged the importance and autonomy of smaller states and their impact on the course of events.[58]

Theoretically, the neorealist ideas employed in different fashions by Gaddis and Leffler make a crucial contribution. First, the emphasis on the explanatory relevance of the structure of the international system is hugely important. Whatever internal factors may or may not shape the choices of policy-makers, those choices are not made or implemented in an international vacuum. Foreign policies must be shaped by, and respond to, stimuli external to the state. The international system does indeed constitute the environment within which states exist and to which they have no choice but to respond.[59]

The elements of system structure that neorealism emphasises – anarchy and polarity – have elegant and plausible explanatory power. Multipolar and bipolar systems do indeed exhibit different characteristics and states do behave according to a self-help logic that decrees that ultimately, only their own actions can ensure their survival. Neorealist logic, to give an example, provides a compelling and parsimonious explanation of the division of Germany and one that is found, beneath the empirical elaboration, in both Leffler and Gaddis. That explanation says that, at the end of the Second World War, a bipolar world emerged. The only potential threat each superpower faced was the other. Between the two, in Western Europe, lay a source of potential military-industrial power sufficient to tip the balance in the direction of whichever of the two controlled it. At the core of Western Europe, and the key to it, was Germany. The Second World War had created a power vacuum in Germany into which both superpowers had entered and which both feared the other would seek to exploit. Since each superpower felt that a unified Germany under the domination of the other would fatally weaken their position in Europe, they ended up dividing it between them as the least dangerous option. Anarchy, polarity and power calculations combine to explain the actions of both powers in compelling fashion.

Despite these significant achievements, however, post-revisionism also contains major weaknesses, both empirical and theoretical. In the first place, while the post-revisionists have been most assiduous in their unearthing and utilisation of new archival material, not all the arguments they derive from this data stand up to scrutiny. Indeed, the argument, primarily, though not exclusively, found in early post-revisionism, that key aspects of US policy were explained by domestic political pressures is notable for the absence of data used to support it. Polling data may be cited to indicate public attitudes, and policy-makers' actions interpreted as responses to those attitudes, but the connection is rarely convincingly demonstrated.[60] Others, having examined the evidence, come to the conclusion that 'public opinion and the Congress proved malleable, compliant and permissive in the making of America's Cold War foreign policy',[61] and that it was the policy-making elite, not the public, that drove American anti-communism.[62]

A second evidence-related problem has to do with Gaddis's assertion that the new evidence coming from Soviet archives is demonstrating the truth of the traditionalist claim that Stalin was the cause of the Cold War. Initially Gaddis based this assertion on Mastny's *Russia's Road to the Cold War*, which he described as a 'comprehensive' account of Soviet foreign policy.[63] That claim was a wild exaggeration. The book was written in 1979 and as such had access to hardly more evidence from inside the Soviet Union than those writing in 1950. As a result, there are frequent evidential gaps in the text that Mastny is forced to fill with speculation. That speculation, without exception, takes the blackest possible interpretation of Soviet motives available. Today, Gaddis is able to support his claim by pointing to the increased number of documents that have become available with the collapse of the Soviet Union. The fact is, however, that other people reading the same new documents do not agree with his or Mastny's interpretation.[64] The new archival evidence is simply not decisive and as a result the Gaddis – Mastny interpretation of Soviet foreign policy remains at best one of several competing versions.

A brief discussion of the normative aspects of post-revisionism also needs to be included here. With the obvious exception of the later Gaddis, whom we will return to shortly, it has been common, as we have seen, for post-revisionists to make play of their efforts to avoid the 'value-laden' approaches of their predecessors and to seek only an 'understanding of what happened and why'.[65] In making that claim to impartiality, post-revisionists are engaged, wittingly or unwittingly, in their own act of containment. To contrast one's own approach of seeking 'understanding' with the 'value-laden' efforts of those who went before is, of course, to imply, quite unjustly, that those who went before did not in fact seek to understand events. It is a claim for the superiority of one's own scholarship and the inadequacy of that of others, but one based not on evidence or argument so much as on a highly contentious and arguably spurious distinction between methods.

Of course, to be quite open about the normative element in one's work is not therefore to shield it effectively from criticism on those grounds. Gaddis, in recent years, has engaged as much in a normative justification of US foreign policy as in an attempt to explain it. While he is entirely within his rights to do so, his argument invites at least two broad criticisms. First, he suggests that scholars should pay more attention to the nature of the two regimes in conflict in the Cold War. To the extent that he is saying that the Soviet Union had a more unpleasant regime than the USA, he is stating the obvious and is unlikely to find much disagreement. What he will find, however, is a lot of people saying 'so what?' What seems to be implicit in Gaddis's position is the claim that, because the Americans were the good guys, if they occasionally had to do bad things (oppose self-determination, support colonial regimes, violate their own principles), this was defensible on the basis of America's long-term good intentions. In addition, US actions are justified on the grounds that the actions of the Soviet Union were worse. This logic is weak. Moral judgements are made against universal standards or, at least, against the standards one sets oneself. To assert that, whatever the moral failings of the United States, they are somehow nullified, or even partially mitigated, by the wickedness of the Soviets, is sophistry. Whatever one thinks of his explanation of the origins of the Cold War, the insistence of William Appleman Williams that Americans should judge themselves against their own high moral standards and not against the actions or principles of others is infinitely to be preferred.[66]

The second problem is that Gaddis combines this normative defence of US foreign policy with the remnants of his neorealist framework. Despite his having apparently repudiated neorealism in the early 1990s, its influence is still evident in *We Now Know*, written in 1997. In the opening pages of that book he states that, 'when a power vacuum separates great powers . . . they are unlikely to fill it without bumping up against and bruising each other's interests'.[67] Gaddis is careful to insist, nevertheless, that the Cold War was not therefore inevitable, and that both the USA and USSR had choices. Such an insistence on a balance between structure and agency is perfectly reasonable, but what is problematic is the inconsistent fashion in which Gaddis uses it and the manner in which explanation and moral judgement are combined.

On occasions where the US committed actions that violated its proclaimed principles, Gaddis uses system structure and security imperatives as a moral escape clause. The USA was forced into these actions by the imperatives of the Soviet threat and is thus exculpated from responsibility.[68] This combination of neorealism and moralism is profoundly incoherent. At an explanatory level it produces the problem (for Gaddis) that if US actions can be thus explained then so too must those of the USSR. Systemic imperatives must apply equally to both powers, in which case the Cold War cannot simply be attributed to Stalin's malevolence or paranoia. At a normative level Gaddis's reasoning is also easily inverted. If the bad things the USA did were a response to systemic pressures, then the same must also be true, to some extent, of the good things (or are we expected to believe that all America's noble actions were voluntary and all the bad ones compelled?). In which case, what basis is there for a normative defence of US actions? One can hardly take credit for actions that are compelled by systemic pressures any more than one can be expected to take the blame for them. Ethical responsibility requires free will and agency; neorealism does not.

Finally, and most importantly, there is the matter of the neorealist – national-security framework employed by Gaddis and Leffler. The attractions of an explanation that invokes the structure of the international system – its simplicity and ability to provide compellingly plausible explanations – have already been noted, but it also has its weaknesses. First, the claim that system structure determines actions has an unavoidably metaphysical quality about it. The system in question is not a concrete reality; rather it is the alleged relationship between states, the only material parts of the system. To say that state behaviour is determined by the structure of the international system is thus to say that it is determined by something that cannot be shown to exist. The 'system' is merely hypothetical. That states behave in a manner consistent with the supposed imperatives of system structure implies the effects of that structure but it does not demonstrate cause and effect. The danger, therefore, is that neorealism possesses a logic that provides a plausible explanation of events but may bear no relationship to what actually happened.[69] This situation, in turn, exacerbates the danger that the historian will unconsciously tend to select the facts to fit the theory, rather than vice versa. This is not to say that system structure is not a useful hypothesis upon which to base an explanation, merely that historians should be careful not to assume what needs to be demonstrated.

The other great weakness of neorealism is that a theory that seeks to explain everything that happens in the international system as the result of that system's structure makes no sense. Above all, it cannot explain changes in the structure of the system itself. Over time we have had multipolar and bipolar systems and different distributions of power and dominance between states – the structure of the system has changed. But it makes no more sense to say that a change in the structure of the international system was caused by a change in the structure of the international system than it does to say that your car broke down because your car broke down. Just as your car (system) broke down because some element within it failed (changed), so any change in the structure of the international system must be explained by a change in some element within the system. Since the only other element of the system that can cause change is the states and factors within the states, it is therefore clear that they cannot be treated as merely responding to the structure of the international system but must be seen as having a degree of autonomy and being independent sources of change in the system.[70] For example, the emergence of a bipolar world might be explained in part as a result of the Second World War which itself might be explained in terms of anarchy and multipolarity, but it also requires that we take into account the internal political, social and economic processes that created two such powerful states in the first place.

Even Kenneth Waltz has been forced to concede that 'structures shape and shove. They do not determine behaviours and outcomes, not only because unit-level [states] and structural causes interact, but also because the shaping and shoving of structures may be successfully resisted'.[71] Gaddis and Leffler, happily, agree. As we have seen, Gaddis has come increasingly to stress the limits of systemic determination, and in his latest book on the Cold War explicitly asserts that, while system structure made conflict between the USA and USSR likely, the Cold War was not inevitable.[72] For Leffler, US foreign policy is a product of the interaction of external threats and internal core values. Neither, therefore, succumbs to the trap of crude systemic determinism. Instead they rightly insist that US foreign policy must be understood as the product of an interaction between systemic structures and factors internal to the American state.

The real weakness in both Gaddis's and Leffler's conceptual frameworks is that, while they recognise the significance of the domestic sphere to explaining US foreign policy in principle, they neglect to develop that insight in any systematic or thorough fashion. In *A Preponderance of Power*, for example, we certainly find reference to the 'core values' US policy-makers sought to defend – democracy, the free market, the American 'way of life' – but there is little or no discussion of those values, how they were produced, or how they came to dominate the world view of the US government. They are, in fact, treated essentially as givens about which no discussion is required. Nor is there any real evidence of debate about how they are to be protected. That task is deemed to require the establishment of a favourable balance of power, which objective then becomes the whole focus of the book. While ostensibly including the internal processes of the state in the explanatory framework, therefore, Leffler actually reduces those processes very quickly to the tactical calculations of executive branch policy-makers about how to respond to the external threat in order to create a favourable balance of power.[73]

What this reflects, and much the same could be said of Gaddis and most other post-revisionists, is that they think that the core values that states seek to defend – security, prosperity, their 'way of life' – are pretty obvious and universal. While claiming that it is important to acknowledge the internal processes that make up part of the explanatory framework, therefore, they actually reduce them to a consensual banality. To say that states act to protect core values is in practice little different from the realist claim that states act to preserve and expand their power and security. The logical effect of this is to return all explanatory power to the external threats to those values, since they are the only things that change.

This disregard for the significance of internal processes is also reflected in the way that they are treated by post-revisionists not as systematic sources and explanations of foreign policy but as ad hoc devices utilised when systemic imperatives fail to provide a satisfactory explanation.[74] The post-revisionist position on Eastern Europe is a good example. Neorealist logic says the USA should have accepted a Soviet sphere of influence in the region and not have provoked a conflict when it had no hope of affecting the outcome of events there. Domestic political pressures are thus invoked in order to explain away the otherwise incomprehensible behaviour of US policy-makers in demanding self-determination for the countries of the region. The implicit logic is that systemic causes are the primary ones, but occasionally domestic factors interfere with their effects.

This anaemic conception of the domestic sources of policy produces an implausible explanation of US foreign policy. What the post-revisionist approach to core values implies is that they are obvious and consensual and that it is a relatively simple task to agree upon how to respond to external threats to them. In practice, even the most cursory reflection indicates that this is not the case. Not everyone in the United States in the late 1940s responded to Soviet actions in the same way; not everyone supported the shift to containment, which came under attack both from the liberal left and the conservative right. The reason for this is that not all groups in American society perceived Soviet actions and their implications in the same way. They did not all share a common understanding of the core values at stake or how best to preserve them. To put it bluntly, people disagreed and disagree about the appropriate response to external threats. And, if that is the case, it is simply not possible to treat core values as some kind of universally shared and obvious given.[75] Recognition of that fact leads necessarily to the conclusion that the internal processes of the state require a much more extensive examination than the post-revisionists engage in. If what is to be defended and how is not, in fact, obvious and uncontested, then who controls the levers of policy and how they came to control those levers matter. The whole process by which core values come to be defined, how certain values become dominant while others are excluded, why some groups are heard and others are ignored, become questions of fundamental importance. Post-revisionism simply does not engage with these questions in any systematic fashion.

This point can be reinforced by consideration of the post-revisionist treatment of two themes central to revisionism – namely, ideology and economics. As he has shifted away from neorealism, Gaddis has attributed US actions increasingly to the influence of ideology. In his discussion of the 'new Cold War history' in *We Now Know* he asserts that one of the lessons historians need to learn is the need to 'take ideas seriously'.[76] Yet Gaddis's own treatment of ideology is superficial and seems designed largely to reinforce his normative claims about responsibility for the Cold War. US ideology is reduced to hostility to authoritarianism and a benevolent Wilsonian desire to spread democracy, freedom and capitalism.[77] The roots of these alleged ideologies and their relationship to US domestic politics, interests and groups remains largely unexamined. As with Leffler's core values, Gaddis's ideology is treated as a given. In Leffler's case ideology is depicted merely as a possible factor shaping core values.[78] In neither case is ideology truly treated as a systematic, deep-rooted factor shaping foreign policy.

The same is true of economics. Gaddis regards economic interests as largely insignificant and entirely secondary to political considerations. Leffler discusses economics extensively, but only as an end of US foreign policy and a source of national power. In neither case is economics or capitalism treated as a systemic or domestic structure or constraint within which policy-makers have to function on a daily basis and which determines US policy objectives in its own right. What is missing, in short, is a recognition that, just as the structure of the international system systematically shapes the environment of US policy-makers and the decisions they make, so do ideology and economics. The latter are simply not accorded the sustained analytical consideration afforded geopolitics by the post-revisionists.

In fact, neither Leffler nor Gaddis has developed any kind of systematic conceptualisation of the domestic sources of foreign policy whatsoever Gaddis, in retreating from what he now regards as the inflated claims of neorealism, has warned that this must not result in a 'mindless eclecticism' that simply lumps various explanatory factors together (as in early post-revisionism). Moreover, he asserts that there is no reason why a proper synthesis cannot contain multiple causal factors if political scientists, for example, can regularly incorporate multiple variables in their analyses.[79] As of this moment, however, this remains no more than a rhetorical commitment. In *We Now Know*, for example, there is no sense of Gaddis seeking to pursue such a systematic multi-causal analysis incorporating a systematic and theoretically informed discussion of ideological, social or economic factors.

In Leffler's case, his view of the domestic aspects of foreign policy is best encapsulated in his 1990 article on 'National security', in which he proposes an extensive conception of core values. These are to be identified by looking inside the state at the key actors, organisations and interests; they emerge from the internal processes of negotiation, trade-offs and competition and they encompass ideological and cultural as well as material elements. He acknowledges that there are many different theoretical approaches that one could use to identify those core interests. He thus proposes an extensive examination of the processes by which core values come into existence.[80]

However, while this approach appears to give much more appropriate weight to domestic sources of foreign policy, it does so at the price of becoming theoretically innocuous. Leffler says, for example, that the national-security approach could incorporate a Marxist analysis of the origins of American core values since all that it does is examine how policy-makers react to threats to those values, however they are determined. But in that case, it seems, Gabriel Kolko was conducting a national-security analysis of US foreign policy, he just did not realise it. Indeed the national-security' approach appears capable of incorporating any cause and any theory within its capacious bounds. 'Core values' just becomes a catch-all term for the ideology, beliefs or interests of policy-makers without providing any guidance as to how these are to be identified. It thus amounts, like Gaddis's multiple variables, to an exhortation to consider domestic factors without any substantive proposition about how that should actually be done.

Despite their professed efforts to take the domestic sources of foreign policy seriously, both Gaddis and Leffler retain an essentially realist conception of the state. In their analyses what has to be defended is a set of consensual values or interests that are shared by a society that is treated as a unified actor and taken as manifested in the individuals who man the ship of state. With those consensual values and interests remaining essentially unchanged over time, all the explanatory power reverts to the international system.

CONCLUSIONS

Post-revisionism, therefore, does not achieve Gaddis's goal of integrating the strongest elements of traditionalism and revisionism into a coherent synthesis. To the extent that it does achieve a synthesis, it does so only at the cost of systematically downplaying the significance of factors such as ideology and economics that are emphasised in revisionist accounts. The way economics, for example, is integrated into the post-revisionist analysis is by reducing it to a secondary factor, without independent causal power, which is significant only in terms of its contribution to power and security. They make economics a mere tool of politics. Such an approach may be theoretically coherent, but it achieves that end at the price of reducing the potential explanatory richness of capitalism as a system to nothing. Ideology is given similarly short shrift.

In fact, this treatment of domestic sources of foreign policy is an inevitable result of the post-revisionist preoccupation with geopolitics. Once you admit policy-makers have systematic ideologies, for example, you immediately undercut the significance of external factors in explaining policy. What becomes important is not the external stimulus *per se* but how it is interpreted through the ideology of the policy-maker. Leffler and Gaddis see the Soviet threat as a self-explanatory given that triggers a consensual response from US policy-makers. An analysis focused on the role of ideology would see ambiguous Soviet actions that produce a unified US response due to the ideological consensus binding US policy-makers.[81] They are thus not readily compatible approaches to understanding US foreign policy so much as they are alternative ways of understanding that policy.[82] Similarly, a national-security approach that privileges geopolitical calculations of power cannot readily incorporate an approach that stresses the explanatory role of the capitalist system, because it would simply amount to two alternative ways of explaining the same policies.

Nevertheless, this discussion should not lead us to neglect the vital contribution of post-revisionism to our understanding of US foreign policy in the Cold War. This is constituted, above all, by the insistence upon the importance of geopolitics and the structure of the international system as vital factors in any complete explanation of that policy. Revisionism focused, with justification, upon the domestic sources of US foreign policy, but it failed to recognise that that foreign policy was also influenced profoundly by stimuli that emanated from outside the state and from an international state system with particular characteristics and structures that in turn created patterns of constraints and incentives that materially shaped US foreign policy.

Whereas revisionists therefore see the end of the Cold War as fairly insignificant in terms of its implications for US foreign policy, post-revisionists are much more likely to see it as a development with profound implications. Gaddis, for example, asserted that the period 1989–91 was a 'turning point' in history comparable to the 'geopolitical earthquakes' of 1789–94, 1917–81 and 1945–7.[83] From the geopolitical standpoint that is post-revisionism's main theoretical contribution to our understanding of US foreign policy, the most profound consequence of that turning point is the transition from a bipolar to a unipolar world order. While neither Gaddis nor Leffler has written about this, the logic of the post-revisionist emphasis on system structure implies that it is the implications of unipolarity that would lie at the heart of a post-revisionist account of post-Cold War US foreign policy.

A post-revisionist account of the foreign policy of George W. Bush, for example, would start from the observation that the collapse of the Soviet Union removed the only significant global obstacle to the exercise of US military power. With Saddam Hussein's key ally eliminated, and no danger of military intervention leading to global nuclear conflagration, the USA was free to act in a way that simply was not possible during the bipolar Cold War confrontation. The structure of the international system, in short, had changed, with profound implications for the exercise of US power. This is an important, not to say vital, insight, but, as both Gaddis and Leffler acknowledge, it is insufficient on its own. Change in the structure of the international system made the invasion of Iraq possible, but does not explain in itself why that possibility was seized upon. That is where ideology, core values and other factors enter the equation and where the post-revisionists still need to do some work.

NOTES

1. Gaddis, 'On moral equivalency', p. 137.
2. Stephanson, 'The United States', pp. 35–6.
3. Kimball, 'Response to John Lewis Gaddis', 198. See also Bernstein, 'Cold War orthodoxy restated'; Cumings, ' "Revising postrevisionism" '.
4. The foremost representative of the former approach is John Lewis Gaddis, and of the latter, Melvyn P. Leffler.
5. Stephanson, 'Commentary: Ideology and neo-realist mirrors', p. 285.
6. Gaddis, *Russia, the Soviet Union and the United States*, p. 153.
7. Ibid. p. 177.
8. See, for example, Davis, *The Cold War Begins*; Paterson, *On Every Front*, Yergin, *Shattered Peace*. Also, in an early incarnation, Leffler, 'The American conception of national security'.
9. This is true of Gaddis in his later work: Gaddis, 'The emerging post-revisionist synthesis'; Gaddis, *The Long Peace*; Gaddis, *The United States and the End of the Cold War*; Gaddis, 'The tragedy of Cold War history'; Gaddis, *We Now Know*. See also Kuniholm, *The Origins of the Cold War in the Near East*, Mastny, *Russia's Road to the Cold War*.
10. This is basically the position of Leffler's *magnum opus*: Leffler, *A Preponderance of Power*.
11. This difference is clearest in the debate between the two in the *American Historical Review*: Leffler, 'The American conception of national security'; Kuniholm, 'Comment'; Leffler, 'Reply'.
12. The argument is most extensively developed in Lundestad, *The American Non-Policy*, but it is found in some variation in almost every post-revisionist account. See Mark, 'American policy towards Eastern Europe'; Gaddis, *The United States and the Origins of the Cold War*, pp. 133–73, 263–5; Gaddis, *We Now Know*, pp. 15–20; Leffler, 'The American conception of national security'; Mastny, *Russia's Road to the Cold War*.
13. Gaddis, 'The emerging post-revisionist synthesis', pp. 174–5.
14. Gaddis, *The Long Peace*, pp. 14, 42; Leffler, *A Preponderance of Power*, pp. 160–1.
15. Pollard, *Economic Security and the Origins of the Cold War*.
16. See also Gaddis, *The United States and the Origins of the Cold War*, pp. 18–22; Kuniholm, *The Origins of the Cold War in the Near East*, p. 428.
17. This is a pervasive phenomenon in post-revisionism, but it is particularly explicit in these examples: Gaddis, *We Now Know*, pp. 191–4; Jones and Woods, 'Origins of the Cold War in the Near East'; Kuniholm, *The Origins of the Cold War in the Near East*, pp. 274–301; Leffler, *A Preponderance of Power*, pp. 10–14.
18. Mastny, *Russia's Road to the Cold War*, p. xiii.
19. Jones and Woods, 'Origins of the Cold War in the Near East', 253.
20. Davis, *The Cold War Begins*, p. 7; Gaddis, 'New conceptual approaches', pp. 409–10; Kuniholm, 'The origins of the first Cold War', pp. 40–1; Leffler, 'New approaches, old interpretations', 178–9; Paterson, *On Every Front*, p. x.
21. Gaddis, *The United States and the Origins of the Cold War*, pp. 133–73; Kuniholm, 'The Origins of the first Cold War', pp. 49–52.
22. Seminal accounts include Allison, *Essence of Decision*; Allison and Halperin, 'Bureaucratic politics'; and Halperin, *Bureaucratic Politics and Foreign Policy*.
23. Gaddis, *The United States and the Origins of the Cold War*, pp. 96–104.
24. Davis, *The Cold War Begins*.

25. Gaddis, 'The emerging post-revisionist synthesis'.
26. Hogan, 'The search for synthesis'; McCormick, ' "Drift or mastery?" '; Stephanson, 'The United States', p. 37.
27. Paterson, *On Every Front*, p. 173.
28. Stephanson, 'The United States', p. 37.
29. Waltz, *Theory of International Politics*.
30. Gaddis, *The United States and the Origins of the Cold War*; Gaddis, *We Now Know*, pp. 1–25.
31. Gaddis, *The United States and the Origins of the Cold War*, p. 3.
32. Waltz, *Theory of International Politics*; there is a good brief summary and critique of the Waltzian argument in Hollis and Smith, *Explaining and Understanding International Relations*, chapter 5.
33. Gaddis, 'The emerging post-revisionist synthesis', p. 173.
34. Gaddis, 'New conceptual approaches', p. 419.
35. Gaddis, 'The emerging post-revisionist synthesis', p.181–2; Gaddis, *Russia, the Soviet Union and the United States*, pp. 227–62; Gaddis, *We Now Know*, pp. 152–7.
36. Probably the best short example of this new approach is the chapter entitled 'The insecurities of victory: The United States and the perception of the Soviet threat after World War Two', in Gaddis, *The Long Peace*, pp. 20–47.
37. Mastny, *Russia's Road to the Cold War*. The quote is at p. 4. See also Mastny, *The Cold War and Soviet Insecurity*.
38. Lundestad, 'Empire by invitation?'
39. Gaddis, *The United States and the Origins of the Cold War*, pp. 353–60.
40. Gaddis, *We Now Know*, p. 292.
41. Gaddis, 'History, science and the study of international relations'; Gaddis, 'International relations theory'.
42. Gaddis, 'International relations theory', p. 34.
43. Gaddis, 'History, science and the study of interantional relations', p. 45.
44. Gaddis, *We Now Know*, chapters 2 and 3, for example.
45. Gaddis, 'On moral equivalency'; Gaddis, 'The tragedy of Cold War history'.
46. Gaddis, *The United States and the End of the Cold War*, p. 61.
47. Leffler gives a very clear summary of his argument in the introduction: Leffler, *A Preponderance of Power*, pp. 3–23.
48. Ibid. pp. 7–12.
49. Ibid. pp. 160–5.
50. See Chapter 5.
51. Leffler, *A Preponderance of Power*, pp. 160–3.
52. Leffler, 'National security', 143.
53. Leffler, *A Preponderance of Power*, pp. 511–16; Leffler, 'Inside enemy archives'; Leffler, *The Specter of Communism*, pp. 34–43.
54. Leffler, *The Specter of Communism*, p. 49.
55. Leffler, *A Preponderance of Power*, pp. 495–8.
56. See e.g. the following exchange: Leffler, 'The American conception of National Security'; Gaddis, ' Comment'; Leffler, 'Reply'; also Leffler, 'Inside enemy archives'.
57. Stephanson, 'The United States', p. 47.
58. Lundestad can be seen as part of a larger school of 'European revisionists' who have emphasised the independent role of the West European states, especially the United Kingdom, in shaping the early Cold War. In the view of some of these historians, it was the UK, rather than the USA or USSR, that started the Cold War. While this is

an important insight into the origins of the Cold War, however, it is only peripheral to explaining US foreign policy. See Deighton, *The Impossible Peace*; Harbutt, *Iron Curtain*; Ovendale (ed.), *The Foreign Policy of the British Labour Governments*; Reynolds, 'The origins of the Cold War'; Reynolds, *The Origins of the Cold War in Europe*; Watt, 'Rethinking the Cold War'; Young, *France, the Cold War and the Western Alliance*. It is also only fair to point out that Kuniholm, *The Origins of the Cold War in the Near East*, performed a similar role to Lundestad's several years before him but with regard to Greece, Turkey and Iran.

59. Paterson, *On Every Front*, also deserves some credit for this insight.
60. Bernstein, 'Cold War orthodoxy restated', p. 458; Cumings, ' "Revising postrevisionism" ', p. 35; Gaddis, *The United States and the Origins of the Cold War*, is perhaps the most obvious example of this tendency.
61. Paterson, *On Every Front*, p. 137; see also Leffler, *Preponderance of Power*, pp. 14–15.
62. Quester, 'Origins of the Cold War'.
63. Gaddis, 'The emerging post-revisionist synthesis', p. 175.
64. See, in particular, Leffler, 'The Cold War: What do "We Now Know?'; also Buzzanco, 'Whatever happened to the New Left?', p. 584; Leffler, 'Inside enemy archives'; Roberts, 'Ideology, calculation and improvisation'.
65. Jones and Woods, 'Origins of the Cold War in the Near East', p. 253.
66. For further criticism of Gaddis's normative claims, see Cumings, ' "Revising postrevisionism" '.
67. Gaddis, *We Now Know*, p. 11.
68. Ibid. p. 157.
69. See, for a critique along these lines, Schraeder, 'Historical reality vs Neo-Realist theory'.
70. This point is made by Ruggie, 'Continuity and transformation in the world polity'. The neo-traditionalist John Lewis Gaddis of the 1990s makes the same point: Gaddis, 'International relations theory', p. 34.
71. Waltz, *Theory of International Politics*, pp. 343–4.
72. Gaddis, *We Now Know*, pp. 11–12.
73. See Fordham, *Building the Cold War Consensus*, pp. 13–21; Walker, 'Melvyn P. Leffler'.
74. Fordham, *Building the Cold War Consensus*, p. 16.
75. Ibid. pp. 72–4.
76. Gaddis, *We Now Know*, p. 283.
77. Gaddis, *Russia, the Soviet Union and the United States*, pp. 26–56; Gaddis, *We Now Know*, pp. 12–13.
78. Leffler, 'National security', pp. 144–5.
79. Gaddis, 'New conceptual approaches', pp. 409–10.
80. Leffler, 'National security', pp. 145–6.
81. Bernstein, 'Cold War orthodoxy restated', p. 460; Walker, 'Melvyn P. Leffler', pp. 669–71.
82. For a slightly different take on the absence of ideology in postrevisionism, see Stephanson, 'The United States', pp. 48–51.
83. Gaddis, 'The Cold War', p. 22.

FOUR

Corporatism

M ore than any of the other schools of thought discussed in this book, corporatism has the potential to confuse simply on account of its name. Students new to the study of US foreign policy might not have heard of traditionalism or post-revisionism, but the words corporatism or corporatist are likely to be at least vaguely familiar. This is hardly surprising when one considers the number of phenomena to which the term has been applied. 'Corporatism' has been a nineteenth-century social doctrine that proposed the organisation of industrial society around functional economic groups; a stage in the development of capitalism;[1] a political and social doctrine associated with fascist regimes in the 1930s; an alternative to pluralist theories and descriptions of modern industrial democracy[2] and, finally, a school of US diplomatic history.

Despite this apparent diversity, there are a number of themes and ideas that remain central to corporatism. First, in all its forms it is rooted in the evolution of capitalism as a mode of production. Secondly, the key actors at its core are always groups defined in terms of economic function, rather than individuals or classes. Thirdly, it is primarily concerned with questions of how harmonious relationships can be and are forged among those groups and political conflict thus avoided. Finally, and inextricably linked to the last point, it is always an attempt, or understood as an attempt, to find a 'third way' between the twin evils of unrestrained individualism (laissez-faire) and excessive statism (socialism).

From that description it should be no surprise to discover that corporatism as a perspective in diplomatic history shares with revisionism a focus on the domestic economic sources of foreign policy. Advocates of this perspective, however, have been keen to stress that it is not only different from, but also analytically superior to, revisionism. This is due, its proponents argue, to a more sophisticated conceptualisation of the domestic political-economy and an ability to synthesize a wider variety of factors into the explanatory framework. In agreeing with the revisionists on the fundamental primacy of the domestic political-economy, nevertheless, corporatists clearly reject the primacy accorded to geopolitics in post-revisionism. In fact corporatists see themselves as moving beyond both revisionism and post-revisionism while synthesising the best elements of both. Corporatism roots its explanation of US foreign policy in the evolution of the US political-economy while also seeking to incorporate external factors, such as the behaviour of the Soviet Union.

Despite some of the sweeping claims originally made for it, however, this perspective has produced a rather limited body of work, in terms of both quantity and scope. It appears now to have been abandoned by its original exponents in favour of alternative approaches. The reasons for this are to be found, in part, in problems inherent in the perspective itself. But it is also, to a significant extent, the result of a failure on the part of those who originally developed the approach to exploit its strengths to the full. The view offered here is that corporatism as a perspective remains underdeveloped and under-utilised, at least in part because those who advocated it failed to explore its full potential.

EXPLANATORY FRAMEWORK

The two scholars primarily responsible for the articulation of the 'corporatist synthesis' are Michael J. Hogan and Thomas J. McCormick. They drew up corporatist frameworks that are similar in most essentials and, in Hogan's case, sought to demonstrate the usefulness of such a framework through an extensive study of American efforts to recast the international economic order between 1920 and 1950.[3] Directly or indirectly, their work draws upon a wide and eclectic range of sources, but the starting point is the identification by a number of scholars of a discrepancy between the conventional wisdom about the development of the American political economy and the historical reality.

Standard accounts of American economic development stress its conformity to liberal economic theory. More than any other country in history, the United States, it is assumed, maintained the distinction between the private sphere of economic activity and the public sphere of political activity. In fact, critics of this interpretation argue, in the first half of the twentieth century the United States saw the steady erosion of this public–private distinction. In its place emerged increasing business-government cooperation and the development, bridging the private and public sectors, of an 'organisational sector'. In this sector the distinction between the public and the private became increasingly hard to identify. On the one hand, there was greater 'public' intervention in the 'private' sphere of the economy – regulation, macro-economic management and the beginnings of a welfare state. On the other, there was greater 'private' penetration of the 'public' sphere as business elites were incorporated into the policy-making process and delegated public authority to regulate themselves and their sectors of the economy.[4]

The source of this development was deemed to be the transition of the US economy from the era of 'laissez-faire,' when economic activity had been dominated by individuals and small businesses, to the era of 'corporate capitalism', when the giant business corporation became the dominant economic form.[5] This shift produced an increasing concentration of economic power and a consequent decline in the capacity of market forces alone effectively to regulate economic activity. There was therefore a growing disjuncture between economic reality and the dominant laissez-faire ideology. Political leaders such as Woodrow Wilson and Herbert Hoover recognised this problem but saw the new form of capitalism as inevitable and unavoid-able.[6] They therefore cast about for a means to reconcile the 'imperatives of an organized capitalism' with America's liberal ideology and institutions.[7]

They were assisted in this task by the emergence of a small but growing section of the corporate elite who were prepared to surrender a degree of economic freedom for the sake of their long-term interests. These 'corporate liberals' were ready to abandon laissez-faire economics for at least two reasons. In the first place, they had begun to see laissez-faire as wasteful. Corporate capitalism was a system that required management, planning and scientific organisation to make it work most efficiently. Repeated cycles of boom and bust were a hindrance to that task.[8] Secondly, they saw laissez-faire as dangerous. It produced economic and social dislocation through the bankruptcies, unemployment and poverty that resulted from economic slumps. That dislocation, in turn, produced widespread public unrest and resentment. Their greatest fear was that such resentment, expressed at the ballot box, might result in extensive governmental control of the economy in an effort to eliminate the negative consequences of the free market.[9]

Parts of both the political and the economic elites were therefore in agreement on the need to reform the management and operation of the US economy. The emergence of the corporate stage of capitalism had made the perpetuation of laissez-faire economics anachronistic and potentially socially explosive. Yet, while seeking to ameliorate those characteristics of corporate capitalism that generated resentment and demands for radical change amongst the masses, the corporate liberals wished to retain the essentially private character of the US economy and the dominant role of the big corporations. The resulting 'corporatist' polices represented an attempt to find a 'middle way' between the flaws of laissez-faire and the dangers of excessive state intervention.[10]

Corporatism was a 'political-economic system' characterised by 'certain organizational forms, by a certain ideology and by a certain trend in the development of public policy'.[11] The organisational forms in question return us to the blurring of the public–private boundary noted at the start of this section. The corporate liberals sought to ameliorate the political conflicts that resulted from the operation of the market but to do so through a form of regulation that kept the direct role of the state to a minimum. Organisationally, the solution they arrived at was to create a system of 'officially recognized economic or functional groups' (primarily business, agriculture and labour) that would, along with public officials, form an integrated mechanism for the management of the economy. Instead of the individualistic actions of laissez-faire, 'institutional, regulatory, coordinating and planning mechanisms [would] integrate these groups into an organic whole'.[12] Political conflicts over economic questions would be prevented by forging compromises between the key groups in the economic system and by regulating economic activity in ways supportive of those compromises.

In order to prevent the excessive statism feared by both economic and political elites, this process of integration and coordination was not to be achieved primarily through an expansion of state control. While there was, inevitably, a degree of such expansion, the principal emphasis was on the extension of the private sector into the realm of the state. More precisely, much of the new regulatory authority would be vested not in public agencies but in the representatives of the private sector. Trade associations, farmers' groups, unions and other organisations representing the various sectors of the economy would be delegated the authority of the state in order that they could, in effect, regulate themselves. A bargain was struck; in return for exercising a degree of self-restraint, the functional economic groups would be allowed to keep their own houses in order rather than have that order imposed by the heavy hand of the state. Thus was produced the blurring of the boundaries between public policy and private power identified above.[13]

Ideologically, these institutional arrangements were buttressed by a growing body of liberal thought that sought to legitimate the pursuit of a 'third way' between laissez-faire and statism. Central to the ideology, as with all economic ideologies, was the claim that the economy could be organised in such a way that the needs of all would be met and social harmony prevail as a consequence. Corporatist scholars have termed this aspect of the ideology 'productionism'. The ideology of productionism asserted that sustained economic growth would serve as a kind of 'magic bullet' for resolving class conflict. According to this analysis, class conflict was the result of insufficient aggregate material wealth producing redistributive struggles as the different groups within the economy sought to make gains at the expense of each other. Workers fought for higher wages at the expense of businessmen's profits and vice versa. If economic growth could be sustained, without the recurrent slumps in economic activity that stimulated such redistributive struggles, then it should be possible for all groups in the economy to make absolute material gains without the need to redistribute wealth between them (as would occur under excessive statism/socialism). Workers could have higher wages and businessmen could make higher profits at the same time.[14]

Productionism was thus a legitimating ideology for the policies of corporatism and a concrete objective of those policies. Which point brings us to the trends in public policy identified by Hogan as the third leg of the corporatist political-economic system. While the functional economic groups would manage the basic processes of production, the role of the state was to shape complementary public policies. If the objective of maintaining harmony through sustained economic growth and the forging of compromises between functional groups was to succeed, certain kinds of public policies had to be adopted. Specifically, the key to sustaining growth was to engage in counter-cyclical fiscal, monetary and other macroeconomic policies in order to avoid the pattern of boom and slump characteristic of a laissez-faire system. In addition, international economic policies that maintained access for American business to overseas opportunities for trade and investment would help to sustain growth. Finally, some recognition of trade-union rights, and the instigation of limited social welfare policies designed to cushion the impact of any economic downturn, would help secure the allegiance of the working class to the corporatist system.[15]

Corporatism, in sum, was a 'sort of . . . pro-capitalist reformism'.[16] In response to the evolution of a new stage of capitalist development and the perceived inefficiencies and dangers of laissez-faire economics, far-sighted political and economic elites sought to ameliorate the most politically and socially destructive aspects of the capitalist system in order to avoid more radical, statist solutions gaining popularity. Reform was pursued in order to avoid revolution. These reforms took the form of a 'corporatist' integration of economic groups into an 'organic' whole; the development of an ideology of productionism that legitimated the harmonious relationship of those groups; and public policies designed to provide the material wherewithal to sustain that harmony.

But what does any of this have to do with foreign policy and the Cold War? The answer to that question, according to Thomas McCormick, lies in the 'simple proposition that people do not think one way about their national society and a different way about the world society. Instead they tend to project and internationalize conceptual frameworks first articulated at home.'[17] Thus, according to this perspective, US policy-makers tended to draw analogies between the domestic and international arenas that influenced their policies in the latter. Specifically, they perceived that the primary sources of conflict in both domestic and international politics had their roots in economics. Economic nationalism, protectionism, state trading and autarky all had very similar effects to unmanaged laissez-faire at home, producing conflicts over the distribution of wealth. The solution, logically, was to create an international economic system that mirrored the US domestic corporatist compromise. The primary objective of US foreign policy thus became the shaping of a basically liberal international economic system with limited economic planning, international coordinating institutions, public–private cooperation and elements of welfare grafted on. Internationally, as at home, sustained economic growth was to be the cure for all ills. US foreign policy became, in effect, a kind of globalised corporatism.[18]

Michael J. Hogan

We can gain a better understanding of the corporatist perspective by examining the work of Michael Hogan in more detail. In a series of articles and an important book, he has sought to demonstrate how, between 1920 and 1950, US policy-makers attempted to refashion the international economic system along corporatist lines. The first step in his project was to demonstrate how the USA itself developed a corporatist political-economy. In that effort Hogan relied heavily on an important article by Thomas Ferguson.[19] Ferguson was not concerned with the phenomenon of corporatism as such; rather he sought to demonstrate how shifts in the US industrial infrastructure brought to power the New Deal coalition in the 1930s. The key to this development, he argued, was the fragmentation of US industry. Before the First World War, the Republican Party's dominance of the political system rested on the support of a unified American industrial and financial bloc. Largely labour-intensive and domestically oriented, this bloc was deeply hostile to organised labour and favoured policies of laissez-faire at home and protection from international competition.

After the war, however, a division emerged with the development of a 'multinational bloc' of industries and banks. Their interests diverged from the 'national bloc' along two lines. First, they were internationally competitive, and thus supported free trade rather than protectionism. Secondly, they were capital- rather than labour-intensive. The relatively low labour costs they incurred as a result inclined them to accommodate their workforces rather than confront them, as was the tendency of the labour-intensive national bloc. According to Ferguson, the Democratic Party was able to establish a political hegemony in the USA from the 1930s until the 1960s because it was able to forge a coalition between these capital-intensive, internationally competitive industries and banks and large sections of the working class. Though Ferguson himself does not use the term, Hogan sees that coalition as embodying the corporatist compromise. The New Deal coalition was composed of the 'corporate liberals' from the competitive capital sector, the industrial working class and sections of the agricultural community plus various other groups. It was based upon a deal in which the big corporations retained their dominance of the economy and a fundamentally liberal economic orientation, while counter-cyclical, 'Keynesian' macroeconomic policies were adopted and labour was afforded limited welfarism, 'productionism' and union rights.[20]

In its essence, Hogan's argument is that the transition to a corporatist political economy described by Ferguson was paralleled in America's approach to the international political economy. In place of the older version of US foreign policy from 1920 to 1950, which posited a series of shifts from international engagement to isolation and back to internationalism again, Hogan argues that there was an underlying continuity in US foreign policy based upon an attempt to reconfigure the international economy along corporatist lines.[21] He claims that US policy-makers in 1945 viewed the problems facing them and the answers to them in fundamentally the same light as their predecessors in 1918. Both world wars were perceived to have been produced by European policies of economic nationalism that had undermined growth, fostered German hegemony in Europe and led, ultimately, to war. The solution to the problem was to promote European economic integration, and thus simultaneously boost economic growth, undermine economic nationalism and reintegrate and contain German power within Europe.[22]

In the 1920s American policy-makers, led by Herbert Hoover – first as Secretary of Commerce and then as President – sought to reconfigure the European economy along proto-corporatist lines. While opposing what they regarded as excessive European state intervention in the economy and depending largely upon private capital to underwrite economic recovery,

> Republican policy-makers also promoted a business collectivism and self-regulation, devised transnational coordinators to supplement market forces, and then offered these strategies and their faith in technical expertise as the best way to resolve disputes, prevent excessive government intervention, and encourage a rational and productive integration.[23]

This first American effort to recast Europe failed, as history recalls. In part at least, Hogan argues, this was because the US government failed to commit itself sufficiently to the degree and kind of intervention in European affairs required. That failure, in turn, he explains in terms of the transitional nature of the US political economy at this point. The corporatist coalition of competitive capital and organised labour had not yet been forged. The 'corporate liberals' who favoured it were not yet dominant within the US capitalist elite, and the domestically oriented national bloc retained significant political power. As a result, while Hoover went beyond the nostrums of laissez-faire, he lacked the domestic political base to pursue a full-blown corporatist solution to Europe's (and the world's) economic and political problems.[24]

By 1945, however, the situation was quite different. The multinational bloc had firmly entrenched itself in power through its alliance with the Democratic Party and organised labour, and corporatism was the dominant political ideology within the United States. America, moreover, stood at the height of its global dominance. The wind was now set fair for the reconstruction of the international economic order upon corporatist lines. Globally, the primary goal was to entrench modified free trade and economic multilateralism and through them to generate the 'magic bullet' of economic growth. The restoration of international economic liberalism was to be coordinated and regulated by institutions, such as the IMF and the World Bank, and agreements like the GATT. Foreign aid and technical assistance would be provided to help others adopt the American way of doing things. Business and government would work hand in hand to spread the corporatist gospel.

Hogan's major work[25] is an attempt to provide a detailed study of this process through an analysis of its most famous example. The Marshall Plan was a vehicle for exporting corporatist policies and practices to Western Europe in order to forge economic integration and peaceful cooperation. Economic recovery was not to be left to the whim of the market. Instead, economic liberalism was tempered by extensive planning, regulation and aid. Throughout, the US public and private sectors worked hand in hand. The Marshall Plan was implemented by a newly established and independent agency, the Economic Cooperation Administration (ECA), headed not by a government official but by Paul G. Hoffman of the Studebaker Corporation. Its management was dominated by businessmen, as were its advisory committees, which also incorporated representatives of agriculture and organised labour. Representatives of the latter were dispatched to Western Europe to persuade their counterparts in the European labour movement of the benefits of 'productionism' and wean them away from dangerous Marxist doctrines. The Marshall Plan, in short, was an exercise in remaking Western Europe in America's corporatist image.

Hogan claims to provide a fresh perspective on the Marshall Plan and US foreign policy in the early Cold War by explaining it as the extension of a long-term project to reform the international system, rather than merely as a product of the immediate circumstances of the late 1940s and, in particular, of the actions of the USSR.[26] This, in turn, reflects a broader claim Hogan and McCormick make for the corporatist perspective – namely, its utility in analysing and explaining change over time. The great weakness of most diplomatic history (including post-revisionism) in this view is a bias towards isolated incidents and crises and a related failure to place them in the context of long-term change and evolution. The result is an alleged absence of systematic analysis, generalisation and theorising. By rooting its explanation in the development of the US political economy, in contrast, corporatism focuses on the broad structures and forces affecting policy-makers and their development over time.[27] At the same time corporatists believe that their perspective, while rooted in these long-term structural causes, is also capable of successfully integrating other factors into the explanation. Like the post-revisionists before them, they claim to have found the Holy Grail – the explanatory perspective that is able both to accommodate complex and multiple causes and the synthesise them into a single, coherent explanation. As the post-revisionists felt they had transcended traditionalism and revisionism while extracting the best of both, so the corporatists believe they have done the same with revisionism and post-revisionism.

CRITIQUE

The relevance of economic interests to foreign policy has already been discussed in the chapter on revisionism, but the point is worth repeating here. The maintenance of prosperity is a, if not the, central *raison d'être* of the modern state and essential to the continuance in power of democratically elected governments. Since foreign policy is an extension of domestic policy, inasmuch as it is directed towards the maintenance of the state's prosperity and survival, economic concerns will play a central role in the foreign policy of any state and especially that of a democratic one. The revisionists, of course, share this basic insight, but the corporatist perspective represents a distinct advance on revisionism because of its more sophisticated conceptualisation of the economic roots of foreign policy. Revisionism of the Kolko variety tended towards an economic reductionism that treated the capitalist elite as largely undifferentiated, and the state as a tool of that elite. Corporatism seeks to present a much more nuanced picture of both the capitalist class and its relationship to the state.

The first important distinction between corporatism and revisionism is the former's rejection of class divisions as the only important explanatory cleavages in the political-economy. Corporatism's central emphasis is on sectoral divisions that can cut across class lines. The inability of workers to move easily from one sector of the economy to another (factor immobility), for example, means that cross-class alliances are possible. Workers in uncompetitive domestic industries are likely to share with their employers an enthusiasm for measures to protect them from foreign competition, while those in internationally competitive sectors will support free-trade policies that will secure their jobs and boost their wages. Sectoral economic divisions are thus as important, if not more so, than class divisions. This insight is at the core of the corporatist argument, since the basis for the emergence of corporatism as a political-economic system is the ability of one section of the capitalist class to accommodate sufficient interests of the working class and other social groups to form an alliance, allowing them to dominate the political system at the expense of another sector of the capitalist class.[28] The corporatist perspective thus retains revisionism's emphasis on the importance of economic interests, but posits a more complex and flexible model of how those interests interact to shape foreign policy.

The other key difference between revisionism and corporatism is the latter's insistence upon the autonomy of the state. No doubt influenced by earlier critiques of revisionism, corporatists rejected the notion that the state could simply be reduced to a tool of the capitalist elite. While they would agree that business is the dominant partner in the relationship, the state is regarded as an autonomous actor with its own interests which pursues the creation of a corporatist political economy for its own reasons and not simply in response to the demands of capitalists.[29] Corporatist foreign policy, likewise, is understood as resulting from the interaction of the state, competitive capital and the other functional economic groups in the corporatist coalition. The result is a more complex conceptualisation of the relationship between the state and the capitalist class, which sees it as an interaction between two autonomous (if not necessarily equally powerful) groups, rather than the simplistic determination of the actions of one by the other.

Corporatism's innovations in turn enable it to evade the charge of economic determinism that can be levelled at some revisionist accounts. While corporatism as a historical phenomenon is clearly depicted as a product of changes within the capitalist mode of production, it is also a product of the choices of human agents in the form, primarily, of the state and certain business elites. It is the product of an interaction between structural economic change and the response to it of key groups in society who were able, eventually, to forge a democratic majority for their chosen course of action. There is no suggestion in corporatist accounts of the inevitability of corporatism. Moreover, by focusing on sectoral cleavages within the US political economy, corporatist analyses can avoid the kind of irrefutable functionalist accounts of US foreign policy that follow from a crude revisionist analysis. By identifying the different interests of various sectional groups, it is possible to construct more specific hypotheses about the kind of foreign policy that is in their interests. These are then testable by examining which sectoral interests are dominant within government, what foreign policies are being pursued, and which groups are opposing them. For example, corporatism can explain the cleavages over containment policy in the late 1940s between the Truman administration and its Republican-led critics in a way that revisionism (and post-revisionism with its differently derived unitary national interest) simply cannot.[30]

Foreign policy, however, does not have solely domestic sources. One of the post-revisionist objections to revisionism, of course, centred on the latter's failure to treat anything external to the state as a primary cause of US foreign policy. For their own account, the post-revisionists claimed that they had managed to emphasise the importance of external policy stimuli while also incorporating domestic factors into a multi-causal argument. The corporatists, however, believe that their account is an advance on both revisionism and post-revisionism. In the corporatist view, while the post-revisionists 'may duly note materialist [economic] factors, they then hide them away in an undifferentiated and unconnected shopping list of variables. The operative premise is that multiplicity, rather than articulation, is equivalent to sophistication.'[31] In other words, the post-revisionists do not really take the domestic causes of foreign policy seriously, and, to the extent that they acknowledge multiple sources of policy, they merely aggregate them instead of articulating their interconnections in a synthesis. This criticism, as we have seen, is a largely valid one, at least as regards early post-revisionism.

It is the claim that they have found the means to forge a genuine synthesis of internal political-economic and external geopolitical sources of foreign policy that is the capstone of the corporatist claim to explanatory superiority. Revisionists fail to address external sources of US foreign policy; post-revisionists fail to place the state and policy-makers within their domestic political-economic context. Corporatism, its proponents claim, recognises the importance of policy-making elites and external stimuli, but roots its explanation in the domestic context.[32] The phrase that best sums up the corporatist view of how these elements are to be integrated is this one: 'definitions of national security and national interests were not shaped in isolation from the nature of the society they were meant to defend.'[33] Policy-makers react to external stimuli, but how they do so is shaped by their relationship to and position within the domestic political-economy.

Despite this claim, in practice, the corporatist synthesis does not represent an advance on post-revisionism so much as an inversion of its inability adequately to reconcile the domestic/economic and the geopolitical. In the first place, what we find in Hogan's account of the Marshall Plan is a failure actually to discuss the geopolitical aspects of foreign policy in any significant detail or depth.[34] For much of his discussion, one could be forgiven for forgetting that there was a Cold War, so rarely does the Soviet Union play a significant role in the analysis. To the extent that national-security imperatives or geopolitics are mentioned, there is no sustained effort to relate them to the dynamic generated by the corporatist nature of US foreign policy. It clarifies little to claim that 'it was the strategy of integration [corporatism] as much as the strategy of containment [geopolitics] that shaped American policy'.[35] Similarly, the assertions that geopolitical designs were 'linked' to the nature of the US political economy and that strategic and economic goals were 'intertwined'[36] are very similar to the language used in some postrevisionist accounts to obscure the failure actually to explain how these interconnections functioned.

Geopolitics, in other words, is very much an afterthought in Hogan's corporatist analysis. Nor is this surprising, since behind the claim of the economic and the geopolitical being linked or intertwined is the reality that geopolitics actually plays little or no explanatory role in corporatist analyses. In concrete terms, the primary objective of US foreign policy after 1945, according to Hogan, was the creation of a corporatist international economic order, continuing an effort going back to the 1920s. The emergence of the 'Soviet threat' after 1945 lead to changes in the means by which that goal was pursued – most obviously a militarisation of foreign policy – but no change in the fundamental ends of policy.[37] Though he himself never says this, it is implicit in Hogan's argument that the USA would have sought to do what it did in the Marshall Plan regardless of the existence of any 'Soviet threat'. If US efforts to reshape the world and Europe in its corporatist image went back to the 1920s, and US policy after 1945 was a continuation of that effort, based on an analysis of global problems going back to 1918, then the emergence of a 'Soviet threat' after 1945 has very little to do with the basic direction of US foreign policy.

Protestations to the contrary aside, therefore, geopolitics plays little or no role in corporatist arguments. The source of foreign policy is rooted firmly in the US domestic political economy. US policy-makers from the 1920s to the 1940s were driven by a fundamentally economic view of the world. Just as the main threats to peace at home were clashes over the distribution of wealth, so they were in the international sphere. Boom and slump were the problems at home, and economic nationalism and autarky were the problems abroad. In both cases the solution was the corporatist compromise. While this certainly represents a coherent argument, it deprives the geopolitical elements of any significant explanatory role. The only function that the USSR plays in this analysis is as a potential threat to objectives that have already been determined by the corporatist economic world view. There is no place here for anarchy or the polarity of the international system as independent explanatory variables.

This point is perhaps most clearly demonstrated by Hogan's claim that the difference between the 1920s and the 1940s is that the dominance of the corporatist coalition in the 1940s ensured the pursuit of internationalism, while its relative weakness in the 1920s led to the lurch back into isolationism. This neglects the rather obvious geopolitical argument that the difference between the two is actually the existence of the Soviet threat in the 1940s. This is a synthesis of the political-economic and the geopolitical, therefore, which is an inversion of post-revisionism in its neorealist version. Where post-revisionism reduced economics to a mere tool of geopolitics, corporatism turns geopolitics into a handmaiden of goals determined by economics. Again, synthesis is achieved only at the expense of the trivialisation of the secondary factor.

Given this failure to treat geopolitics seriously, corporatism cannot be considered to have successfully bridged the economics–politics/internal–external divides that separate the perspectives we have discussed so far. Nevertheless, its relatively sophisticated conception of the domestic political-economic context, as compared to revisionism and post-revisionism, can still be argued to represent a significant step in the right direction. In that regard the two key elements of the corporatist argument are its emphasis upon the importance of sectoral divisions in the economy and its conception of an autonomous state interacting with capitalist elites and other groups to make policy.

While they have asserted the importance of these innovations in principle, however, corporatist scholars have generally failed to demonstrate them effectively in practice. We can see this if we start by looking at the question of the autonomy of the state, an issue that, as we saw in the chapter on revisionism, is crucial to any sophisticated explanation of US foreign policy that seeks to link it to the interests of US capitalism. A state with its own interests and objectives is alleged to be a key element distinguishing corporatism from crude revisionism. Rather than the depiction of policy-makers as mere puppets of the capitalist elite, corporatism is supposed to provide a more sophisticated understanding of the interplay between these two groups. The corporatist political-economic system is to be understood as a compromise between the various groups involved – the state, competitive capital, sections of the working class and agricultural sectors – 'in which each party obtains something it needs but also gives up something it would rather have in exchange'.[38]

Fully to explain that compromise, it is necessary to have some conception of the interests of each group that is a party to the bargain in order to understand what they are surrendering and what they are gaining. We do have a clear idea of those interests in the case of functional economic groups, because they are rooted in their position in the economy. The corporate liberals in the competitive capital sector gave up some degree of economic freedom and accepted a degree of regulation and state intervention in return for securing the long-term future of a basically free-market US economy under their control. Organised labour gave up its interest in greater control of the economy and extensive regulation and welfarism in return for limited degrees of the latter and the promise of steadily increasing wages.

The state, however, is not a functional economic group, and its interests cannot, therefore, be identified in a like fashion. They have to be derived in some other way. At the most general level, we can assume that the state seeks its own survival. More concretely, at the level of the political-economy, the state's interest lies in the maintenance of general prosperity and stability across society. Rather than a particular economic interest, as in the case of the other groups involved, the state's interest is the economic welfare of society as a whole. The problem for the state in relation to the political-economy is that its interest in the general, long-term prosperity of society as a whole may conflict with the short-term interests of particular economic groups within that society. That, in turn, leads to the question of why the state enters into corporatist arrangements. It must be the case that it is gaining something that it otherwise would not have; so what is that? Presumably what it gains is a greater degree of control over the key functional economic groups than would otherwise be the case. Corporatist arrangements offer those groups long-term material rewards in return for surrendering those short-term interests that clash with the state's conception of the general welfare.[39]

What we ought to find in a corporatist explanation of US foreign policy, therefore, is not merely public–private cooperation, a productionist ideology and particular macroeconomic policies. We should also find clear evidence of an autonomous state establishing a degree of control over producer groups that it would not otherwise have, and those groups in turn sacrificing certain interests in return for the support of the state. In practice, however, we do not find this. While there is certainly a great deal of discussion of the state in corporatist accounts, there is also a general tendency to fail adequately to explore the state–capital relationship and to demonstrate any significant degree of state control over big business.[40]

This point can be emphasised by a concrete example – namely, David Painter's work on the relationship between the US government and the oil industry. Painter claims that his study demonstrates the existence of a 'public–private partnership in oil' in which the American government 'chose to utilize private oil corporations to protect and promote the national interest in foreign sources of oil'.[11] The book argues that, as the US government came to recognise America's increasing dependence upon foreign sources of oil, it acted to create a stable and secure international environment in order that the major US oil companies could procure that oil. 'The interests of the major oil companies . . . coincided with the national interest' and they were therefore used as a tool of US foreign policy.[42] What gives this account its corporatist flavour is the emphasis upon the 'national interest', the idea of the state 'utilizing' the oil companies, and the concept of a 'partnership' between the two.

But Painter does not convincingly demonstrate the validity of his claims. He makes no attempt to outline any theory of the state or its interests, though, since his subject is oil, it is not too difficult to identify these things. The US economy needs oil to function, therefore the state has an interest in securing sufficient oil. Without oil, economy, society and state collapse. More importantly, however, Painter fails to demonstrate that the state 'utilized' the oil firms to secure that interest. Indeed, in Painter's account, the ability of the US government to influence the behaviour of the major US oil firms is conspicuous by its absence. In contrast, what is striking is the way that, at each point at which Painter identifies the government or part of the government as coming into conflict with big oil, it is the former that ends up backing down.[43] Even at times of national crisis like the Second World War and the early Cold War, the American state was apparently unable to impose its interests against the wishes of the major oil firms. It is, in consequence, difficult to see how Painter can really talk about the 'utilization' of big oil by the US government.

The problem is that, as the oil companies were at no point compelled to do anything other than that which they wanted to do, and since the policies of the US government consistently aided them in that project, there is nothing in Painter's account that is incompatible with an old-fashioned revisionist explanation that sees US foreign policy as determined by the interests of the capitalist class. He may show that policy-makers at times wished to go about things in a different manner from the big oil firms, but in each and every case they ended up doing what big oil wanted. For Painter to validate corporatism as an explanation, it is not sufficient simply to show that there was close cooperation between government and business, that they occasionally disagreed about things, and that the 'interests' of both state and oil companies were served by the policies followed. It must be shown how the state's interest was generated separately from that of the capitalist elite; that the state was in fact able to some degree to control the activities of big business; and that the latter were forced to make sacrifices to secure the support of the state. That would constitute a corporatist explanation of US foreign policy.

Painter's failure to demonstrate how the US state was able to use the big oil firms exposes a potentially fatal weakness in the corporatist perspective – namely, the possibility that the USA simply never was corporatist. By the calculations of most scholars who have examined the question, the United States is the least corporatist of all the industrialised democracies.[44] The primary reason for this, and one of the most obvious characteristics of the USA as a society, is the relative weakness of the state. The United States is 'a polity in which virtually all scholars agree that there is less structural basis for such [state] autonomy than in any other modern, liberal capitalist regime'.[45] The USA inherited no institutionalised bureaucratic structure from pre-democratic days; it has no elite, high-status civil service; no authoritative planning agencies or public ownership of important sectors of the economy; and political authority is deeply fragmented by federalism and the separation of powers.[46] As Anders Stephanson has suggested, the United States has historically been characterised not by the intervention of the state into society but by the penetration of the state by the dominant sectors of that society.[47] For example, if we follow Painter and look at oil, during the Second World War the oil industry sponsored a Petroleum Administration for War. This resulted in 3,000 industry executives staffing that and other parts of the bureaucracy, and massive profit making. After the war the oil and gas divisions of the Department of the Interior were virtually run by the National Petroleum Council and oil industry executives.[48]

The corporatists might argue that that interpenetration of the public and private sectors is precisely their point. They might also argue, as McCormick does, that he and other corporatists are not trying to demonstrate the relevance of a strict 'neo-corporatist' model so much as they are adapting elements of that model and other ideas to create a 'specific subtype of societal corporatism' that attributes greater power to capital than other varieties.[49] Nevertheless, it remains the case that, if corporatist scholars are unable convincingly to demonstrate that the state is able to assert its interests and control or ignore big business to a significant degree, then a fundamental aspect of what is required for corporatism to be an alternative perspective to revisionism is missing. Unless the authority and power of the state can be demonstrated, 'why call it corporatism? Why not simply call it monopoly capitalism?'[50]

It must be recalled at this point, nevertheless, that, as was discussed in the chapter on revisionism, simple socio-economic determination of state actions is theoretically and empirically unsustainable. Even if the USA is rightly seen as possessing a particularly weak state in relation to societal interests, it does not follow that the state is entirely without autonomy.[51] If the corporatists have failed to demonstrate that autonomy, therefore, it is not because it does not exist but because they have failed to find it. And one possible reason they may have failed to find it is that they have not been looking in the right place. Here, the twin failings of corporatism with regard to the state and geopolitics intersect, because the autonomy of a state does not depend solely upon its relationship to its own society. The state acts in two dimensions, the domestic and the international, and the state may be empowered in relation to domestic interests by inputs from the international system. In the case of the Cold War, for example, the perception of a grave Soviet threat can be argued to have greatly enhanced the power and autonomy of the office of the President and the various organs of the national-security bureaucracy vis-à-vis domestic societal interests.[52] Instead of the state being a neutral balancer between domestic socio-economic coalitions, it might be demonstrated that its representatives utilised pressures from the international system to manipulate and influence those coalitions. By taking geopolitics more seriously, therefore, corporatists may also be able to conceptualise the autonomy of the state more effectively.

Even if the corporatists have not yet been able convincingly to demonstrate the autonomy of the US state from the US corporate elite, their emphasis on sectoral economic divisions as an explanatory factor still distinguishes them from the revisionists. However, we do not have much in the way of evidence as to the utility of this approach, because corporatist scholars have largely failed to implement it in practice. In fact, the work of Hogan and Painter is characterised by a notable absence of explanation and a tendency to description.[53] This weakness is found initially in the articles in which corporatist scholars defined their perspective. If one examines the three characteristics of corporatism as defined by Hogan − public–private partnership, the ideology of productionism and specific kinds of public policy − what one finds is corporatism defined primarily as a set of material and ideological circumstances rather than as an explanation of why they came about. The causes of corporatism are largely left to footnotes that credit the single article by Thomas Ferguson. Thomas McCormick pays more attention to the roots of corporatism in state–capital relations, but he has failed to elaborate on them in any substantive work.[54]

This tendency towards description at the expense of explanation carries over into the substantive work. The vast majority of Hogan's book on the Marshall Plan, for example, is concerned with the detail of its implementation; with demonstrating that the policies and practices adopted conformed to his tripartite model of corporatism, and with how things were done. The why question is dealt with in the introduction; corporatist foreign policy follows from corporatist domestic policy, which follows from changes in the economic infrastructure analysed by Thomas Ferguson. David Painter spends even less time discussing the causes of corporatism in his eagerness to demonstrate the reality of a public–private partnership in foreign oil policy.

In a sense, the weaknesses of this perspective, as employed by Hogan and Painter, are encapsulated in the choice of the word 'corporatism' to describe it. Corporatism is a specific set of institutional arrangements, ideologies and public policies. It describes a singular historical phenomenon rather than a method for explaining that phenomenon. It is an effect, not a cause. What Hogan and Painter do is to elaborate in detail upon the implementation of these elements rather than focus upon the explanation for their emergence. The underlying shifts in the economic infrastructure of the United States and the responses of policy-makers to them are where the explanatory elements lie, but this aspect of the perspective is underdeveloped. Hogan's work on this aspect relies largely on others, and Painter does not deal with it at all. For all the emphasis on the importance of the interconnections between the state and functional economic groups, these are not actually systematically explored.[55] What is done by Hogan and Painter is fine as far as it goes, but it does not go far enough. Certainly, it does little to indicate what the potential of this perspective might be, since it renders it into a static description of a particular foreign policy at a particular time. This is especially ironic given the corporatists' emphasis upon the ability of their perspective to explain change over time. It may indeed have that potential, but only if the emphasis is shifted from 'corporatism' – which is simply one possible result of shifts in industrial structure and the interaction of sectoral economic interests and the state – to an emphasis upon those changes and interests themselves.

CONCLUSIONS

To a significant extent, the failings of corporatism as a perspective lay not so much in fundamental flaws in its explanatory framework as in the failure of self-proclaimed corporatists actually to apply them. In the work of Hogan and Painter, what we find is a description of the implementation of some rather specific aspects of US foreign economic policy, rather than a thorough and sweeping explanation of the roots of US foreign policy per se. If one treats corporatism not as a specific US foreign policy, however, but as an explanatory framework emphasising the relationship between sectoral economic divisions, the state and foreign policy, one has a broad approach with extensive potential applications that unquestionably represents a significant advance on revisionist accounts that treat the US capitalist class in an undifferentiated fashion. Corporatism, in a sense, is a perspective that is still waiting to happen.

By way of elaborating this point, we might consider how a 'corporatist' would approach the problem of explaining US foreign policy since the end of the Cold War. If one takes corporatism as a given, as in the work of Hogan and Painter, then it has nothing to tell us. Time has moved on, the corporatist compromise is dead and US foreign policy is not an expression of it. If, however, we were to focus on the underlying framework of transitions and divisions in the US political-economy, then a more encouraging picture emerges. A corporatist analysis of contemporary US foreign policy, I suggest, would start from an analysis of the collapse of the New Deal coalition and the corporatist compromise in the 1970s. It would focus on the way that a series of long- and short-term economic pressures undermined the alliance of inter-

nationally oriented capital and organised labour and resulted in the dominance of a new bloc that combined elements of both the old national capital
and internationally oriented capital. It would then go on to examine how this
transition underpinned a general shift to the right in US politics and
Republican dominance of the presidency from 1980 to the present day.
Finally, it would explore how those underlying changes influenced the shape
of US foreign policy.[56]

What is missing from that analysis, of course, is geopolitics, and those who
regard geopolitics as fundamental to any explanation of US foreign policy are
bound to find corporatism as it stands an unsatisfactory framework for further
exploration. For them corporatism might provide a plausible description of
US foreign economic policy and even an explanation of the specific nature of
that foreign economic policy. They would, however, regard it as wholly
inadequate for addressing the larger nature of US Cold War foreign policy,
since to them it would merely demonstrate how certain aspects of foreign
policy were pursued while missing the fundamental explanation of why they
were pursued.[57] For the post-revisionists, the Marshall Plan was ultimately
about power and security. It was an economic means to a geopolitical end that
was determined primarily by the Soviet threat to the national interest. That it
sought to put in place a particular form of political–economic cooperation is
for them an essentially trivial fact. For the corporatists, the Marshall Plan was
driven by an economic vision of the world and rooted in a domestic political–
economic compromise. For them, the Soviet threat is essentially secondary to
the basic explanation.

The problem is that both explanations are adequate on their own terms.
Each of them, in the abstract, provides a plausible explanation of the foreign
policy it seeks to account for. But we have also seen that an over-reliance on
geopolitics to explain US foreign policy is deeply flawed, particularly because
it is wholly unable to account for the existence of domestic divisions and
conflicts over the appropriate response to external stimuli/threats. Corporatism, in contrast, because it roots its explanation in such divisions, sheds light
on aspects of US foreign policy that geopolitical approaches ignore, yet, in
neglecting geopolitics and failing to operationalise the autonomy of the state,
it does not advance as far beyond revisionism and towards synthesis as was
hoped. What is required, therefore, is an explanatory framework that gives
due weight to factors from both domestic society and the international system
while allowing the state some degree of autonomy, even as it also acts as the
arena in which these various factors combine. The pursuit of such a complex
and multicausal perspective, however, heightens the risk of lurching into
atheoretical eclecticism, and the difficulty of pursuing a useful synthesis, is
readily apparent. This problem will be addressed again in the next chapter
and in the Conclusion.

NOTES

1. Sklar, *The United States as a Developing Country*; Williams, *Contours*.
2. This version is sometimes known as 'neo-corporatism' in an attempt to distinguish it from earlier versions and to escape the taint of the term's association with fascism. Schmitter, 'Still the century of corporatism', is the seminal article; see also Cawson, *Corporatism and Political Theory*; Williamson, *Corporatism in Perspective*.
3. Hogan, *Informal Entente*; Hogan, 'The search for a creative peace'; McCormick, ' "Drift or mastery?" ' McCormick, 'Corporatism: A reply to Rossi'; Hogan, 'Revival and reform'; Hogan, 'American Marshall planners'; Hogan, 'Corporatism: A positive appraisal'; Hogan, *The Marshall Plan*; Hogan, 'Corporatism'.
4. Hawley, 'The discovery and study of a "corporate liberalism" '.
5. Sklar, *The United States as a Developing Country*; Williams, *Contours*, pp. 343–78.
6. Sklar, *The United States as a Developing Country*, pp. 106–17.
7. Hogan, 'Corporatism: A positive appraisal', p. 363.
8. Williams, *Contours*, pp. 350–1.
9. Ibid, pp. 350–6; Wolfe, *The Limits of Legitimacy*, pp. 108–18.
10. Hogan, *The Marshall Plan*, pp. 4–5.
11. Hogan, 'Corporatism: A positive appraisal', p. 363.
12. Ibid.
13. Hogan, *The Marshall Plan*, p. 4. For this aspect of their perspective the corporatists draw on the non-American 'neo-corporatist' literature that emerged in the 1970s, which emphasised this integration of functional groups into the policy-making process. See Cawson, *Corporatism and Political Theory*, and Williamson, *Corporatism in Perspective*.
14. Maier, 'The politics of productivity'.
15. Hogan, 'Corporatism: A positive appraisal', pp. 364–5; Hogan, *The Marshall Plan*, pp. 17–18.
16. McCormick, ' "Drift or mastery?" ', p. 324.
17. Ibid. p. 326.
18. Ibid. pp. 326–7; Hogan, 'Corporatism: A positive appraisal', pp. 366–7.
19. Hogan, *The Marshall Plan*, pp. 13–14.
20. Ferguson, 'From normalcy to New Deal'; see also McQuaid, 'Corporate liberalism'.
21. Hogan, 'Revival and reform', p. 288.
22. Ibid. p. 289.
23. Ibid. p. 297. Hogan's thinking on the proto-corporatism or 'associationalism' of the 1920s draws upon an extensive range of literature, including: Hawley, 'Herbert Hoover'; Hawley, 'Herbert Hoover and American corporatism'; Hawley (ed.), *Herbert Hoover as Secretary of Commerce*; Leffler, *The Elusive Quest*; Maier, *Recasting Bourgeois Europe*; Maier, 'The two postwar eras'; J. H. Wilson, *American Business and Foreign Policy* J.H. Wilson, *Herbert Hoover: Forgotten Progressive*.
24. Hogan, 'Revival and reform', pp. 298–9.
25. Hogan, *The Marshall Plan*.
26. Ibid. pp. 18–19; Hogan, 'Revival and reform'.
27. McCormick, ' "Drift or mastery?" ' pp. 319–20; Hogan, 'Corporatism: A positive appraisal', p. 367.
28. Hogan, 'Corporatism', p. 227.
29. McCormick, 'Corporatism: A reply to Rossi', p. 57.
30. Hogan, 'Corporatism: A positive appraisal', p. 371.

31. McCormick, ' "Drift or mastery?" ' pp. 318–9; see also Hogan, 'Corporatism', p. 226.
32. Hogan, 'Corporatism', p. 226; Hogan, 'Corporatism: A positive appraisal', pp. 370–1; McCormick, ' "Drift or mastery?" '
33. Painter, *Private Power and Public Policy*, p. 209. Hogan identifies this as a key insight: Hogan, 'The search for synthesis', p. 496.
34. Gaddis, 'The corporatist synthesis', p. 360–1.
35. Hogan, *The Marshall Plan*, p. 33.
36. Hogan, 'The search for synthesis', p. 497.
37. This logic is most obvious in Hogan, 'Revival and reform'.
38. Wolfe, *The Limits of Legitimacy*, p. 154.
39. Williamson, *Corporatism in Perspective*, pp. 134–9.
40. Rossi, ' "A silent partnership?" '
41. Painter, *Private Power and Public Policy*, p. 1.
42. Ibid. p. 208.
43. Ibid. pp. 32–47, 52–9, 99–100, 136–52, 156–7.
44. Salisbury, 'Why no corporatism in America?'; Williamson, *Corporatism in Perspective*, p. 150; G. Wilson, 'Why is there no corporatism in the United States?'; Wolfe, *The Limits of Legitimacy*, pp. 128–9.
45. Skocpol, 'Bringing the state back in', p. 12.
46. Ibid.
47. Stephanson, 'The United States', p. 43.
48. Wolfe, *The Limits of Legitimacy*, p. 131.
49. McCormick, 'Corporatism· A reply to Rossi', p. 54.
50. This was the question McCormick was asked by a group of Japanese students: McCormick, 'Corporatism: A reply to Rossi', p. 54.
51. Skocpol, 'Bringing the state back in', pp. 12–13.
52. Halliday, *Rethinking International Relations*, pp. 84–7.
53. Stephanson, 'The United States', p. 43.
54. McCormick, ' "Drift or mastery?" '; McCormick, 'Corporatism: A reply to Rossi'.
55. Rossi, ' "A silent partnership?" ' pp. 46–7.
56. See, for an indication of what this might look like, Ferguson, *Golden Rule*
57. Stephanson, 'The United States', p. 43.

FIVE

World-systems Theory

W orld-systems theory represents the latest stage in the evolution of that strand of analysis, starting with revisionism (Kolko version) and passing through corporatism, that roots its explanation of US foreign policy in socio-economic factors. It is also influenced, however, by the post-revisionist critique of revisionism and corporatism and their failure to place US foreign policy within the context of the global system. Nevertheless, whereas the post-revisionists define the global system primarily in geopolitical terms of anarchy and the distribution of power, world-systems theorists characterise it in terms of the market and the distribution of wealth. What world-systems theory provides, in short, is an analysis of US foreign policy that explains that policy primarily in terms of the effects of global capitalism as a structured system and the position of the USA within that system.

In a similar fashion to post-revisionism, there is a core of common concepts and ideas to world-systems theory, but there are also two quite distinct versions of it. The first of these, drawing heavily on the ideas of Immanuel Wallerstein, has been articulated by Thomas McCormick. Abandoning his earlier flirtation with corporatism, McCormick has taken his pursuit of the social and economic bases of US foreign policy in a quite different direction. If corporatism was an essentially 'bottom-up' approach to understanding US foreign policy, then McCormick's take on world-systems theory is very definitely a 'top-down' analysis. Abandoning his concern with social and economic change inside the USA, he has shifted to a form of analysis that focuses on the structures and workings of capitalism at the broadest possible level – the global economy. In that sense McCormick's approach contains certain parallels with Gaddis's neorealist-influenced version of post-revisionism, with the structure of global capitalism replacing that of the anarchic state system as the locus of explanation. It also possesses similar weaknesses of implicit determinism and reductionism.

Bruce Cumings's version of world-systems theory does not abandon the insights of corporatism. It seeks rather to integrate them into an analytical framework that also incorporates a systemic level of explanation in the form of the global capitalist system. Whereas McCormick chooses 'top-down' over 'bottom-up', Cumings attempts to hang on to both ends of the rope at the same time. This produces a much richer and more complex explanatory framework than McCormick's but one that also poses some fundamental questions about the limits of theory when applied to historical explanation.

THOMAS J. McCORMICK

In *America's Half Century*[1] McCormick presents us with a sweeping overview of American foreign policy in the second half of the twentieth century. His analysis is based on a modified version of Wallersteinian world-systems theory. While a fuller account will be given below, a brief summary of the basic elements of Wallerstein's framework is necessary if the reader is to appreciate McCormick's argument. The core of Wallerstein's theory is that capitalism is a global system into which virtually all states are integrated. That system is characterised by a global division of labour between core (industrialised), peripheral (underdeveloped) and semi-peripheral (semi-industrialised) areas. The key to understanding the global role of any country is to locate its position within this system. In the case of US foreign policy after 1945, argues McCormick, the key is to recognise that the position of the USA in the system was that of dominant core state or hegemon.

Hegemons are important, according to McCormick, because the modern world system contains a contradiction. The economic dimension of the system is truly global, and its successful functioning requires the free flow of goods and capital. The political dimension of the system, however, is organised around the nation state. Nation states pursue their own prosperity, security and interests rather than those of the system, and in so doing they often pursue economic policies such as mercantilism and protectionism that obstruct the free flow of goods and capital. The resulting contradiction between the interests of the global capitalist system and the nation state can be softened, however, by the existence of a hegemon, which is an economically dominant core power sufficiently strong to exert its will on the other states within the system. It uses that power to ensure the free flow of goods and capital and to undermine economic nationalism.[2]

McCormick's historical narrative begins by describing the effects of the decline of British hegemony in the first half of the twentieth century. Without a hegemon to maintain the liberal capitalist system, that period was characterised by conflict as a number of then semi-peripheral powers – the USA, Japan, Germany and Russia – bid for core status and hegemony. In their efforts to advance their own national power at the expense of their rivals, these states pursued mercantilist/protectionist economic policies. Politically, the rivalry manifested itself first in imperialist competition for control of the periphery, and ultimately in the German bid for hegemony that precipitated the First World War. In the continued absence of a hegemon, this competitive and ultimately destructive pattern of behaviour repeated itself after that conflict. The lack of a power capable of constraining economic nationalism allowed 'beggar-my-neighbour' protectionism and mercantilism to precipitate the Great Depression. A further round of imperialist competition culminated in Germany's second and final bid for hegemony in 1939.

By the early 1940s, however, the USA was in a position to make a decisive bid for hegemony and to stabilise the world capitalist system. During and immediately after the Second World War, American policy-makers planned their 'hegemonic project' – a 'world order of economic internationalism and collective security'.[3] In concrete terms this translated first into the recon-struction of the core economies of Western Europe and the semi-peripheral economy of Japan. This was to be accompanied by the reintegration of the underdeveloped periphery with the economies of the USA, Western Europe and Japan in order to reconstruct a functioning world capitalist system. The principal potential threat to this vision was the USSR. It controlled, in Eastern Europe, an area of historic economic importance to Western Europe; it had links to Communist parties and trade unions in the latter area; and it had significant military power. Taken together these factors might induce West European governments to accommodate themselves to Soviet power rather than America's plans.

The USA did not act to contain the USSR immediately the Second World War came to an end. The key question for US policy-makers was whether 'Russia would organize its territorial bloc into an autarkic bloc or enter into America's internationalist system'.[4] While the Soviets saw definite advantages in cooperation with the USA after 1945, however, the price was perceived to be too high. American influence in Eastern Europe could not be tolerated, given the vital importance of the region to Soviet security. An ideological belief in the inevitably of future conflicts among the capitalist powers also persuaded Stalin to isolate his empire from the rest of the world. The proximate cause of the resulting US-Soviet conflict was Germany, which was vital to both superpowers' post-war visions. To the Soviets, control of Germany was vital for security; to the Americans, it was central to their economic plans for Western Europe and the world.

In practice, the primary threat to the achievement of the American global vision was not the USSR, which was relatively easily contained, but the inability of the governments of Western Europe to restore their economies to anything approximating rude health. This problem manifested itself primarily in the form of the 'dollar gap'. Western Europe needed US manufactured goods, raw materials and food to rebuild its economic base, but without that economic base it could not earn the dollars to pay for them. If the resulting vicious circle could not be broken, the Europeans might lapse back into policies of economic nationalism and even seek to accommodate themselves politically and economically to the USSR. This, in turn, would undermine America's prosperity and, ultimately, its political system.

This is the context within which McCormick explains the key American policy initiatives of 1947–50. The Truman Doctrine helped reduce the dollar drain on the British economy, stabilized the eastern Mediterranean (and therefore Western Europe's oil lifeline) and prepared domestic public opinion for the subsequent Marshall Plan. The latter was the Truman administration's medium-term response to the crisis of the world system. It provided the influx of dollars needed to get the West European economy moving and 'attempted to move Europe irrevocably away from nationalism and autarky toward internationalism and free convertibility'.[5] By late 1949, however, the system faced renewed crisis. In Japan, the deflationary Dodge Plan had led to the collapse of domestic demand, a growing trade deficit and fears of impending economic catastrophe. In Europe, meanwhile, the dollar gap persisted despite the inflow of Marshall aid. The reintegration of the periphery into the world system was also lagging, and the lack of growth in trade between Western Europe and the periphery was contributing to the former's stuttering economic recovery. Domestically, the US economy went into recession in early 1949 and Congress was increasingly reluctant to extend American economic benevolence abroad. To compound all this, that year also saw the victory in China of Mao Zedong's Communist forces and the explosion of the first Soviet atomic bomb.

The combined effect of these developments, many US policy-makers believed, would be a renewed crisis of confidence in Western Europe and Japan and a consequently enlarged temptation to negotiate with the Soviet Union. In order to address that potential threat, they devised their final, long-term, answer to the dollar gap – military-Keynesianism. Manifested firstly in the shape of NATO and the US–Japanese peace treaty, this programme was less than ideal in economic terms. Politically, however, it was the most attractive of the available options. By shifting US aid from the economic to the security sphere, it would boost demand in the USA and transfer dollars to Europe in a manner acceptable to right-wing Republicans otherwise hostile to handouts to foreigners. It would also reassure those in Western Europe and Japan who feared Soviet military attack, and help to contain any possible resurgence of German military power. In so doing it would refocus the attention of the West Europeans on the primary objectives of economic development and integration.

The massive programme of militarisation that resulted also created the wherewithal to assist in the integration of the periphery with the core states – the project that became the primary objective of US foreign policy after 1950. However, while the spending programme proved successful in finally overcoming the dollar gap, and in so doing contributed to a period of unprecedented global economic growth from 1950 to 1970, the cost to the hegemon was a heavy one. The two major wars in which the USA became engaged in Korea and Vietnam represented the price of a 'general strategy to integrate the periphery more effectively into core economies and . . . a specific strategy to sustain Japan's economic recovery, [and] insure its participation in the world system'.[6]

The domestic crisis that resulted from the latter of these wars was indicative of the weakening of American hegemony. While Vietnam was the proximate cause, however, hegemony always contains the seeds of its own demise. The excessive military spending necessary to maintain both the hegemon's position and the world capitalist system that it dominates undermines the civilian economy. That, in turn, allows rival core powers to catch up (as Japan and Western Europe were doing by 1970). No longer able to afford the cost of policing the world system, the hegemon seeks to offload parts of its burden, and may even resort to nationalistic economic practices of the kind it hitherto sought to quash, as it attempts to retain its pre-eminence. Increasing conflict characterises the relationship among the core powers.

All of this, McCormick argues, we can see in US foreign policy after 1970. The key underlying reality of US foreign policy, from then until the end of the Cold War, was one of long-term structural crisis. One of the earliest indications of this was Richard Nixon's unilateralist abandonment of the Bretton Woods agreement in 1971. The 1970s also saw the transformation of the US economy. Traditional heavy and manufacturing industry declined, as did the domestic rate of profit, leading more and more investment to go abroad in search of a better rate. The USA increasingly became a rentier nation, earning profits on foreign direct investment (FDI) and with manufacturing subcontracted to the newly industrialising countries (NICs) of the semi-periphery. Producing less and consuming more, the USA depended on these rents and a steady inflow of FDI from Europe and Japan to finance an inverted version of the dollar gap of the late 1940s. The effect of these economic changes, when added to the continued costs of hegemony, was to create structural deformities in the US economy. Massive military spending, plus overseas FDI, starved the US civilian economy of investment. The result was a decline in productivity and competitiveness and a steep decline in the income growth of the American working and middle classes.

Explaining US foreign policy against this background, McCormick argues that the détente of the early 1970s and the world-order policies of Jimmy Carter should be understood as attempts to come to terms with hegemonic decline. Both involved efforts to cut the military costs of hegemony and to seek new, cooperative, solutions to the management of the Cold War and the global order. The first-term policies of the Reagan administration, in contrast, represented the desires of those elements within the USA who sought to restore hegemony. Those ambitions were undercut by the long-term structural economic changes, and the new détente of the late 1980s and the end of the Cold War were fundamentally the consequence of the inability of either superpower to sustain the cost of the Cold War any longer.

In McCormick's view, the early post-Cold War period is one of transition, with the future of the world order uncertain and dependent upon the robustness of global interdependence, global economic growth and the stability of the former Soviet Union. US hegemony is still in decline, nevertheless. This is indicated, he suggests, by the rise of ethnic and nationalist conflicts in the early 1990s and the inability or unwillingness of the USA to control or resolve them. The first Persian Gulf War was a bid to perpetuate the credibility of US hegemony, tying in US allies and reinforcing their dependence on US military power, while putting potential trouble-makers on notice of American intent. He would no doubt explain the invasion of Iraq in 2003 in similar terms.

The scholar whose historical account McCormick's most closely resembles is Gabriel Kolko. In both cases we find the same focus on the American preoccupation with restoring the transatlantic nexus of global capitalism and the explanation of the various policy initiatives of 1947–50 as devices to that end. Nevertheless, there are two crucial differences between the two accounts. In the first place, the impact of post-revisionism is clear in the depiction of the US–Soviet relationship. Kolko at times depicts US policy-makers as engaged in an almost conspiratorial exploitation of anti-communist fears for purely economic ends. McCormick provides a much more nuanced account that emphasises US policy-makers' genuine fears of Soviet power and influence. Secondly, and more importantly, whereas Kolko rooted US foreign policy in the specific needs of the US capitalist economy, McCormick explains the same policy by reference to the position of the USA within the structure of the world capitalist system. This is his major theoretical contribution, and it is to a more detailed explanation of that which we now turn.

Explanatory Framework

As we have noted already, the theoretical framework that underpins McCormick's panoramic survey of US foreign policy is the world-systems theory of

Immanuel Wallerstein. In order to evaluate McCormick's contribution it is therefore necessary to engage in a more detailed elaboration of Wallerstein's basic propositions.

Over many years, and in a massive body of work, Wallerstein has sought systematically to explain the origins of the capitalist world system and how that system works.[7] His focus upon the capitalist world system is indicative of the two fundamental theoretical commitments that underpin his argument. The focus is on capitalism because Wallerstein is a Marxist, and as such he privileges economics as the fundamental determinant of social and historical change. Capitalism is to be studied as a world system because Wallerstein also believes in the necessity of explaining at the level of the system as a whole. That is, rather than explaining the behaviour of the units of the system – states or classes in his case – by factors internal to them, he explains their behaviour by an external factor, their position in, and relationship to, the world capitalist system.

Wallerstein argues that any state will fall into one of three positions within the world system. It will be in either the core, the semi-periphery or the periphery. Though states may, historically, move from one zone to another, the existence of the three zones is a necessary and defining characteristic of the world system.[8] These different zones of the system are defined not by what is produced in them but by how it is produced. Core areas are defined by high-wage, high-profit, capital-intensive tasks and peripheral areas by low-wage, labour-intensive tasks, while semi-peripheral areas are somewhere in between.

The world capitalist system is also characterised by an inherent tendency to geographical expansion and, most importantly, by the transfer of wealth from the periphery to the core. Capitalism's dynamism is a product of trade and exchange among the various regions that comprise it. Most of the profit produced in this process, however, ends up in the core states, since capitalism as a system tends to reward accumulated capital (money and skills) more than raw labour power (ability to work). Therefore those who have capital get more and those who do not get less. Wealth created in the periphery is transferred to the core through a process of unequal exchange

The wealth of the core is thus a result of its exploitation of the periphery. Understanding this allows us also to understand the significance of systemic explanation. The argument in Wallerstein is clearly a modified version of some of the earlier Marxist arguments found in Kolko and others that attribute US foreign policy to economic necessity.[9] But, whereas they tended to focus on the interests of US capitalists in isolation, Wallerstein argues that it is the position of the USA as a core economy in the world system, and its dependence for its prosperity upon the continued integration of the periphery into that system, that is the real explanation. What appears in Kolko as a property of the US capitalist economy is really a property of the global capitalist system as a whole.

Occasionally, a core state will become hegemonic. Hegemonic powers tend to be advocates of liberalism both economically (the strongest economy benefits most from free trade) and politically. Hegemony itself is a consequence of the role of the state in the functioning of capitalism – namely, to assist the capitalist class in its never-ending accumulation of capital. The logical corollary of this is that the state seeks a position of global hegemony, whereby the state's capitalists have a competitive advantage in every area (that is, the goal of hegemony is inherent in the logic of capitalist accumulation). Thus, core states will seek ever-expanding world power in order to assist their capitalists' accumulation of capital. When hegemony is achieved, this also facilitates a cooperative relationship between the classes within the hegemon, which all benefit from hegemony (there is sufficient wealth to provide absolute material gains for all). However, the liberalism of the hegemon leads to its demise. It prevents it from stopping the spread of technology and getting caught by later developers, while the internal policies of liberalism – steady increases in real wages of workers and the bureaucrats who service the hegemon – lead to a decline in competitiveness.

Critique

Wallerstein's arguments have been the subject of wide-ranging critiques over the years. Only a fraction of these, however, have direct relevance to the application and adaptation of his theory as practised by McCormick. Three key problems in particular will be the focus of our attention. First, Wallerstein's theorization of capitalism as a system and his assumptions about the dynamic elements within that system; secondly, his analysis of the nature and role of the state; and, finally, the problematic implications of his insistence upon locating all key explanatory variables at the systemic level.

One of the most powerful criticisms of Wallerstein's world-systems theory is that it incorporates a fundamentally flawed understanding of how capitalism works. Wallerstein attributes the dynamism of capitalism to the combination of geographical expansion and the regional division of labour. Trade and exchange are depicted as the key characteristic of capitalism and the basis of its expansion and the transfer of wealth from the periphery to the core. This argument, however, runs into major problems at both an empirical and a theoretical level. Empirically, the most obvious weakness of the argument is that the central Wallersteinian assumption that the wealth of the core comes at the cost of the impoverishment of the periphery is difficult to substantiate. The period since 1945, for example, when capitalism has been at its most dynamic, is also a period when the standard of living in the periphery has actually risen, and indeed when the latter may have experienced historically unprecedented economic growth.[10] Rather than underdeveloping the periphery, in other words, the core has been developing it, albeit in a typically brutal and iniquitous fashion.[11] The second main empirical problem we have already noted in regard to the arguments of Gabriel Kolko – namely that, while there is a transfer of wealth from the periphery to the core, in the form of profits on FDI, for example, it represents too small a fraction of overall corporate profits easily to explain the expansive global role of the USA after 1945.[12]

These empirical objections are reinforced by the theoretical critique of Wallerstein's conceptualisation of capitalism. Rather than exchange, this critique argues, the most important characteristic of capitalism is its inherent tendency towards technological innovation and increases in productivity. Wallerstein argues that these qualities are a response to cyclical economic downturns, but it is apparent to virtually any observer of capitalist economies that they are in fact inherent and constant characteristics of capitalism. Wallerstein is unable to account for this fact, according to his critics, because of his failure to recognize that capitalism is defined not by production for profit in the market, but by a particular system of class relations and especially the existence of free wage labour.

The latter in particular is vital in explaining the tendency to innovation in capitalist economies. In a mode of production based upon slavery or serfdom, the dominant class increases the surplus it extracts by making the slaves/serfs work longer/harder or by taking a greater share of what is produced. In a system with free wage labour, however, these courses of action are not so desirable/possible. Making the workers work harder is difficult without the coercive power of the slave-owner/serf-lord. Making them work longer does not help, because you pay wages for the extra work and so make only a small extra profit. Taking a greater share of what is produced (cutting wages) reduces demand for what is produced (since workers are also consumers of the goods produced) and therefore reduces profits. On the other hand, increases in productivity (producing more with the same or less labour time) allow the capitalist to maintain or to increase wages (and therefore demand) whilst making more profit. Capitalists thus invest heavily in order to produce technological innovation and productivity increases and it is this that produces the dynamism of capitalism as an economic system.[13]

Taken together, the empirical and theoretical weaknesses of Wallerstein's conceptualisation of capitalism have significant implications for McCormick's analysis. Above all, they appear to undermine the argument that the transfer of wealth from the periphery to the core is a fundamental or even necessary feature of the world system. Historically, that transfer is relatively small, and is not actively making the periphery poorer. The reason for this, we can surmise from the theoretical critique, is that such transfer is not fundamental to the system because the driving force of capitalism is not exchange but innovation and productivity increases within the core states. Neither point, of course, proves that wealth is not transferred from the periphery to the core, or that the relationship between the core and the periphery is not, in some sense, exploitative. Nor do they prove that US foreign policy after 1945 was not driven by an interest in the maintenance of the global capitalist system. What they do demonstrate is that, if the latter is the case, the explanation for that foreign policy posited by McCormick is wrong. If the USA was driven by a systemic imperative, it was not the transfer of wealth from the periphery to the core. On that basis, McCormick offers us a description of US foreign policy after 1945 but not a convincing explanation.

The second major problem with Wallerstein's analysis is his conceptualisation of the nature and role of the state. On the one hand, he gives the state, or at least the core state, a crucial role in the functioning of the world system through its enforcement of the system's imperatives upon the periphery. Simultaneously, however, he argues that the capitalist world system so fundamentally shapes the social and political structures within it that they can be treated as products of that system. Classes are constituted within the world system and they, in turn, constitute the state as they attempt to maintain their power. The actions and relations of classes and states are therefore mere expressions of the global economy. Wallerstein thus reduces the actions of the state to a simple expression of ruling-class interests, which are in turn determined by the world capitalist system. He employs a crude economic determinism that gives no autonomy to the state apparatus whatsoever.[14]

This trivialisation of the state exposes two quite fundamental weaknesses in Wallerstein's argument. First, whether economic determinism is rooted in the US capitalist system or the global capitalist system, it is, as has already been demonstrated in the chapter on revisionism, unsustainable. Secondly, in rooting the explanation of state behaviour in the systemic level in this fashion, Wallerstein commits the same error as the neorealists discussed in the chapter on post-revisionism.[15] It becomes impossible to explain change in the system because the only possible source of change is the system itself.

We should note, however, that there are important differences between Wallerstein's treatment of the state and that of McCormick. In part, at least, this is a result of differences of focus. Wallerstein is interested in the system as a whole, while McCormick is interested in the foreign policy of the United States. This individualising focus inevitably brings the American state to the fore. McCormick's divergence from Wallerstein goes deeper than that, however, and is most clearly revealed in his treatment of the concept of hegemony. Unlike Wallerstein, McCormick places the concept of hegemony at the heart of his argument, and appears to regard it as a more or less necessary feature of the world capitalist system.[16] The reason for this is the conflict he identifies between the internationalist drive of the world capitalist system and the nationalistic imperative of states. This positing of a funda- mental conflict between these two imperatives is an important deviation from Wallerstein. The latter acknowledges an antimony between the state system and the world capitalist system, but he does not see it as irreconcilable in the way McCormick does because he regards state behaviour as ultimately reducible to an expression of systemic imperatives. He therefore sees the antimony as being resolved by the normal operation of the world system and not only by the creation of hegemons.

McCormick's formulation, in contrast, does not appear to treat state behaviour as reducible to a function of the world system, but rather regards it as having a dynamic of its own – nationalism – that threatens the functioning of that system. He thus gives autonomy and causal power to a unit of the system, rather than restricting these qualities to the system as a whole. In principle, this is a significant improvement upon Wallerstein's formulation. It eliminates the crude economic determinism found in Waller- stein and, in seeking to blend the agency of states with systemic constraints and imperatives, avoids the impossible task of explaining change in a system with only one level at which causal agency can be found.

However, this is the case only if this theoretical synthesis is developed and then applied throughout McCormick's analysis, and in practice this is not the case. What we actually find in *America's Half Century* is a typical inference of systemic determinism with only an occasional nod to the agency of states and political elites. For example, McCormick argues that, after the First World War, the USA possessed the material attributes of a hegemon but, for various reasons, chose not to take on that role. Indeed, he is quite specific in asserting that hegemony requires not only material power but also the will to use it, a formulation that clearly implies state agency.[17] Shortly afterwards, however, he asserts that the resolution of the crisis of capitalism in the 1930s through geographical expansion represented an inevitable and necessary development, implying systemic de- terminism.[18] So at one point McCormick implies policy-makers have a choice but a few pages later argues that they do not. It is difficult to see how these two positions can be reconciled. It would be possible to argue that in one case system structure offers a range of opportunities and in another very few, but not to allow state agency in one case but not in the other. Perhaps McCormick believes that hegemons, as uniquely powerful states, have more freedom than others, but they must still, ultimately, be bound by systemic constraints under this argument. As it stands, therefore, the argument is contradictory.

McCormick's acknowledgement of the agency of states is half-hearted. He typically resorts to the same kind of determinist explanation as Wallerstein, with all the inherent problems therein. While he takes a step in the right direction, he fails to carry it through. Like Kolko and the corporatists, he fails to take the state seriously enough. To avoid the pitfalls of Wallersteinian theory he would have had to retain the importance of system structure while also incorporating the agency of states and the groups within them in a much more systematic fashion. In *America's Half Century*, the agency of states is not a systematic part of the explanation so much as a residual factor of explanation resorted to when systemic determinism breaks down. It is not an elaboration and development of world-systems theory but rather an attempt to disguise its weaknesses.

Finally, although we have already touched on this question, we have the problem of systemic determinism. Wallerstein's reductionist conception of the state is a logical consequence of his insistence that it is the system as a whole that is the unit of analysis, and that the explanation of the behaviour of the units of that system lies in their relationship to the system. The theoretical power and originality of world-systems theory derives from this assumption. If Wallerstein were to give autonomy and causal power to the state, then the behaviour of the state would not be predicted by the theory as it is at present and the power of the theory would be undermined. No doubt this is a large part of the reason why McCormick, despite his recognition of its flaws, finds it so difficult to abandon systemic determinism.

Nevertheless, besides the problems already identified, systemic explanation also has an inherent tendency towards functionalism. The easiest way to understand this problem is through the oft-used analogy of the human body, where an understanding of the function of any part within the system is best understood by its relationship to other parts and, especially, by its contribution to the maintenance of the system (life) as a whole; thus, we know what the heart (unit) is for and why it does what it does by understanding its function in keeping the body (system) alive. Taking this analogy to its logical conclusion, one arrives at the view that, just as a body has needs that must be met for it to function, so do other systems such as the world capitalist system.

While this form of reasoning is attractive, and allows the theorist to develop powerful arguments, it also contains significant flaws. First, functionalist reasoning is teleological; that is, it argues that the parts of the system and their actions exist because of their benefits for the system as a whole. The objection to this, however, is that it treats an effect (the benefit to the system) as a cause (of the parts of the system and their actions), but this is not logically possible because causes must precede effects. The only way around this dilemma is to specify a 'feedback mechanism' that explains how an effect can precede a cause. Human intention, for example, would constitute such a mechanism if one could show that policy-makers took a certain action because of its perceived benefits for system maintenance.[19]

Functional explanation also tends towards determinism, as unit behaviour is depicted as determined by the needs of the system. This reification of the system is unacceptable, because only conscious human agents can possess such needs and systems must ultimately be conceived of as the outcome of the total effect of individual human actions. That is not to say that systems and structures do not impose constraints on human actions, but it is to deny that they determine them. Rather, what exists is a deeply complex interaction of system and units that is best understood as a process of co-determination, with each shaping the other.

Wallerstein commits the sins of system reification and functionalism throughout his writings. As a result, his theory is of very doubtful utility as a tool of historical analysis because there is nothing left for the historian to explain. If you accept the theoretical premises of world-systems theory, then you know why everything happened already and there is no requirement for further exploration. As long as the historical events in question appear to conform to the logic of the theory, then they are to be considered explained. Historical evidence is merely drawn upon to illustrate the theory's explanatory power, not to test it.[20] But almost any theory, even the weakest, can easily be sustained by looking for plausible correlations between events and the theory's premises and ignoring the evidence that does not fit.[21]

This form of teleological explanation is also very clear in McCormick, who knows how the world system functions and what it requires. Armed with this knowledge, and the advantage of hindsight, he explains US foreign policies in terms of their functional benefit for the system. With such an approach there is no real need for a detailed analysis of the historical record or of alternative explanations (and none is provided). As long as US policies can be shown to serve the needs of the world capitalist system, it is assumed, rather than demonstrated, that this is an adequate explanation for them. Given our knowledge of the methodological and theoretical flaws inherent in world-systems theory, however, there is really no good reason for us to accept that those policies are in fact thus explained.

Ultimately, there are two ways of treating McCormick's ambitious attempt to use world-systems theory to explain US Cold War foreign policy, both of which can be justified. The negative conclusion would treat it as an expression of Wallersteinian certainty – this is how the world works and this is why US foreign policy was the way it was. As we have discussed at length, we have very good reasons to reject this claim, not only because of the theoretical and methodological weaknesses of world-systems theory as formulated by Wallerstein and adapted by McCormick, but also because, ultimately, it is not a fruitful basis for historical investigation. If we accept world-systems theory as a given, we know all the answers and there is nothing left to do. Read thus, *America's Half Century* announces, in effect, 'the end of diplomatic history'.[22]

It is possible, however, to extract a more positive conclusion from the critique that has been offered. In the first place, while thoroughgoing systemic determinism should be rejected, the importance of systemic analysis should not. Regardless of the weaknesses in Wallerstein's understanding of its functioning, there is a world capitalist system that does have its own inherent logic and that coexists with a system of nation states that have their own purposes and interests.[23] Wallerstein and McCormick may not have adequately addressed the relationship between those two dynamics, but in drawing our attention to the systemic level they emphasise a point of great importance:

> If the essential determinant of a structure or process is the connection of the social unit in which it appears to a whole system of social relationships, the connection frequently produces effects which seem to be autonomous properties of the social unit itself.[24]

A policy that we see emanating from inside a state, in other words, may in fact be caused by the relationship between that state and groups inside it and the wider international system. If you look inside the state to explain a policy, you may be looking in the wrong place. What appear to be autonomous choices made by policy-makers or economic elites may actually be responses to powerful systemic constraints over which they have little if any control.

Secondly, even if we must reject the implication that Wallerstein and McCormick have given a true account of history because the theoretical framework from which they extrapolate their conclusions is flawed, it does not follow that their arguments contain no vestige of truth. Rather than accept world-systems theory as a whole, we can take various of its concepts and the historical arguments generated by them and treat them as hypotheses to be tested, rather than givens.[25] And world-systems theory and its application by McCormick do generate some extremely interesting arguments. The concept of hegemony, in particular, provides a powerful and plausible explanation of the nature of US foreign policy post-1945 and its preoccupation with the construction of an open international economic system.[26]

At a more specific level, the emphasis on the nature and needs of the world capitalist system and the role of the hegemon therein allows McCormick to generate a series of important arguments about specific policies such as the Truman Doctrine, the Marshall Plan and the militarization of containment policy during and after the Korean War. In particular, his application of world-systems theory generates interesting arguments about some issues with which other schools of thought have had difficulty. Revisionism, for example, had problems explaining the Vietnam War because of the lack of a significant direct US economic interest there. By stressing the importance of South-East

Asia (periphery) to Japan (semi-periphery), and of Japan to the USA (core) and the world system as a whole, McCormick is able to provide a plausible explanation of Vietnam that retains the economic focus of revisionism but within a more plausible theoretical framework.[27] Similarly, many orthodox and post-revisionist scholars have had difficulties explaining away the apparent inability of US policy-makers to draw distinctions among pro-Soviet, nationalist communist and nationalist and leftist regimes and their tendency to treat all of them as equally threatening. McCormick's analysis provides a plausible answer – any regime, pro-Soviet or not, that threatens to withdraw an area from the world system threatens the functioning of the system, and that is why it must be opposed.

BRUCE CUMINGS

The other important diplomatic historian who espouses a world-systems approach is Bruce Cumings. However, despite a common emphasis upon the central explanatory role of the world capitalist system, and a tripartite division of that system into core, semi-periphery and periphery, the approaches of the two scholars are very different. Rather than following Wallerstein closely, Cumings borrows some key ideas from him but integrates them into a explanatory framework that is all his own. In framing his methodological commitments he draws heavily on the work of Karl Polanyi, while he borrows from Franz Schurman and corporatism for insights into the domestic sources of US foreign policy. Perhaps more importantly, whereas McCormick has a strong tendency towards systemic determinism, Cumings demonstrates an acute sensitivity to the problematic interaction of structure and agency. What results is a highly nuanced and complex analysis in which explanatory levels and factors are layered one on top of the other in a multifaceted argument. This is one of the most complicated and challenging, but also one of the most rewarding, perspectives on US foreign policy and the Cold War.

Whereas most of the writers in this study have tended to focus their attention primarily upon US policy towards Western Europe, Cumings's focus and area of expertise is North-East Asia, and primarily Korea.[28] This fact is of little significance for our purposes, however, since Cumings develops a general framework for explaining US foreign policy of which his study of US policy towards Korea is merely a specific application. As was noted above, that framework is a multilayered one, explaining US foreign policy as a product of the interplay of factors located at the systemic, state, societal and individual levels.

A crude summary of the argument in Cumings's two-volume history of the origins of the Korean War (very crude, because this is a long and massively detailed work) would begin with the position of the USA within the world capitalist system at the end of 1945. Here Cumings's argument is quite similar to that of Wallerstein and McCormick. The USA was the hegemonic power in the system and as such sought to demarcate a 'grand area' within which nations oriented themselves towards Washington and its preferred political and economic organising principles. In the specific case of North-East Asia, this objective centred on the semi-peripheral economy of Japan, which was vital to the revitalisation of the economy of the whole region and its reintegration into the world capitalist system. Ultimately, US intervention in the Korean War was driven by the need to ensure this objective and to draw the boundaries of the grand area in North-East Asia.[29]

Within that broad structural imperative, however, Cumings allows significant latitude for other factors to come into play and to dictate the specific course of US policy. Of these, the most important by far is the conflict between two political coalitions rooted in America's socio-economic divisions. Here Cumings's analysis is the same, in its essentials, as that of the corporatists. The 1930s were a turning point in US society in which class conflict engendered new political alignments centred on the split in US capital. A dominant New Deal coalition of international capital and organised labour faced the Republican-led national capital bloc.[30] It is the conflict between these two blocs and the foreign-policy expressions of their domestic interests that dominates Cumings's account of US foreign policy in the early Cold War.

Following Franz Schurman,[31] Cumings does not label these two streams as internationalism and isolationism but as imperialism/internationalism and expansionism/nationalism. The former was characterised economically by support for the Keynesian compromise at home and for modified global free trade (regulated by International Financial Institutions) abroad. It pursued a multilateralist liberalism and sought to create an integrated world capitalist system, including the USSR, based upon those principles. Optimistic and confident of its vision, this strand of thought was dominant in the policies of the Roosevelt administration as it planned for the end of the Second World War. The expansionist/nationalist stream, rooted in the weaker national capital bloc, feared global free trade as a threat to its economic base. It favoured laissez-faire and the minimal state at home combined with protectionism and mercantilism abroad. It was not isolationist, but focused on Latin America and Asia, rather than Europe. US economic relations with those areas, moreover, would be based not on free and open competition but on exclusive US access, secured by force if necessary. Fearful of the USSR, this stream wished to exclude it from, rather than integrate it into, the world system. Moreover, it soon came to advocate not merely the containment of the USSR but the active 'rollback' of communism in Eastern Europe and East Asia.

Cumings explains US foreign policy from 1945 to 1950 as the product of the struggle between these two currents, operating within the framework of constraints imposed by the world system. That struggle finally resulted in the triumph of a modified internationalism in the shape of the policy of containment. Initially, the optimistic world view of Rooseveltian internationalism was abandoned by the Truman administration in favour of the doctrine of containment. The reason for this transition was quite simply that the Soviet Union proved resistant to, and hostile towards, integration into the world system, while the system proved itself incapable of restoring itself without extensive US intervention. This development necessitated a shift on the part of the USA. From a plan to integrate the whole world via global laissez-faire, and with minimalist international institutions and little or no military role for the USA, Truman moved towards integration of a US sphere (excluding the communist bloc) with a far more interventionist economic regime and institutions, and a significant security apparatus based on US military power.

After 1945, therefore, the struggle over US foreign policy was not between internationalism and nationalism but between containment and nationalism. An internationalist stream remained, represented by individuals such as former Vice-President and Secretary of Commerce Henry Wallace, but it was increasingly marginalised. In contrast, the late 1940s saw the growing influence of the nationalist 'rollback' stream. Cumings identifies a variety of reasons for this growing influence, including changes in senior government personnel (especially the appointment of Secretary of Defense Louis Johnson), bureaucratic interests concerned with seeking an economic hinterland for Japan and external events such as the explosion of the Soviet atomic bomb and the fall of China.

Before the Korean War, as a result, US foreign policy was an uneasy blend of containment and rollback policies, as is clearly indicated, in the Asian context, by the document known as NSC-48, and, in a global context, by NSC-68. The US decision to intervene in Korea reflected that compromise, with different groups from the nationalist and containment streams agreed on the need for intervention for different reasons. Some nationalists saw an opportunity to secure US security guarantees for the Chinese nationalist regime on Taiwan as well as to push back the boundaries of communist influence in Asia. Leaders of the containment stream, like Secretary of State Dean Acheson, focused on the need to secure Japan's economic hinterland as well as the need to protect themselves from McCarthyism and the fallout from the 'loss' of China. Both streams agreed on the need to preserve the credibility of American power and commitments.

The significance of the Korean War for Cumings is not only the direct impact of that intervention on Korea, but also its role in resolving the struggle between the containment and nationalist/rollback camps inside the United States. The decision of the Truman administration to cross the 38th parallel and attempt to unify Korea represented the highpoint of rollback nationalism in the post-war era. The disastrous failure of that policy, and the subsequent heaping of blame on the shoulders of such representatives of the rollback tendency as General Douglas MacArthur, allowed the containment stream decisively to seize the upper hand and consigned rollback to permanent marginality. Nevertheless, containment remained a compromise; a complete victory for the internationalist bloc would have included incorporation of the USSR into the global system and no Cold War. The nationalist bloc remained sufficiently powerful to prevent that and force the compromise of containment.

Explanatory Framework

We have already outlined some of the elements of Cumings's interpretative framework above. Here we will give a more systematic account of the methodological and theoretical commitments that underpin the above narrative. To do this the following account will start with Cumings's broad methodology and his commitment to a form of 'total history' and then explore how he attempts to operationalise this in his more specific theorisation of US foreign policy.[32]

The most important element of Cumings's methodological approach to explaining US foreign policy is undoubtedly his desire to write a 'totalizing history' that recognises the multiplicity of causes and circumstances that contribute to any historical event or development. He has something in common with Wallerstein and McCormick in his insistence that US foreign policy has to be understood in relation to the broadest possible structural framework – the world capitalist system. However, the primary influence on Cumings in regard to method is not Wallerstein but Karl Polanyi. Indeed, Polanyi has a good claim to have been a world-systems theorist before Wallerstein.[33] In *The Great Transformation*, Polanyi traces the development of the world system from the early nineteenth century until the advent of the Second World War. The key theme of the book is the ongoing conflict between the imperatives of the global capitalist economy and states' pursuit of national welfare.[34] In contrast to the abstraction and economic determinism of Wallersteinian theory, however, Polanyi insists on the need for this totality to be grasped concretely and to seek the structural relationships of the various parts of the system to each other without ultimately reducing them to the determination of one level or factor. In practical terms, this meant Polanyi pursued a complex analysis employing multiple levels – world market system, states and society – and sought to demonstrate how the interaction of all three levels transformed the international system without denying the autonomy, or the importance, of any of them.[35]

Polanyi's influence on Cumings's method is very clear and manifests itself primarily in the latter's preoccupation with questions of structure and agency. The problem, as he puts it, is that 'each political event is both structured and random',[36] the product both of constraining structural forces and individual human initiative. The best summary statement of that reality, he observes, is Marx's famous comment that men (*sic*) make their own history, but not in circumstances of their own choosing.[37] Historical explanation, therefore, is a matter, among other things, of doing justice to both structure and agency and the full complexity of their interaction. This requires the application of an approach, like Polanyi's, that has room for both the shaping influence of structures and the agency of individuals and that incorporates explanation on several levels of analysis without giving a priori determinacy to any single one. The levels in question are the same ones used by Polanyi apart from Cumings's introduction of a regional level of explanation between the state and the world system. For the purposes of analysis, however, it makes sense to group the world and regional levels together. We can therefore divide our discussion of Cumings's specific theoretical commitments into three sections: world and regional system, state and society.

At the highest level of analysis therefore, is the world market system and its regional subsystem in North-East Asia. It is fundamental to Cumings's argument that the basic direction of US foreign policy after 1945 cannot be understood 'apart from the structural position of America in a distinct world system that had its own identifiable imperative'.[38] That system, as we have noted, was (and is) composed, like Wallerstein's, of core, semi-peripheral and peripheral states. The structural position of the USA within it, as argued by McCormick, was that of hegemon. And, as the global and regional hegemon, the USA behaved in an appropriately hegemonic fashion, defined by Cumings as 'the demarcation of outer limits in economics, politics and international-security relationships, the transgression of which carries grave risks for any non-hegemonic nation'.[39]

In concrete terms, Washington sought the demarcation of a 'grand area' within which states would orient themselves and their economic and security policies towards the American project. That project, ideally, was organised around principles of free trade, open systems and liberal democracy, though pragmatism allowed the incorporation of states with neo-mercantilistic and authoritarian characteristics. The liberal-internationalist ideology of the US hegemon was not, as McCormick argued, an inevitable product of the hegemon's structural position but a specific reflection of the history, culture and ideology of the USA.[40]

North-East Asia is a regional subsystem of the world capitalist system with its own particular dynamic, centred around the triangular relationship of the American core, the Japanese semi-periphery and the Korean, Chinese and South-East Asian periphery. In simple terms Japan, as the only significant industrial economy in East Asia, was vital to the revival of the regional, and ultimately world, political economy. The American plan, therefore, was to eliminate the military and political strength of Japan while supporting its evolution into a vital pole of global economic growth. That plan was threatened, however, by the fact that Japan's North-East Asian economic hinterland in China and North Korea had been placed beyond its reach by communism. The success of America's regional and global plans thus depended on securing a viable economic hinterland for the Japanese economy in the East Asian periphery by whatever means necessary. The Korean and Vietnamese wars were part of the effort to secure that peripheral hinterland.[41]

Whilst US policy-makers were thus subject to systemic imperatives at both a global and a regional level, their precise response to them was not wholly determined by those imperatives. Rather, in order to understand the specific nature of their policy choices, Cumings argues, we have to look at American society and the American state. With regard to the latter Cumings is influenced again by Polanyi but also by Franz Schurman. Following Schurman, Cumings attributes a significant degree of autonomy to the American president. This autonomy is explained by the president's need to represent broad societal interests and the national will. Even if elected and backed by relatively narrow interests, he/she must reach beyond them to govern. In Polanyian terms, presidents must have this autonomy from narrow interests because long-term system maintenance may require short-term sacrifices from powerful economic interests. Yet the president must also serve the interests of those powerful capitalists, since they are the source of the material wealth upon which the long-term survival of state and society depend. The state is thus pulled in two directions simultaneously, needing to serve the broader interests of society but also the narrow interests of powerful economic groups. The autonomy of the president from narrow economic interests is significant but ultimately constrained by the broader structural requirements of the national and global capitalist systems.[42]

Thirdly, below the level of the state, we have the level of American society, which influences the state and the specific US response to its position in the world system. As we have seen above, Cumings's analysis of that society is fundamentally the same as that of the corporatists, with society divided between the dominant internationalist bloc based on competitive capital and labour and represented politically by the Democrats and a weaker nationalist bloc rooted in national capital and represented politically by the right-wing of the Republican Party. Underpinning Cumings's analysis here is the concept of the 'product cycle'.[43] This conception argues that industries and industrial sectors pass through a number of clearly defined phases beginning with their innovation of a product and consequent competitive dominance in global markets and ending with the manufacture of the product more cheaply in foreign countries and its export back to the original home country and the decline in competitiveness of the industry there.

From a policy point of view, the key implication of this argument is that industries will prefer different kinds of public policies depending upon which stage of the product cycle they are at. In crude terms, an industry at the first stage will want free markets and free trade because it has a competitive advantage while one in the last stage will seek protectionist policies to defend it against foreign competition. A great deal about domestic and foreign policy can thus be learned by grasping which industries are politically dominant at any given time and at what stage of the product cycle they are.[44] The broadly liberal free trade policies pursued by the USA after 1945 reflect the dominance of a coalition of industries in the early stages of the product cycle.

Theoretically, the main point of this analysis is that the response of a state to the imperatives of the world capitalist system depends in large part on the balance of power within its domestic political-economy. The imperatives of the system may have driven the USA to act in a hegemonic fashion and to seek to maintain the system, but they did not determine how. Had the nationalist bloc been able to grasp control of the levers of the American state, US foreign policy after 1945 would have been much less liberal and multilateralist, more aggressive and militaristic, and oriented towards Asia rather than Europe. It would still have sought to maintain hegemony, but in a quite different way.

In sum, Cumings explains US foreign policy in the Cold War through a multilevel framework of analysis that seeks to balance the imperatives of structural constraints with the agency of states, groups, classes and individuals at lower levels. The world capitalist system had its own dynamic and the hegemonic position of the USA within that system impelled it towards certain objectives. How it pursued those objectives, however, can be fully explained and understood only by grasping the nature of the American state and presidency and the particular coalitions of forces within US society and the balance of political power between them. Cumings's approach is thus rather the opposite of that employed by Wallerstein and McCormick. Although the latter both have an ostensible commitment to holism, in practice they reduce the various levels of analysis to the determining power of a single one – the world capitalist system. Likewise, whereas Cumings insists on the close analysis of concrete institutions and societies, they tend to assume the truth of their theory and fit the details to it.

Critique

There is a huge amount to admire in this ambitious, complex and subtle analysis. Cumings demonstrates a greater sensitivity to the structure–agency problem and the difficulties of combining different levels of analysis than any other historian discussed in this book. The strengths of his analysis are perhaps best perceived by comparing his work to the three previous models discussed – post-revisionism, corporatism and the world-systems theory of Wallerstein/McCormick. What Cumings does rather successfully is to incorporate the strengths of these various approaches while avoiding their more obvious weaknesses. The post-revisionists and Wallerstein/McCormick both emphasised the importance of system structure to explanation, but in so doing they tended towards reductionism and the neglect or oversimplifcation of factors below that level. The corporatists, on the other hand, developed a sophisticated conception of the American political-economy that helped them to explain why the USA responded to external events in a particular fashion, but lacked any conception of the systemic structures from which those external stimuli originated. Cumings, in contrast, stresses the importance of the systemic without reducing other factors to it and seeks to give full play to factors internal to the United States without neglecting the systemic constraints to which they were subject.

In a very real sense, therefore, Cumings does achieve his objective of a 'totalizing history' that combines structure and agency, multiple levels of analysis and the theoretical and the empirical. This success comes at a price, however, but it is different from the one that we have typically found thus far. Whereas, in most of the perspectives we have examined, the theoretical weakness has tended towards reductionism and determinism, with Cumings, rather, the opposite is the case. It is a constant struggle for him to hold all the various aspects of his explanatory framework together and to reconcile the inevitable tensions between them. Nevertheless, his determination to do so without being reductionist leads, on the one hand, to a certain ambiguity and uncertainty about how the various levels interact and, on the other, to a surprisingly limited role for theory in his actual explanation of historical events.

Cumings gives little guidance as to how the various levels of his analysis are to be integrated or how we are to conceptualise the interaction between them. He enjoins us to engage in a constant 'back and forth' between observed facts (actions of human agents) and theory (underlying structure) in order to do justice to both and not to prejudge the explanatory power of the latter.[45] In practice, however, this is easier said than done, because Cumings is dealing with one of the most intractable problems of social and political theory. At an abstract level, his insistence on the co-determining nature of structure and agency and the refusal to reduce one to the other is admirable and a position that most social theorists would agree with. At a practical explanatory level, however, this methodological position is fraught with difficulties. The problem, as Cumings implicitly acknowledges, is that structure and agency are an 'indissoluble unity';[46] they cannot be separated analytically. Structures are, ultimately, composed of the activities of all the human agents within them, and those agents' actions, in turn, are in part a product of the structures their actions create. Structures and agents thus form a unified whole, an unbreakable circle with no point at which we can enter to start our analysis. But if we cannot separate the two analytically, how can we analyse their interaction? We may recognise the essential truth of Cumings's assertion, therefore, but it affords us little guidance when it comes to the concrete analysis of US foreign policy.[47]

This ambiguity about how we are actually to conceive of and to explain the interaction of the different levels in Cumings's explanatory framework carries through into his concrete analysis. In the first place, Cumings's commitment to the interaction of his various levels without reductionism is not as absolute as it might at first appear. Though he does not say so in either of his volumes on the origins of the Korean War, Cumings must be an economic 'determinist in the last instance'[48] if his insistence upon the fundamental importance of the world system is not to collapse. The world capitalist system can be a vital explanatory factor only if it imposes certain necessary actions upon the states and policy-makers who operate within its bounds. At some point, if they wish to maintain their capitalist economies and the global capitalist economy, they have to act in a certain way. Despite his desire to avoid reductionism, therefore, Cumings remains, and must remain, an economic determinist, albeit of a rather sophisticated kind.

On the other hand, however, the actual extent to, and manner in which, the world capitalist system ultimately constrains/determines US foreign policy remains unclear. Cumings talks about it as having its own 'identifiable imperative', but exactly how that imperative affects those subject to it is not spelled out. In fact, the operation of the world capitalist system and its imperatives is rather under-theorised in Cumings's analysis. Clearly, he rejects the mechanistic model utilised by Wallerstein and McCormick; he does not insist upon the transfer of wealth from the periphery to the core, accepts the possibility of peripheral and semi-peripheral states developing within the system and does not treat the liberal ideology of the American hegemon as a necessary product of its structural position in the system. The problem is that what that leaves us with is rather abstract. Essentially, all Cumings gives us is the fact that there is a world capitalist system made up of core, semi-periphery and periphery and that the integration of those three areas is necessary to its effective functioning. The USA, as hegemonic power, had to ensure that integration in order to secure the system and its own interests. This is a cogent and compelling argument, but it leaves a great deal of work to be done by the levels of analysis below that of the world system. Let us take, for example, Cumings's argument that the liberal ideology of the USA was a product not of its position as hegemon but of its own particular culture and history. This is a convincing argument,[49] but it means that the determining effects of the world system do not even stretch as far as how hegemony is practised.

In his insistence on being an economic determinist only in the last instance, therefore, Cumings limits the explanatory role of the structure of the world system to such an extent that it becomes of virtually no use to a historian studying anything but the broadest and most general patterns of historical events. This is demonstrated by his analysis of the origins of the Korean War. Apart from his theoretical discussion at the beginning of the second volume, the imperatives of the world system are almost entirely absent from the narrative. Beyond the fact (not insignificant in itself) that systemic imperatives require the USA to seek to integrate the various regions of the world economy, the systemic level tells us nothing about the events discussed. All the work of explaining events falls on the levels of state and society within Korea and the United States. The specifics of how the USA practised hegemony are a product of its own internal dynamics.

Despite the injunction to see structure and agency as an indissoluble whole, therefore, there is in practice a failure actually to integrate structure and agency in the argument. There is no back and forth between structure and agency or theory and facts. Rather, what we find is a framework in which the world capitalist system acts as a determinant in the last instance – a kind of boundary to the space within which the agency of states and societal groups determines the course of events. As long as states and societies operate within those boundaries, the world system remains absent from the analysis. Structure and agency, in other words, are not so much integrated as separated. Rather than a constant back and forth between structure and agency, we have two separate levels of analysis that barely connect. On one level we have a structural explanation, expressible in a few paragraphs, which says that US intervention in the Korean War was a necessary requirement of its role as hegemon. On another we have a long and complex historical argument running to over 1,000 pages, demonstrating how the interactions of states, classes, groups and individuals produced the specific course of events. The interaction is there, of course, in that the specifics of the second analysis ultimately depend in some sense upon the structural imperatives of the first, but those imperatives are so vague and abstracted as to play virtually no role in the explanation.

Arguably, the other major weakness of Cumings's theoretical approach lies in his treatment of politics. For all the attempt to incorporate the full multiplicity of causal factors into the analysis while granting each its own integrity and autonomy, politics is given very short shrift in Cumings's explanatory framework. This is true at both the systemic and the state level. At the level of the state, politics is treated as a function of the basic division in the underlying political-economy. Of course, Cumings is not actually as crudely reductionist as that, and other factors are incorporated into the analysis to explain political events. But those factors are essentially ad hoc and particularistic. This neglect of politics is tied to a related neglect of the role of the state. In this regard, Cumings is much the same as the corporatists with whom he shares much of his explanatory framework. An ostensible commitment to the importance of the state as an autonomous actor comes to little in practice. It is striking, for example, that, after stressing the importance and autonomy of the presidency, Cumings finds virtually no role for Harry Truman in his two volumes. Secretary of State Dean Acheson, in contrast, looms large, but essentially as lead representative of the containment stream rather than as an agent of the autonomous state. Politics is allowed no dynamic of its own and is fundamentally driven by underlying socio-economic factors.

At the level of the world system, Cumings has very little to say about the operation of geopolitics or security imperatives. To the extent that he does, a typical formulation is to argue that American hegemony 'fuses security and economic considerations . . . inextricably' or that containment 'synthesized' economic and security concerns.[50] What these security concerns or considerations were, however, tends to remain somewhat vague. The reason for this, it is clear, is that Cumings here runs into the same problem that defeated both the post-revisionists and the corporatists before him – namely, how to incorporate the geopolitical and the economic into a coherent synthesis without reducing either to a function of the other. What the above linguistic constructions reveal is that he does not succeed where they failed. Ultimate economic determinist that he is, Cumings cannot give autonomy to geopolitics. If the geopolitical system has its own autonomous imperative, then the role of the world capitalist system as determining in the final instance becomes open to question because you have two systems operating in parallel at the global level. If, on the other hand, US foreign policy is ultimately determined by the need to maintain the functioning of the world system, then geopolitical and security considerations are, in the final analysis, derivative of that purpose. Cumings's references to the fusion of economic and security concerns cannot disguise the fact that he has chosen the latter course. In the case of politics, therefore, his argument is reductionist.

Not only does Cumings not allow geopolitics a dynamic of its own, but he also has a very constricted conception of the role of political events external to the USA in the US policy-making process in general. According to Cumings, the basic process is that an external event 'detonates' the raw mat domestic conflict, which in turn produces changes in foreign policy.[51] noted in the discussion of post-revisionism, this argument has much v One cannot place all the explanatory weight on the external stimuli of US foreign policy because that makes it impossible to explain the different responses of different groups inside the state. However, there is a danger of going too far in the opposite direction and giving virtually no explanatory role to those external factors. For example, in his explanation of the transition from the internationalist foreign policy of Roosevelt to the containment policy of Truman, Cumings emphasises the struggle between the nationalist and internationalist blocs as the fundamental source of the shift. What is virtually excluded from the explanation is the significance of the Soviet refusal to go along with internationalist plans for a worldwide capitalist system. Similarly, Cumings attributes the ultimate triumph of the containment stream to its base in the hegemonic socio-economic bloc. This discounts the vital role of the defeat of the rollback effort in Korea in explaining containment's ultimate victory.

Of course one needs to be careful here. Cumings accepts that these external events did cause the US foreign-policy response to some degree, and thus the argument is over the slippery question of what degree of influence should be attributed to them. The objection being made here is that Cumings does not seem to accept that these external events not only 'detonated' internal conflicts but also significantly affected their outcome and the resulting foreign policy. This point can be made only counterfactually, but it is unlikely, for example, that the policy of containment would have evolved had the Soviets gone along with Roosevelt's internationalist vision. And if rollback had succeeded in uniting Korea, would containment have triumphed even if it was rooted in the dominant socio-economic bloc? External events may, in short, have more causal power than Cumings attributes to them.

CONCLUSIONS

Individually and collectively, McCormick and Cumings have made a major contribution to our understanding of US foreign policy during the Cold War. They have pushed that strand of thinking that roots explanation in socio-economic factors in important new directions. Most obviously, they have shifted the focus outwards from an earlier preoccupation with structures and processes internal to the USA to the wider world capitalist system. This is an important move for a number of reasons. In the first place it is so simply because global capitalism is a system – a set of structures and processes with its own dynamic – within which the American state, like any other, is compelled to act. Understanding this allows us to see that behaviour previously attributed to causes emanating from within the USA may actually have its ultimate source at a global level. In addition, setting up a systemic level of explanation creates the potential for a fruitful examination of the interaction between causal factors operating at different levels and thus a more complex understanding of the policy process.

Along with the emphasis on the importance of world capitalism as a system goes the idea of hegemony. While this is not the exclusive insight of world-systems theorists by any means, only Cumings and McCormick among diplomatic historians have applied this insight systematically. In so doing, they have produced a powerful and compelling explanation for the pursuit by the USA of certain key policy objectives after 1945. The position of the USA in the global capitalist economy and its consequent interest in the reconstruction and reintegration of that economy are nowhere better explained than in these accounts. Of the two, however, Cumings's is superior in that he does not attribute the particular nature and ideology of US hegemony to the world system, thus avoiding an implausible reductionism.

As well as sharing strengths, the two writers have one or two weaknesses in common. Along with virtually every other economically oriented historian we have discussed, they possess an inadequate and reductionist conceptualisation of politics. While McCormick's account is clearly the more reductionist of the two in this regard, both he and Cumings give the political, whether it be domestic politics or geopolitics, no autonomy. At best it is an ad hoc phenomenon, as with nationalism in McCormick's account, which is used to fill in the explanatory gaps left by the broader theory. More characteristically, it is treated as a derivative expression of more fundamental socio-economic forces. In addition, neither author gives a very satisfactory account of how the capitalist system actually works. The Wallerstein/McCormick account of the relationship between core and periphery and the necessary transfer of wealth between the two is subject to some compelling critiques, while Cumings never clearly spells out the mechanics of the relationship. This does not mean that their basic assumption about the necessity of integration is wrong. Indeed there is every reason to believe it is right given the evolution of the world system since 1945. It does mean that that process is inadequately explained in these accounts.

Alongside the similarities between these two perspectives there are also vital differences. Where these exist, they, without exception, favour the work of Cumings over that of McCormick. For all its capacity to generate powerful hypotheses about the roots of US foreign policy, McCormick's Wallersteinian framework is too flawed to represent a useful basis upon which others might build. The combination of extreme reductionism and economic determinism based on a profoundly flawed understanding of how capitalism actually works, plus an assumption of a priori understanding so total it leaves the historian nothing to do except illustrate revealed truth, is distinctly unpromising. McCormick's *America's Half Century* is the most extreme example of systemic determinism discussed in this book.

Cumings, in contrast, provides us with a much more open conceptual framework and thus with one with far greater potential for development and adaptation. His explanation of the origins of the Korean War is a sophisticated attempt to write a 'total history' of US foreign policy in the early Cold War – total, that is, in terms of the desire to grasp the full complexity of causes and connections. Fundamentally, what this involves is a continual effort to hold in balance a series of tensions between opposing poles without collapsing either into the other. Thus, Cumings insists upon the importance of theory while also acknowledging the reality of historical contingency that theory cannot capture. And he seeks to explain at the broadest structural level possible (the world system), but without reducing the layers of activity below that level to mere epiphenomena.

On the whole he achieves his objective with remarkable skill, but even with that skill his work demonstrates some problems, or rather limitations, to such an ambitious project. In the first place, the determination to avoid reductionism to the systemic level leads Cumings to circumscribe the explanatory role of the world system to such an extent that it plays virtually no role in the narrative at all. The dynamic of world capitalism is somehow both fundamental to the explanation and absent from it at the same time. The question this raises is whether Cumings's version of world-systems theory has much explanatory utility below a very general and long-term historical perspective.

That question could be avoided if Cumings had indicated how the systemic imperatives of global capitalism played themselves out inside the US society and state. The reason the world system plays so little role in the narrative is that, while Cumings regards it as ultimately determinative of the US drive to reintegrate global capitalism, he does not show how that determination shaped specific policies, which are treated as the product of dynamics operating at lower levels. What Cumings posits in his claim that structure and agency are an indissoluble unity is a relationship between the structure of the world system and the state/society levels in which each shapes the other in a continuous interaction. What we actually have, however, is the world system as a kind of playing field, bounding the action/policies, which are treated as entirely the product of factors operating below the systemic level, with no sense of how the two have shaped each other. What is supposed to be indissoluble is thus in fact dissolved. The structural imperatives of the world system and the agency of states, societies and individuals are unpacked for the purpose of analysis but not then put back together. The result is to undermine the explanatory utility of the systemic level and, ultimately, to fail to explain how the various levels of the explanation combine to produce the total history Cumings is seeking to achieve.

NOTES

1. McCormick, *America's Half Century*.
2. Ibid. pp. 1–7. See also McCormick, ' "Every system needs a center sometimes" ';
   McCormick, 'World systems'.
3. McCormick, *America's Half Century*, p. xiii.
4. Ibid. pp. 38–9.
5. Ibid. p. 78.
6. Ibid. p. 111.
7. Wallerstein, *The Modern World System*; Wallerstein, *The Modern World System II*;
   Wallerstein, *The Modern World System III*; Wallerstein, *The Capitalist World
   Economy*; Wallerstein, *The Politics of the World Economy*; Wallerstein, *Geopolitics and
   Geoculture*.
8. Wallerstein, *The Modern World System*, pp. 349–50.
9. Burman, *America in the Modern World*, pp. 90–2.
10. Warren, *Imperialism*.
11. Evans, *Dependent Development*; Cardoso and Faletto, *Dependency and Development*.
12. See above, Chapter 2, p. 51.
13. Brenner, 'The origins of capitalist development', pp. 27–33.
14. Skocpol, 'Wallerstein's world capitalist system'; Rupert, 'Producing hegemony'.
15. See Chapter 3.
16. He is ambiguous as to whether hegemony is necessary or not; see McCormick,
    ' "Every system needs a center sometimes" ', pp. 198–9.
17. McCormick, *America's Half Century*, p. 8.
18. Ibid. p. 30
19. On functionalism, see the debate in *Theory and Society*, 11 (1982), 453–540; Elster,
    Ulysses and the Sirens, chapter 1; Giddens, *Studies in Social and Political Theory*,
    chapter 2.
20. Rogin and Chirot, 'The world system of Immanuel Wallerstein', p. 305.
21. Skocpol, 'Wallerstein's world capitalist system', p. 1088.
22. Ninkovich, 'The end of diplomatic history?'.
23. McCormick, 'World systems', p. 92.
24. Tilly, *Big Structures*, p. 146.
25. Rogin and Chirot, 'The world system of Immanuel Wallerstein', p. 305.
26. The significance of hegemony is not an insight exclusive to world-systems theory,
    however. It also plays a significant role in neorealist political economy: Gilpin, *The
    Political Economy of International Relations*, pp. 72–80; Keohane, *After Hegemony*;
    Kindleberger, 'Dominance and leadership in the international political economy';
    Ruggie, 'International regimes, transactions and change'. This parallel reflects the fact
    that both neorealism and world-systems theory are preoccupied with explanation at
    the systemic level.
27. Kolko, of course, developed an argument that was similar in many ways to this, but
    that lacked the coherent treatment of the systemic aspect that we find in
    McCormick.

28. Cumings, *The Origins of the Korean War*; Cumings, 'Power and plenty in Northeast Asia'; Cumings, *The Origins of the Korean War, Volume 2*; Cumings, 'Japan and the Asian periphery'.
29. Cumings, 'Japan and the Asian periphery', p. 227.
30. See Chapter 4.
31. Schurmann, *The Logic of World Power*, pp. 48–65.
32. Cumings's articulation of his methodology and theory can be found in Cumings, *The Origins of the Korean War, Volume II*, pp. 4–22.
33. Agh, 'The hundred years peace'.
34. Polanyi, *The Great Transformation*.
35. For a good summary of Polanyi's method, see Block and Somers, 'Beyond the economistic fallacy'.
36. Cumings, *The Origins of the Korean War, Volume II*, p. 4.
37. Ibid. p. 5.
38. Ibid. p. 12.
39. Cumings, 'Japan and the Asian periphery', p. 218.
40. Ibid. pp. 218–19.
41. Ibid. pp. 225–7.
42. Cumings, *The Origins of the Korean War, Volume II*, pp. 20–2; Schurmann, *The Logic of World Power*, pp. 20–7; Block and Somers, 'Beyond the economistic fallacy', p. 67.
43. See Vernon, *Sovereignty at Bay*.
44. Kurth, 'The political consequences of the product cycle'.
45. Cumings, *The Origins of the Korean War, Volume II*, pp. 7–8.
46. Ibid.
47. For attempts to deal with this dilemma, see; Carlsnaes, 'The agency–structure problem'; Giddens, *Central Problems in Social Theory*, pp. 69–73; and the debate between Martin Hollis, Steve Smith and Alexander Wendt in the *Review of International Studies*: Wendt, 'Bridging the theory/meta-theory gap'; Hollis and Smith, 'Beware of gurus'; Wendt, 'Levels of analysis vs agents and structures'; Hollis and Smith, 'Structure and action'.
48. See Cumings, 'Archaeology, descent, emergence', p. 87.
49. Frank Ninkovich has stressed the illogic of Thomas McCormick's argument that economic liberalism is a product of hegemonic status by noting the implausibility of Nazi Germany becoming a liberal hegemon had it won the Second World War; Ninkovich, 'The end of diplomatic history?' p. 442.
50. Cumings, 'Power and plenty in Northeast Asia', p. 80; Cumings, *Origins of the Korean War, Volume II*, p. 36
51. Cumings, *The Origins of the Korean War, Volume II*, p. 17.

SIX

Post-structuralism and Culture

The perspectives discussed in the first five chapters of this book constitute a fairly coherent body of work. The analyses covered in this chapter, however, take arguments about US foreign policy and the Cold War in an entirely new direction. The perspectives discussed in the previous chapters disagreed about many things – what happened, why it happened, how it happened, what caused it, who was to blame and so on – but those disagreements occurred within a broad consensus as to what the objective of study was and how those studies were to be pursued. They all sought to establish what happened, to identify the causes of US foreign policy, and thus to provide the right, or at least the best possible, explanation. Moreover, they were all in broad agreement about how this was to be done, at least in terms of methods. Initial hypotheses or intuitive judgements about the sources of US foreign policy were to be tested against the evidence, which was to be found primarily (though not exclusively) in official documents and other primary sources.[1] To use an analogy, they were like people arguing about the best way to win at poker. They all disagreed about what the best strategy was, but they all agreed on the objective of the game and the rules by which it was played. Indeed, and importantly, it was precisely because they agreed on those basic elements that they were able to argue with each other at all.

The problem posed by post-structuralist and 'culturalist' approaches is that, to continue the analogy, not only do they reject the poker strategies proposed by the other perspectives but they also, in most cases, reject the accepted view of the objective of the game and its rules. To put it in more formal terms, they present not merely or even primarily an alternative perspective/theory on US foreign policy but an alternative epistemology or theory of knowledge. They are concerned, that is, not only with what happened but with how and whether we can know what happened. All post-structuralist, and many culturalist, historians believe that different perspectives have different rules and that there is no objective basis upon which it is possible to choose between, or even compare, either perspectives or rules. They believe in an 'undecidability' of perspectives and therefore of 'truths' in which there can never be a true or even best explanation of US foreign policy. One of the most important things to understand about this perspective, therefore, is that, as a result of these assumptions, post-structuralist historians are not pursuing the same objectives as the historians assessed in the previous five chapters.

In the first place, these historians will offer partial and/or possible accounts of the events that they are studying. History retains its subject matter, more or less. This is done, however, with no claim that the account is exhaustive or superior to others and without the claim that it is, in the commonly understood sense, true. To understand why such accounts are written at all one must grasp the primary purpose of all post-structuralist and much culturalist diplomatic history, which is in one sense the same as, and, in another, completely the opposite of, the purpose of most traditional history. Inasmuch as history has often been written in the hope that an understanding of the past will enlighten us about the present, the purpose is the same. The difference is that, whereas traditionally it has been hoped that establishing the truth about the past would serve that purpose, post-structuralist history seeks to achieve the same end by demonstrating that there is no objective truth about the past.

What post-structuralist methods demonstrate, it is claimed, is the impossibility of certainty. As we are unable to establish objective knowledge about the past, it is impossible for us to identify a singular historical truth. All that can be discovered are alternative and competing 'truths', none of which has any greater claim to our adherence than the others. Given that fact, the task of the historian becomes not to seek the truth but rather to expose the mistaken nature of the attempt to do so. Above all, what post-structuralist scholars wish to do is to undermine the dominant modes of thought and common-sense assertions that are widely held to be true. They seek to expose them as arbitrary and without foundation by showing how it is always possible to write different but equally 'true' stories about the same events. In thus 'denaturalising' and 'destabilising' the dominant perspectives, they seek to open up the field for a diversity of views and to promote pluralism, diversity and tolerance of doubt.

This aspect of these perspectives presents a problem in terms of the criteria by which they are to be judged. On the one hand, given their rejection of the basic premises and purposes of traditional modes of historical enquiry, simply to critique them from that same traditional perspective would somehow be to miss the point. Moreover, an immanent critique (one that works from the inside) is often the most compelling. So one task must be to ask whether this perspective satisfactorily achieves the goals it sets itself. On the other hand, however, it will not do simply to accept at face value the argument that traditional modes of doing history are defunct and deluded. Alongside the first line of enquiry, therefore, is the question of whether the case for rejecting traditional methods is compellingly made and whether the proposed alternative actually provides a satisfactory or useful way of doing diplomatic history.

The analysis that follows will take its lead from what has been written specifically about the Cold War and will focus on its fitness for that task. Inevitably this leads at times to more generalised comments about theory and epistemology, though certainly not to any kind of comprehensive analysis of post-structuralism. The works in question have been divided into two sections. First I examine the most extensive post-structuralist account of US foreign policy in the early Cold War written so far, David Campbell's *Writing Security*.[2] Secondly, the chapter looks at diplomatic historians who describe themselves as concerned with 'culture' but who are also, and more importantly, influenced by post-structuralist ideas.

DAVID CAMPBELL

There is only one book-length account of US foreign policy in the early Cold War that displays a fully developed post-structuralist sensibility. David Campbell's *Writing Security* seeks to provide a wholly new and deliberately subversive account of US foreign policy. The essence of his argument can be summed up in the claim that 'United States foreign policy can be understood as a political practice central to the constitution, production and maintenance of American political identity'.[3]

According to Campbell, US foreign policy is not necessarily about pursuing national interests, servicing the needs of the capitalist system or responding to foreign threats. Rather, to invert the last notion, it is also about the creation of foreign threats because such threats are needed for the production and reproduction of American identity. Identity, he argues, is a necessary quality of existence, for a state as much as for an individual. Neither can exist without some sense of who/what he/she/it is. Moreover, he asserts, identity does not reside in some essence or material quality of the state. It is not defined merely by geographical boundaries, political systems or historical experience. Rather, identity is fundamentally constituted through a process of differentiation – what we are is defined by what we are not, both physically and, more importantly, in terms of the characteristics we ascribe to ourselves and others. This process of inscripting identity thus necessitates the production of the 'other' – the thing(s) that we are not and against which we define what we are. Finally, because identity is not stable or fixed in some unchanging material reality, the process of identity creation is never finished; identity is – must be – constantly produced and reproduced.

According to Campbell, the primary role of the state is to act as a vehicle for securing the identity both of itself and of its citizens. That process requires not merely the constitution of 'otherness' but the constitution of threats to the state. States need threats to exist – they validate their existence as the means to protect the identity and security of their citizens. Threats are, in the language of post-structuralism, the state's 'condition of possibility' – no threats, no need for states.[4] The state therefore generates 'discourses of danger' that justify its existence and secure the loyalty of its citizens.[5] 'Foreign policy' is about the creation of those discourses and thus, crucially, is directed, not only externally at the outside world, but also internally, for the purpose of reproducing the identity of the state. It is important to note in this regard that Campbell distinguishes between 'foreign policy' – defined as all those processes and practices of differentiation that constitute things as other – and 'Foreign Policy', which is the external policy of the state as conventionally understood. It is the former with which he is primarily concerned.

The process of creating threats and inscribing identity typically operates through the use of metaphors that serve to translate the differences between the state/self and the other into terms familiar to the state's citizens. Characteristic metaphors are those relating to gender, sexuality and illness. These categories are organised around binary divisions such as male/female, natural/unnatural and healthy/sick in which one quality is identified as positive and the other as negative. The process of differentiation then operates by associating the state's identity with the positive qualities and those of the other with the negative ones. In the Cold War, for example, communism was regularly portrayed as a disease, virus or other pathological condition. Support or sympathy for it was associated with feminine weakness, homosexuality and mental illness. Anti-communism was therefore logically associated with the positively valued binary opposites of these characteristics. By thus transcribing its difference from the USSR onto differences taken for granted in US culture, the process of foreign policy naturalises those differences while also serving to demonise the other.

According to Campbell, this process of reproducing identity through differentiation is particularly important in the case of the United States because it is the 'imagined community par excellence'.[6] The USA's sense of itself and what it means to be an American is unusually centred upon ideas as opposed to historical or territorial definitions. Moreover, in the case of America, the process of differentiation takes on a peculiarly apocalyptic tone, which Campbell ascribes to the spiritual elements of American identity and its strong sense of itself as a uniquely virtuous political experiment. Such a moralistic sense of one's own identity leads, inevitably, to a highly judgemental view of those who fail to share in it or recognise its virtue.

For Campbell, therefore, the Cold War can be understood as a result of the need of the United States to reproduce an identity that had been destabilised by the successive crises of the Great Depression and the Second World War. In the space of a decade and a half, both America's domestic political and socio-economic systems and its place in the world had been radically transformed. There was a need, as a result, to redefine what America meant. The USSR came to serve as the other against which this new identity was inscribed, but that process was 'not dependent upon (though clearly influenced by) the Soviet Union for its character'.[7] The process of reproducing identity was necessary; the position of the USSR as the other was not, as there was nothing objective in the character of the USSR or its actions that could explain American fears of it.

The resulting process of reproducing identity through differentiation and othering manifested itself in the domestic anti-communism of the late 1940s and early 1950s. The witch-hunts and loyalty programmes that characterised this era were a practice of 'foreign policy' understood as a process of constituting the boundaries between the domestic and the foreign. By emphasising the 'foreign' nature of communism and attaching to it the varied metaphors of illness, disease, perversion and pathology, the American state was able to reproduce its identity and discipline its citizenry by drawing clear lines between what was American and what was un-American. 'Foreign Policy', in the sense of the actual external policies of the United States, served only to reinforce the domestic processes of foreign policy. US foreign policy in the early Cold War is, in sum, to be understood as a process of redefining more clearly what it was to be an 'American' through constituting and demonising an alien other in the shape of the USSR/communism.

Campbell has little or nothing to say about the end of the Cold War in terms of a conventional explanation of that event. Instead, he argues that discussion of the end of the Cold War 'embodies a misunderstanding' because, although the collapse of communism and the USSR removed it as a 'plausible candidate for enmity', the 'entailments of identity' that it served do not change.[8] The need to continue reproducing identity, in other words, remains even if the USSR does not. And, given that 'discourses of danger' are central to that process, new ones have to be created.

Potential candidates for threatening others are always multiple, but Campbell identifies two in particular that became central to US foreign policy in the late 1980s and early 1990s. The first of these was the 'war on drugs' launched by President George H. W. Bush in 1989. As in the case of anti-communism, Campbell notes, 'the "war on drugs" bears all the hall marks of a morality play designed to instantiate the ethical boundaries of identity'.[9] As much as anything else, he argues, this 'war' was about drawing moral boundaries and defining deviants, who often turned out to be exactly the same groups – women, blacks, foreigners, radicals and sexual deviants – who had born the brunt of domestic anti-communism. The extension of drug-testing regimes across society was an effective 'disciplinary technique' for the enforcement of moral boundaries. In addition, the 'war on drugs' had an external dimension that was used to inscribe national borders and identity. Instead of communism, the USA now faced Latin American 'narco-elites' who threatened to undermine American democracy through a tidal wave of illegal drugs. In order to naturalise this danger, the concept of 'narco-terrorism' was invoked. By linking the drug kingpins to insurgents and leftist revolutionaries, the American state was able to draw on familiar tropes of anti-communism as it sought to persuade the US public of the threat.

The other example Campbell cites is the alleged Japanese economic threat much debated in the USA in the late 1980s and early 1990s.[10] In this case, he notes, analyses of the nature of the supposed threat were premised first and foremost upon the notion that Japan was different – authoritarian, hierarchical, conformist and rigid – and fundamentally alien to the US way of doing things. Such a portrayal, he observes, serves as a rather obvious means of reinscribing American identity and values as the opposite – individualistic, pluralist, laissez-faire and open – of those of the deviant Japanese. That discourse disappeared rather swiftly in the 1990s, but, were he writing in the early twenty-first century, Campbell would no doubt find ample grist for his mill in George W. Bush's 'war on terror' with its rhetoric of good and evil and 'civilisation' versus 'barbarism.'

I have little doubt that many readers will have found the above account quite bizarre and utterly alien to their understanding of the Cold War and US foreign policy. Nor should there be any doubt that that is precisely Campbell's intention. In order to analyse his argument, therefore, the first thing we need to do is to reiterate what it is that he is trying to achieve. Campbell is not attempting to provide a complete, best, or, in the conventional understanding of the word, 'true' account of US foreign policy. Rather, the core of his position is that there is no possibility of providing such an account. He does not regard his account as better than any of the others we have discussed thus far; he merely regards it as no worse and, most crucially, believes that there is no valid way of choosing amongst them.

Explanatory Framework

To explain why Campbell believes this, we need at this point to elaborate a little on the basic premises of the post-structuralist epistemology that underpins his argument. This is a slightly vexed task, since Campbell engages in no extended discussion of his assumptions and because the complexity and diversity of this perspective mean that 'to attempt to isolate a common core or central proposition . . . not only risks, but guarantees, oversimplification'.[11] Nevertheless, we cannot proceed without some attempt to outline these ideas.[12]

At the heart of the post-structuralist perspective is the role played by language in mediating between our understanding of the world and the world itself. Everything that we see, hear or read, all of our sense data, is passed through the filter of language and the names, concepts and theories that we apply as we seek to explain and understand it. There is a 'real' world out there, but we have no way of understanding it except through language. That in itself would not be a problem, of course, if language was a simple reflection of reality and we could assume that there was a simple one-to-one correspondence between words and the objects they referred to. The key to the post-structuralist argument, however, is the rejection of the idea that there is any such consistent connection between language and the world it describes. This view derives originally from the structural linguistics of Ferdinand de Saussure, who argued that meaning in language is not a product of the relationship between the sign (word) and its referent (material object) but rather is the product of the differences between words. Thus, the word cat is not applied to the furry mammal in question because of something inherent in that object; the application is arbitrary; it could just as easily have been called a tree. The meaning of the word cat derives, instead, from the whole structure of the language of which it is a part. We know what cat means by differentiating it from all the other words in the language. Cat is not hat, or bat, or dog. The result of this basic idea and its elaboration by various thinkers was to emphasise the essential arbitrariness of meaning that is constructed within language and detached from any reference to external objects. The key conclusion drawn is that we can never be certain that our words/language accurately reflect the object world.

The next step is to argue that, because of this fact, different languages constitute different realities and there is no way of establishing that one or other of these realities is more true than any other. The reason for this is that, traditionally, the way we seek to corroborate our explanations and understandings of the world has been to test them against the evidence or facts of that world. However, if that evidence or those facts are partially constituted by the language we use to describe them and that language is not a simple reflection of reality, then there is no objective evidence available to us to conduct such tests. We are thus, in a sense, trapped by language. We have no means of escaping our language to some position of pure, unmediated access to objective reality that would allow us to test the validity of our assertions about the world. There is, therefore, no means by which we can accurately identify an objective truth about the world. Truth exists only within a given language or 'discourse' and there are as many truths as there are languages.

This is the basis for Campbell's contention that he is providing an account of US foreign policy in the early Cold War that is no more or less true than any other. More fundamentally, Campbell's point is not that we should accept the validity of his argument so much as that it should lead us to question the claims of other arguments. What Campbell desires, more than anything else, is to destabilise and undermine those discourses (realism above all) that do in fact proclaim their ability to identify the one and only truth. The purpose of constructing an analysis based around the inscription of identity is not to assert its superiority but simply to

> demonstrate that, within each realm of policy discourse, it is possible
> to construct, on its own terms, a competing narrative which
> denaturalises and unsettles the dominant way of constructing the
> world, thus prying open the space for an alternative interpretation
> concerned with the entailment of identity.[13]

Ultimately, Campbell's purpose has nothing to do with historical explanation or US foreign policy in the Cold War at all. Following the example of Michel Foucault, the post-structuralist eminence who is clearly the greatest influence upon him, Campbell regards history as aimed not at establishing the truth of the past but at the enabling of thought and action in the present.[14] Above all, the aim is to promote pluralism and diversity and the tolerance thereof. The chief threat to those values is perceived to lie in those 'totalizing' discourses that claim a monopoly of truth. Such discourses are necessarily oppressive and coercive, since they 'attempt to force difference into the straightjacket of identity'.[15] What revisionist readings of history such as Campbell's are intended to do, therefore, is to destabilise dominant perspectives and demonstrate the impossibility of any single correct interpretation in the belief that only when we recognise the limits of our possible knowledge will the 'ambiguity and indeterminacy of life' come 'to be respected'.[16]

Critique

In one sense, Campbell's argument poses no challenge to the other perspectives discussed so far, since he simply offers a different and additional way of looking at US 'foreign policy'. He himself says that he does not wish to exclude accounts that seek 'to authorise their positions through reference to "external reality"'.[17] He is doing one thing and they are doing another, in which case one would need only to pursue a critique based upon his own stated purposes and objectives. On the other hand, however, Campbell's stated tolerance of other perspectives is rather disingenuous, since later in the book he specifically calls for their rejection.[18] Moreover, the logic of his post-structuralist assumptions about the language-dependent nature of historical evidence, if accepted, fundamentally undermines the basis of the arguments contained in all the other perspectives by reducing them to nothing more than entertaining stories with no valid claim to represent historical truth and no way of choosing between them.

At the heart of Campbell's argument lies the concept of identity, and in that idea lie both the strengths and the weaknesses of that argument.[19] The strengths are undoubted. It is very difficult to come away from reading the book not believing that questions of identity and self-definition played a significant role in the domestic and foreign policies of the United States in the early Cold War. The very existence of a word such as 'un-American' testifies to the accuracy of Campbell's analysis. Communism and the USSR were, unquestionably, an alien other. Equally importantly, Campbell forces us to think again about much that we might have taken as given – the identity and coherence of the state, the material nature of the Soviet threat, 'foreign policy' as a practice that is solely directed outwards – and to look at them from a wholly fresh perspective.

But Campbell's emphasis on identity also has its weaknesses. One of his principal objectives in the book is to question the kind of ahistorical, universalising assumptions that underpin perspectives like the neorealism that influences post-revisionism and posit an invariant pursuit of security or power as the determinant of foreign policy. But, as Regina Graemer has pointed out, in the process of so doing Campbell mirrors the failings that he identifies in those he criticises. He abstracts the process of inscribing identity from any kind of political or historical context and depicts it as a universal necessity, invariant across either geography or time.[20] If the process of inscribing identity is indeed such a universal phenomenon, however, it is also of limited interest or utility to anyone seeking to understand US Cold War foreign policy. If the USA and every other nation are always reproducing their identities through this process of differentiation, then the explanation for all that is unique about the Cold War must lie elsewhere. Rather like unchanging human nature, identity production becomes a necessary, but wholly insufficient, explanation for historical events.

To put it another way, if the USA is engaged in a permanent process of reproducing its identity, then how are we to explain the fact that for most of its existence it managed to do this without producing an antagonism towards another country sufficient to produce a forty-year struggle and almost lead to nuclear war? The fact is that it is quite impossible to account for the Cold War without some reference to the material fact of the Soviet Union and its behaviour or to the material reality of the United States itself. Are we to believe that it was mere chance that it was the Soviet Union rather than, say,

Monaco that became the other of American nightmares? Or that the fact that the United States chose to engage in a global policy of expansion and containment at the zenith of its material power was pure contingency? Of course Campbell has a compelling point when he says that it is not possible to explain the Cold War simply by the objective nature of the Soviet threat, but it is equally impossible to explain US fears of the Soviet other simply as the result of the need to reproduce identity.

This point can be reinforced by noting a problem with Campbell's argument about the consequences of the process of inscripting identity. In the first place, it is worth noting that Campbell himself seems unsure about this. On the one hand, he insists, reasonably enough, that the process of inscripting identity is unavoidable. He further says that that process 'always results in an other being marginalized'. Later on, however, he asserts that the process of othering does not necessarily lead to the 'demonisation' of the other, though it always contains the potential for such a development.[21] The semantics of marginalisation as against demonisation do not serve to conceal a fairly obvious problem with this argument – namely, that the process of differentiation does not necessarily lead to any kind of dislike, antagonism or mistrust of the other at all. Most people are not at daggers drawn with others most of the time; most nations are not at war with each other most of the time. It is perfectly clear that not all Americans in the late 1940s and 1950s, even in the face of the coercive, disciplinary strategy of the 'Red Scare', came to see the Soviet Union as the demonic other. In fact, we are continually differentiating ourselves from all the others around us without this necessarily leading us to fear or hate any one of them.[22] The kind of fear of the Soviet Union demonstrated by Americans at the height of the Cold War is highly unusual, so how far can the mundane, everyday process of inscripting identity really go towards explaining it?

What this point demonstrates, as does the last, is how little Campbell's core concept of identity formation actually tells us about the United States and the Cold War. All the process of identity inscription provides us with is a framework of universals – identity being inscripted by differentiation from others – that implies no necessary consequences and can be operationalised only by the introduction of a mass of specific historical evidence to explain why in one case it leads to a Cold War and in another to nothing more than a bit of mild ribbing. In practice, Campbell's account does contain masses of such historical data and often relies upon material factors as part of its explanatory framework. In so doing, however, he runs up against his own objections about the impossibility of adequately grasping such evidence about the past. What he thus demonstrates is the impossibility of anyone, even a post-structuralist, saying much of anything about the past without assuming that it is possible adequately to identify facts about it.

Campbell would probably object, at this point, that all he sought to demonstrate was that it was possible to tell multiple stories about the past on the basis of the historical evidence available and that he is not claiming that what he is saying is 'true'. So, even if he does rely on the citation of evidence and explanation via material causes, this does not matter, because it implies no commitment to truth. He is simply demonstrating that that 'evidence' can be used to construct a variety of different and equally plausible historical narratives. That defence, however, exposes his argument to probably the most telling criticism of all.

This critique derives directly from the post-structuralist insistence that each discourse has its own realities, rationality and criteria of truth (hence Campbell's point about seeking to demonstrate only that you can tell different stories). If that were the case there would be no grounds for the critique Campbell seeks to make of realism and other totalising discourses, since they must be as true as his. Indeed, such a critique would be quite impossible, since, according to post-structuralist logic, any critique can only operate only from within a discourse and on its own terms. If criteria of truth exist only within a language/discourse, you must share its basic assumptions to say anything telling about it. But if you accept its basic assumptions, what profound criticism can you make? Nor does it make any difference if we focus on the normative purposes of Campbell's argument, for they are also bound by discourse. What is moral or immoral depends upon the values of each discourse. Therefore Campbell can offer us no reason to prefer pluralism or diversity over totalitarianism. In fact, if it were true that it was not possible to step outside the intellectual framework created by one's own discourse, Campbell could not even know that other discourses were totalising or oppressive. If he was inside those discourses, he would share their assumptions, and if he was outside them, they would be unintelligible to him.

Campbell is thus caught between his desire to render a critique of other perspectives or discourses and his insistence that each discourse constructs its own truth. If he insists on affirming the latter line of argument, then his case for pluralism and diversity and his critique of realism have no force and we have no reason to take them seriously. If he wishes to maintain that his critique has meaning, that can be demonstrated only either by an appeal to the material reality that they allegedly distort or by a normative critique based upon universal criteria of judgement, neither of which his premisses allow.[23] Campbell thus finds himself in what the post-structuralists like to call an aporia – a logical contradiction – where his own stated epistemological premisses rob his work of its critical force.

For all its freshness of perspective and the persuasiveness of its insistence on the importance of identity production as a factor in foreign policy, therefore, Campbell's analysis is undermined by the contradictions of its epistemological assumptions. An analysis that denies our ability confidently to grasp the reality of the material world depends profoundly on claims upon that reality, first in order to operationalise what would otherwise be little more than a broad classificatory scheme or conceptual framework and secondly to give the ensuing critique of totalising discourses any persuasive force. Despite his denial of the possibility of describing the real world, without it Campbell has little to say.

CULTURAL STUDIES

Campbell's may be the most fully developed example of a post-structuralist analysis of US foreign policy during the Cold War, but it is not the most typical. Far more common are authors who identify themselves as influenced by the discipline of 'cultural studies' or talk about pursuing a 'cultural' analysis of US foreign policy. In practice, however, these scholars are distinguished primarily by their post-structuralist doubts about the limits of historical knowledge and truth. Whereas Campbell foregrounds the specific issue of identity (re)production, they tend to focus more generally on the issue of how language or discourse serves to legitimate, naturalise and sustain certain interpretations, practices and institutions while marginalising and delegitimating others. They are, in other words, discussing what could be called the ideology of US policy-makers. However, as we shall see, they generally reject that term because of its implicit assumption that ideas are a product of objective, material factors. Their basic objective is the same as Campbell's – namely, to force us to question taken-for-granted assumptions, undermine dominant interpretations and open up the space for a plurality of arguments and interpretations.[24]

To that end, the emphasis upon how language serves to construct reality is deployed in characteristic ways to a variety of ends. Frank Costiglioga, for example, demonstrates how George F. Kennan's analyses of the Soviet Union in the late 1940s are shot through with tropes of gender and pathology. Kennan implicitly genders the various historical actors in such a way that the Russian people are depicted as helpless female victims of a cruelly masculine Soviet power, with the United States, in consequence, becoming the noble (masculine) hero whose task is to defeat the wicked oppressor. Costiglioga also notes how Kennan has a tendency to depict the USSR using medical metaphors that construct it as a psychiatric patient subject to various pathological conditions.

These metaphors, in turn, have various effects. The gendered discourse helps to legitimate the policy of containment by playing upon common cultural stereotypes. It can also be reconfigured in such a way as to stigmatise those who seek continued cooperation with the Soviets as weak/feminine/ homosexual. The medical metaphor has the effect of implicitly placing Kennan in the privileged position of diagnostician and expert and of delegitimating arguments for negotiation and cooperation by suggesting that the Soviet state is subject to a form of psychiatric illness that places it beyond the reach of rational dialogue.[25] Costiglioga thus demonstrates how the writings of one of the supposedly most dispassionate and realistic of analysts and policy-makers are permeated by all kinds of subjective and emotive language and assumptions. Far from representing a cool appraisal of realities, Costiglioga implies, Kennan's work is profoundly rhetorical and relies heavily on various metaphorical tropes for its persuasive force. Once we identify those tropes, we must naturally come to question the depiction of an implacable Soviet threat contained in his writings.[26]

On a more general level, historians influenced by cultural studies seek to demonstrate how various 'cultural' assumptions infuse the decision-making environment in which policy-makers operate. In a different article, Costiglioga demonstrates how the US relationship with its NATO allies and the USSR is commonly configured in such a way as to depict the latter as a brutal male aggressor (rapist?), the Europeans as the threatened female figure and the USA as their manly defender. The common use of such metaphors in policy circles, he argues, indicates how policy-makers' emotional evaluations of others infuse their thinking. Consequently, historians must try to 'discern how emotive meanings can constrain and actually shape rational analysis'.[27]

Elsewhere, Robert Dean, in an analysis of the Kennedy administration, has sought to show how 'internalized ideals of manliness influenced the way leaders perceived threats posed by foreign powers'.[28] He argues that a culture of machismo, traceable to the social, educational, military, professional and historical experiences of the Kennedy men, profoundly shaped JFK's foreign policy. The purpose of such analyses, clearly, is to compel us to rethink the factors shaping US foreign policy, to suggest that there is more to them than the material considerations of economics or power and thus to exhort us to 'open ourselves to broader, more meaningful definitions of the history of foreign relations'.[29]

As well as seeking to broaden our horizons in terms of the influences shaping foreign policy, the 'culturalists' also seek to expand the range of sources used to identify them. Dominic LaCapra has argued that one of the failings of traditional history has been a fixation upon the centrality of primary sources to the neglect of other, equally useful, alternatives.[30] An example of the utilisation of such alternative sources is Emily Rosenberg's article on 'Foreign affairs'[31] in which she demonstrates how two films of the late 1940s and early 1950s can be read to contain certain meanings and messages about the appropriate role of US foreign policy. Focusing on the depiction of gender roles in the films, she seeks to show how 'the ideology of male responsibility' depicted therein can be seen to reflect the contemporary imperatives of US foreign policy. In so doing she aims to 'highlight the value of discursive analysis in illuminating the mutually supportive connections between see-mingly unrelated areas of thought and action'.[32]

Running through all these articles, connecting them and imbuing them with their critical edge, is an emphasis on power. Culturalist approaches insist 'on the power relations implied in cultural meanings . . . the power of dominant narratives, symbols and interpretations to create, position and make possible the elimination of historical memories, social options or groups of people'.[33] It is not simply that culture shapes US foreign policy, or that taken-for-granted interpretations can be shown to be full of subjective rhetoric. Most culturalists take the view that the metaphors and tropes and meanings they analyse work in consistent ways, privileging certain practices, institutions and groups and equally systematically marginalising others. As with Campbell, the essential goal here is to demonstrate that what seems natural or obvious is far from being so and thus to create space for alternative perspectives to be aired.

Unlike Campbell, however, there is a tendency within this group to seek a kind of compromise or truce with more traditional modes of history. Whereas Campbell is using history purely for contemporary ethical and political purposes, these scholars are generally not prepared to consign history to the dustbin just yet. Emily Rosenberg has called for an effort to find some position of accommodation in which dialogue between different perspectives becomes possible.[34] Robert Dean has likewise stressed that the culturalists' works are similar to those of their counterparts from other perspectives in terms of their use of evidence and argument and that, unlike many post-structuralists, he believes that there are better, and worse, explanations of the past. He does not believe, however, that there is a best one, and this belief highlights the limitations to accommodation due to 'disagreements over the nature and purpose of historical explanation itself'.[35] Ultimately, the cultur-alists are firmly wedded to the belief that 'knowledge can be neither universal nor objective because both disciplines and authors are culturally constructed within their own time and circumstances'.[36] That being so, the task of the historian is not to seek the best explanation possible but rather to 'complicate' history, demonstrate the diversity of possible accounts of the past and 'let a thousand flowers bloom'.[37]

Critique

On an empirical and a descriptive level, the vast majority of culturalist accounts are compelling. They provide ample evidence and carefully detailed analysis that will convince all but the most blinkered of readers that the language of policy-makers, scholars and popular culture is permeated with tropes of gender, pathology and sexuality. The argument that such uses of language do in fact serve to legitimate and reinforce certain practices and institutions and to marginalise others is equally persuasive. We are all well aware that how something is described affects our response to it and that the same event or practice can be described in many different ways. What is open to question, however, is, first, how important and useful such insights are for the analysis of US foreign policy and, secondly, whether the price we are asked to pay in terms of what is sacrificed by this approach is worth what we gain.

It is the latter question that I will address first. At the heart of the culturalist position lies an assumption of the autonomy of culture – that is to say, a rejection of the idea that culture is reducible to, or explicable as, a reflection of material factors or events. This group of scholars wants to assert the independent importance of ideas in history. The epistemology of post-structuralism legitimates such an approach by rejecting the belief that language reflects a material reality that we can objectively identify. In doing this it creates an intellectual space in which scholars can discuss the meaning and significance of language and culture without feeling compelled to try and relate them to an objectively ungraspable 'real world'.

The opening-up of this space, however, comes at a significant cost in terms of the limits placed upon the scope of the resulting analysis. In the first place, there is the problem of the reification of culture that results from this approach. By refusing to contemplate the possibility of a determinable relationship between the material world and the world of culture, the culturalists necessarily make the latter inexplicable. Hermetically sealed off from the material world, tropes of gender and pathology just exist. It is not possible to explore how they developed or why.[38] Thus to start by placing the central focus of your study beyond exploration or explanation is hardly promising, but the implications of this insistence upon the autonomy of culture hardly stop there.

The determination to deal with culture as an autonomous domain of study accounts for the absence of explanation in culturalist accounts. As Bruce Kucklick has observed, their writings are characterised by a repetitive pattern; a detailed and persuasively argued first section in which the tropes and metaphors are identified and described is followed by a sudden leap to a claim that these cultural elements shaped foreign policy. This claim, however, is more or less entirely unsupported by evidence or argument.[39] It is simply asserted that internalised ideals of manliness had 'profound foreign policy consequences',[40] or 'helped shape and institutionalise' the Marshall Plan and NATO.[41] This absence of substantive explanation is not the product of mere oversight. If you treat culture and the language through which it is expressed as autonomous and the sole focus of your study, then it stands to reason that not only can you not explore and explain its evolution but you can not explore or explain how it affects the world either.

The culturalist answer to this last criticism is the concept of 'intertextuality'. Practitioners of this perspective typically reject the 'simplistic logic of linear causality' in favour of 'a complexity of interactions that are dynamically in play'.[42] This 'intertextuality' can be broadly understood to imply the existence of webs of connections between language, practices and institutions that are of such complexity and circularity that it is impossible to regard one as the cause of any other or any one as having causal primacy. The implication of this is that it is, in practice, more or less fruitless to try and determine the relationships between these factors, thus legitimating the abandonment of the effort to try to do so and the retreat into assertions of influence.

The concept of 'intertextuality' is an attempt to fudge and evade the profoundly thorny issue of the relationship between the cultural and material. Having rejected the idea that culture can be reduced to material causes, the culturalists have no desire to slip into an equally reductionist cultural determinism that denies the material any effect on culture since they are well aware how implausible such a position would be.[43] They also want to assert that culture shapes events. Through the concept of intertextuality, the culturalists seek to resolve both problems by asserting that culture/language is just one part of an enormous web of factors, the relationships between which are indeterminable. This defence rings hollow, however, in the face of the evidence. The obvious implication of intertextuality is surely the necessity of an awareness of the multiplicity of interconnections between the material and non-material worlds and the importance of exploring them. Yet in practice it is used as an excuse to throw up one's hands at the sheer complexity of it all. Account after culturalist account focuses solely upon culture/language with no attempt to examine other factors whatsoever. In practice, the vast majority of culturalist accounts are thus anything but 'intertextual', if what is meant by that word is an attempt to give some idea of the complexity of connections between a wide range of factors and elements involved in foreign policy. On the contrary, they are largely one-dimensional. Intertextuality as utilised in these accounts is little more than a rhetorical device to evade the charge of cultural determinism and the problem of the relationship between the cultural and the material. As a methodology it is preached but not practised.

The culturalist rejection of causality also has more than a whiff of semantics about it. Time after time what one finds in these accounts is a rejection of the concept at the front door followed by its surreptitious re-entry by the back door. Thus language has 'effects' and it 'influenced policy';[44] culture has 'profound foreign policy consequences';[45] 'dominant cultural narratives . . . shape the definitions of national identity out of which foreign policy is enacted';[46] and the 'interaction of dominant and contesting cultural structures, across national and international boundaries, in turn affects definitions of national security'.[47] What, one might reasonably ask, is the precise difference between something that causes something else and something that 'affects' or 'influences' or 'shapes' it?

Perhaps the culturalists would assert that the words they use imply less certainty about the connection and the absence of any kind of simple, monocausal relationship between a singular cause and a policy effect. Rather, all they are positing is the modest claim that culture had something to do with it. In which case one might reasonably respond, how do you know? The rejection of causality or the possibility of establishing any kind of hierarchy of causes has the inevitable effect of meaning that all possible factors are equally significant or insignificant[48] and that there is absolutely no way of claiming with any confidence that any one of them 'shaped' or 'influenced' policy. If the culturalists had the courage of their convictions, they would surely admit that by their own logic they can have no idea whether culture had any effect on policy or not, but that they think that it might have. Rejecting causality but talking about effects is trying to have your cake and eat it too.

Perhaps more seriously, readers must ask themselves how useful is a form of analysis that does not allow one to establish any kind of causal hierarchy whatsoever? The implications of the culturalist position are quite clear in this regard; there is no possibility of better or worse explanations. An account of US foreign policy that focuses on Dean Acheson's piles (if he suffered from such an affliction) plus the position of the planets would be as valid as one that focused upon culture or economics. Of course the culturalists recognise the absurdity of that position, but there is no way of avoiding it. Robert Dean tries to get round it by arguing that there are better and worse explanations and that the former can be identified by the way that they provide a good match between their theory and an 'empirically persuasive' description of events.[49] But the use of the phrase 'empirically persuasive' is just a way of reintroducing objectivity, since what it implies is a description people find convincing regardless of their particular culture, perspective or discourse. If such a description is indeed possible, then so are a solid grasp of reality and the identification of causes and their ordering. The culturalists must either accept that all explanations are equally valid or that we can gain a much more solid understanding of the material world and its causes and effects than they will allow. There is no compromise position between these two.

A further consequence of the culturalist refusal to deal with questions of explanation or causality in any kind of detail is the essentially one-dimensional and static nature of the history that results. One does not have to read many of the articles influenced by this approach before one can guess with a fair degree of certainty what comes next. If you refuse to deal with the interactions of the cultural and the material and to develop explanations of the relationship between culture and policy, then there is not that much left to do. Each culturalist account amounts to much the same thing – a description of the various tropes and metaphors (almost always gender and illness) – and examples of their existence in different texts – policy documents, historical writings, sources from popular culture – plus an assertion of the influence of those tropes on policy. Given its reluctance to go beyond those basic parameters, the only way in which this perspective can advance is sideways, through the steady subjection of every administration, policy and document to an examination for the same familiar tropes. At the end of this process they will then be able to conclude that those tropes are everywhere[50] and that they have an influence on foreign policy, but they will not be able to explain the existence of these tropes or their influence on policy or to integrate them into any larger explanation unless they are prepared to abandon their reification of culture.

Such narrow culturalism also produces analyses that tend towards reductionism. This can be seen, for example, in the work of Andrew Rotter and Frank Ninkovich. Rotter has been interested in the impact of perceptions of religion and gender on US–South Asian relations.[51] This work is valuable and interesting but it also contains sweeping generalisations about culture – such as the claim that 'Hindu society is imagined as an organic whole in which religious values shape the patterns of everyday life'[52] – that flatten out a multitude of nuances and diversities and impose an implausible uniformity of belief/behaviour on millions of people in the space of a sentence. The lack of alternative explanations also causes problems. When President Eisenhower confounds his basic argument about Americans looking down on Indians because of gendered perceptions of them as weak and unmanly by getting on well with Prime Minister Nehru, Rotter feels the need to construct an explanation in similarly gendered terms, asserting that Eisenhower had proved his manhood in war and thus felt no need to assert it now.[53] While there may or may not be something to that claim, it nevertheless raises the problem of irrefutability. If gender can be used to explain US presidents both getting on and not getting on with Indian leaders, then are there any circumstances in which we could prove that it does not explain policy? And if it explains everything, then the inevitable question is, does it really explain anything? All in all it would have been wiser, surely, to accept that the basic argument laid out in the article did not apply in every instance.

There is also an element of self-fulfilling prophecy and a certain lack of self-reflexivity in this work. Historians who emphasise cultural perceptions as a barrier to understanding set out to find the evidence to demonstrate the fact.

They seem to have very little interest, however, in evidence that might contradict it. Now, of course, historians as a class tend to be guilty quite often of pursuing the unscientific goal of trying to prove rather than disprove their hypotheses, and history is not a science. Nevertheless, cultural historians seem to provide particularly egregious examples of this practice. Cultural differences are assumed to create great chasms of understanding despite the fact that there is a vast wealth of evidence to demonstrate just how well communication actually occurs between cultures.[54] Whenever something can be attributed, however tenuously, to some cultural difference, then it is, regardless of the availability of several other possible and equally plausible explanations. Cultural misunderstandings are real and their importance should not be dismissed, but it is a long way to go from a generalisation about an entire culture to the actions of an individual without considering the factors that could intervene between the two.[55] A little more nuance and caution would make the argument more, rather than less, persuasive.

In Frank Ninkovich's case, the purpose of the employment of post-structuralist ideas is to open up space for the study of 'ideology' rather than 'culture', though the same basic point about the autonomy and importance of ideas is being made.[56] By ruling out the possibility of identifying the material causes of policy, ideology becomes a source of policy in its own right rather than an expression of underlying material interests. Equally, by rejecting the possibility of identifying reality, we cannot treat ideology as a mere distortion of it. Indeed, argues Ninkovich, once we accept that we cannot explain policy by reference to objective interests or compare beliefs to reality, then ideology is all that we have left. History thus becomes an attempt to understand ideology and how policy-makers understood what they were doing through the ideology that shaped their thinking.[57]

Ninkovich takes post-structuralist ideas to their logical conclusions. Ideology (or just ideas) becomes a free-floating and autonomous phenomenon and the only one we can talk about with any confidence. The real world is ungraspable, and critique is impossible because of that fact. Unable to say what is real, we are equally unable to say what is right or wrong in the conduct of foreign policy. The question is, though, does Ninkovich's approach produce good history? The answer, I think, is no. In the first place, his whole approach rests upon a massive logical contradiction. On a strict post-structuralist reading, the ideas of the past are no more objectively available than its material realities. Ninkovich has no way of knowing with confidence what Woodrow Wilson meant or believed any more than he has of knowing what he did. Ideology is no more objectively knowable than material events.

More pertinently, what Ninkovich's approach to history produces is a narrative that is uncritical, unanalytical and reductionist. To take the last point first, by refusing to consider anything but ideology, Ninkovich has no choice but to reduce everything to that single phenomenon. Thus, in his latest book, the entire history of US foreign policy in the twentieth century, in all its diversity, is reduced to a simple expression of the ideology of Wilsonianism. Apart from its reductionism and implausibility, such an approach also reduces 'Wilsonianism' to a conception so capacious and vague as to be effectively meaningless.[58] Secondly, without any other sources of policy except ideology and without any critical purpose, what we are left with is essentially rather dull, descriptive, narrative history. Finally, the effect of denying the possibility of a critique against reality is to turn history into hagiography. Ninkovich asserts that he intends to be 'neither critical nor celebratory',[59] but someone who is as aware of binary opposites as he is should know that if one refuses to be the former then it is going to be difficult to avoid being the latter. Certainly, his description of US foreign policy in the twentieth century has an air of complacency and inevitability about it: policy-makers can never be bad or misguided; whatever was must have been; to try and suggest the possibility of alternatives is to engage in 'historical fantasizing'; to ask if Wilson was right or wrong is to pursue 'irrelevant questions that cannot be answered'. Ultimately, he concludes, if Wilsonianism has managed to survive so successfully for so long, it must have been doing something right.

The culturalist reification of culture also massively vitiates the claim to focus on power by reducing the latter to a mere function of language. While it is unquestionably true that language and the meanings it conveys do have the power to shape 'reality', this is but a fragment of the whole picture. In the first place, if, as the culturalists assert, 'meanings are always open to negotiation, error and interpretation',[60] why do they always find the same dominant meanings, the same tropes of gender and illness, everywhere they look? Is it pure chance that the dominant meanings remain dominant? The culturalists have no answer, because they treat culture as a domain unto itself. They are thus unable to account for one of the most interesting aspects of their entire approach. Those of us less than convinced of culture's isolation might venture to suggest that an analysis that examined the relationship between material manifestations of power in the state, society, economy and culture might be more productive. The problem is that the culturalists have, for all their emphasis upon the concept, a profoundly anaemic and under-theorized conception of power. It is everywhere and it affects everyone but somehow it is not exercised by anyone. Their approach obscures the profoundly important reality that power is controlled and exercised by agents and institutions and that it is organised and structured in rather consistent and repetitive ways that they are quite unable to explain.[61]

A final problem relates to the culturalist desire to expand the range of sources used by diplomatic historians to include popular culture. On the one hand, this can produce compelling arguments. When it is claimed that highlighting certain meanings in films and relating them to foreign policy serves to highlight 'symbolic interrelationships among seemingly unrelated institutions and assumptions',[62] one is inclined to agree. Such analysis is very effective at demonstrating how meanings in domestic popular culture might have helped legitimate foreign policy choices. What it less clear, however, is the extent to which it tells us much, if anything, about those policy choices themselves. Partly this is because, as I have already argued, no case is actually made (as opposed to simply asserted) for the effect of those meanings on policy. But there is also the question of matching sources to the focus of study. In the area of cultural studies and intellectual history, a focus on popular cultural sources is obviously desirable, since this constitutes a central element of what is being studied. While one must not dismiss the potential relevance of popular culture to US foreign policy (for what it tells us about the cultural context in which policy choices were made, for example), the fact of the matter is that it is much more marginal to that practice. As one critic has put it in his analysis of one culturalist article, what has a nineteenth-century play to tell us about US foreign policy in the second half of the twentieth century?[63] A little, perhaps, and that is not to be sniffed at, but there are many other places to look to explain that policy that are likely to prove more fruitful.

CONCLUSIONS

Post-structuralist and culturalist scholars have provided us with a new and fruitful approach to understanding US foreign policy during the Cold War and a variety of important and useful insights. In the first place, post-structuralism is valuable in the way it reminds us of the need to pay attention to language – both our own and that of those whom we study. The ability of language to shape and to construct reality, to privilege certain arguments and interpretations and to exclude others through the invocation of metaphors and unconscious cultural biases is a pervasive phenomenon. It is in no way necessary to accept post-structuralist arguments in their entirety in order to recognise the force of this claim.

Many of the specific arguments that follow from this basic insight are also persuasive. Campbell's assertion that foreign policy is, in some degree, a process of (re)producing national identity through the process of differentiation can hardly be gainsaid. Even the most cursory study of the language of US policy-makers of the late 1940s will reveal the extent to which the Soviet Union was constructed therein as an alien other to be feared not merely for its military power but because of the sheer 'un-Americanness' of its ideology, culture, society and state. The Cold War was, in some part, about the incomprehensibility of communism to the vast majority of Americans.

The culturalist claim that common cultural understandings and tropes of gender and illness are readily transposed into foreign-policy discourse is also persuasively demonstrated in most of their writings. There are simply too many examples of policy-makers resorting to allusions about the 'sickness' of communism, the effeminacy of those who were insufficiently anti-communist and suchlike for us to disregard the utility of this kind of analysis. Finally, the basic point underpinning most culturalist analysis, that the realm of culture and ideas is not a mere epiphenomenon, a derivative of material factors, but an autonomous realm that should be explored in its own right, is a fair one. Culture, popular or otherwise, is a realm that deserves exploration as one part of the context by which foreign policy is shaped.

For all these strengths, however, culturalist arguments are greatly weakened by their epistemologically driven refusal to accept the possibility of making true claims about the way the world actually is (or was). This refusal leads to an absence of explanation in culturalist accounts. Causality is replaced with vague correlations in which the demonstration of the existence of certain cultural assumptions is deemed sufficient to claim an 'effect' on policy. Culturalist accounts also tend to one-dimensionality because of their refusal to engage with the non-cultural. One rapidly tires of the predictable discovery of tropes of gender and pathology in every document or statement studied. The point is well taken, but where does it go from here? The reification of culture can also lead to an over-reliance on it to explain anything and everything, no matter how implausible (Rotter) and to uncritical narrative history (Ninkovich).

More importantly, not only does the reification of culture produce these weaknesses; it is also intellectually unconvincing. Non-engagement with the material and the rejection of truth claims about the world are impossible to sustain. Post-structuralism, 'like any brand of epistemological anti-realism . . . consistently denies the possibility of describing the way the world is, and just as consistently finds itself doing so'.[64] Campbell's arguments about the production of identity become contentless universals unless filled with claims about the historical events of the late 1940s. More seriously, his critique of other perspectives for their assumption of the possibility of identifying objective truths actually makes no sense in the absence of that very assumption and is thus intellectually incoherent. Post-structuralist culturalists also find themselves in the self-evidently implausible position of constantly finding certain meanings and interpretations dominating discourse without being able to explain why because of their reluctance to admit that those meanings are embedded in material relations of power.

Culturalists talk of intertextuality and thus imply the existence of complex connections between the cultural and material worlds. After the first five chapters of this book one should have every sympathy with their insistence that these relationships are complex and that no one factor can simply be reduced to another. Nevertheless, in culturalist accounts, intertextuality is more honoured in the breach than in the observation. It should not just be an excuse for saying that matters are complicated before falling back into a reductionist and insular discussion of culture. Culturalist accounts will be made richer and more persuasive if they engage with the connections between the material and the cultural and accept the necessity and possibility of making true claims about both.

NOTES

1. This is, of course, slightly to exaggerate the consensus among all the historians discussed thus far. William Appleman Williams, for example, stands slightly outside the consensus, because of the way his work draws on nineteenth-century German Idealism, while Bruce Cumings's work on the Korean War is influenced by some of the ideas to be discussed in this chapter. Both, nevertheless, share most of the characteristics described.
2. Campbell, *Writing Security*.
3. Ibid. p. 8.
4. Ibid. p. 12.
5. Ibid. It is important to note that no conspiracy theory is being implied here; this process of identity formation through differentiation is argued to be an inherent and necessary quality of all states.
6. Ibid. p. 105.
7. Ibid. p. 157.
8. Ibid. p. 195.
9. Ibid. p. 210.
10. Prestowitz, *Trading Places*; van Wolferen, *The Enigma of Japanese Power*; Fallows, *More Like Us*.
11. Ninkovich, 'Interests and discourses', 136.
12. In practice most students of social science or history ought to have been introduced to these ideas in their theory and methods courses. For those who wish to pursue a more comprehensive understanding, the literature is huge. The sources I have found most useful in my own studies are: Best and Kellner, *Postmodern Theory*; Caplan, 'Postmodernism, poststructuralism and deconstruction'; Dews, *Logics of Disintegration*; Eagleton, *Literary Theory*; Finlayson and Valentine (eds), *Politics and Post-Structuralism*; Jenkins, *Re-Thinking History*; Ninkovich, 'No post-mortems'; Norris, *Truth and the Ethics of Criticism*; Norris, *Uncritical Theory*; Rosenau, *Post-Modernism*; Tallis, *Not Saussure*. For the application of post-structuralist ideas to history specifically, readers should consult the 'Further Reading' in Evans, *In Defence of History*.
13. Campbell, *Writing Security*, pp. 197–8.
14. Ibid. pp. 245–59.
15. Ibid. p. 5.
16. Ibid. p. 248.
17. Ibid. p. 6.

18. Ibid. p. 248.
19. What follows is not a comprehensive critique of post-structuralism. Readers wanting more extensive critiques should try some or all of the following: Anderson, *In the Tracks of Historical Materialism*; Callinicos, *Against Postmodernism*; Callinicos, *Theories and Narratives*; Cunningham, *In the Reading Gaol*; Davidson, 'On the very idea of a conceptual scheme'; Dews, *Logics of Disintegration*; Eagleton, *The Illusions of Postmodernism*; Evans, *In Defence of History*; Hollis and Lukes, *Rationality and Relativism*; Norris, *Truth and the Ethics of Criticism*; Norris, *Uncritical Theory*; Putnam, *Reason, Truth and History*; Tallis, *In Defence of Realism*; Tallis, *Not Saussure*.
20. Graemer, 'On poststructuralisms'.
21. Campbell, *Writing Security*, pp. 24, 77–8.
22. For an extended critique of the idea that the other is inescapably 'marginalised' or 'demonised', see Kristeva, *Strangers to Ourselves*.
23. This argument is drawn from a variety of sources including: Dews, *Logics of Disintegration*, pp. 181–92; Lichtenberg, 'In defence of objectivity revisited'; Norris, *Truth and the Ethics of Criticism*, pp. 16–35, 54; Rosenau, *Post-Modernism*, pp. 134–6.
24. The principal examples of this approach are: Costiglioga, 'The nuclear family'; Costiglioga, 'Unceasing pressure for penetration'; Dean, 'Masculinity as ideology'; Dean, 'Tradition, cause and effect'; Rosenberg, 'US cultural history'; Rosenberg, 'Foreign affairs'; Rosenberg, 'Revisiting dollar diplomacy'; Smith, 'National security and personal isolation'. Hogan, *A Cross of Iron*, is an example of an attempt to incorporate elements of the approach into a more traditional analysis. General advocacy of the value of the approach, rather than specific applications of it, can be found in some of the commentaries on Emily Rosenberg's 1994 article 'Foreign Affairs'; Jeffords, 'Commentary; Culture and national identity'; Kaplan, 'Commentary: Domesticating foreign policy'; G. S. Smith, 'Commentary: Security, gender and the historical process.'
25. Costiglioga, 'Unceasing pressure for penetration'.
26. A similar analysis, applied not to a policy-maker but to a historian (Melvyn Leffler), is found in Kaplan, 'Commentary: Domesticating foreign policy'.
27. Costiglioga, 'The nuclear family', p. 183.
28. Dean, 'Masculinity as ideology', p. 30.
29. G.S. Smith, 'Commentary: Security, gender and the historical process', p. 88.
30. LaCapra, *History and Criticism*, pp. 18–19.
31. Rosenberg, 'Foreign affairs'.
32. Ibid. pp. 66, 70.
33. Jeffords, 'Commentary: Culture and national identity', p. 93.
34. Rosenberg, 'Revisiting dollar diplomacy', p. 158.
35. Dean, 'Tradition, cause and effect', p. 616.
36. Rosenberg, 'Revisiting dollar diplomacy', p. 155.
37. Dean, 'Tradition, cause and effect', p. 622.
38. Stephanson, 'Commentary: Considerations on culture and theory', p. 111.
39. Kucklick, 'Commentary', p. 122.
40. Dean, 'Masculinity as ideology', p. 52.
41. Rosenberg, 'Foreign affairs', p. 66.
42. Jeffords, 'Commentary; Culture and national identity', p. 92. Readers should note in passing that culturalists are not above a bit of exploitation of binary opposites themselves. For them causality is always 'simple', while cultural studies are about 'complexity', and there is little question which of these is to be preferred.

43. It would be ludicrous, for example, to imply that early twenty-first century American culture is not, to a significant degree, the product of the evolution of the American economy and American society.
44. Costiglioga, 'The nuclear family', p. 165
45. Dean, 'Masculinity as ideology', p. 52.
46. Jeffords, 'Commentary: Culture and national identity', p. 93.
47. G.S. Smith, 'Commentary: Security, gender, and the historical process', p. 88.
48. Evans, *In Defence of History,* pp. 157–8.
49. Dean, 'Tradition, cause and effect', p. 618.
50. There is no evidence thus far of a culturalist diplomatic historian not being able to find such tropes, wherever historians have looked for them.
51. It should be noted that Rotter's analysis is not significantly influenced by post-structuralist ideas. It nevertheless shares with the other writers discussed here a focus on 'culture' to the exclusion of other explanatory factors: Rotter, 'Gender relations, foreign relations'; Rotter, 'Christians, Muslims and Hindus'; Rotter, *Comrades at Odds.*
52. Rotter, 'Christians, Muslims and Hindus', p. 600.
53. Rotter, 'Gender relations, foreign relations', p. 537.
54. Eagleton, *The Illusions of Postmodernism,* p. 124.
55. Buzzanco, '"Where's the Beef?"', p. 628; Eagleton, *The Illusions of Postmodernism,* pp. 127–8.
56. Ninkovich, *The Diplomacy of Ideas*; Ninkovich, 'Interests and discourses'; Ninkovich, 'Ideology, the open door and foreign policy'; Ninkovich, *Modernity and Power*; Ninkovich, 'No post-mortems'; Ninkovich, *The Wilsonian Century.*
57. Ninkovich, *The Wilsonian Century,* pp. 5–9.
58. Keylor, 'Post-mortems for the American century', p. 320.
59. Ninkovich, *The Wilsonian Century,* p. 16.
60. Jeffords, 'Commentary: Culture and national identity', p. 92.
61. This weakness parallels that in the thought of Michel Foucault, a key influence on these 'culturalist' scholars; Best and Kellner, *Postmodern Theory,* pp. 70–1.
62. Rosenberg, 'Foreign affairs', pp. 65–6.
63. Buzzanco, '"Where's the beef?"', p. 627.
64. Eagleton, *The Illusions of Postmodernism,* p. 28.

Conclusions

A t the beginning of the 1980s, Charles Maier complained that US diplomatic history was 'marking time'. The study of US foreign policy, he opined, was mired in outdated methods and concepts. Wagons circled against foreign ideas and dangerous theories, diplomatic historians, it was claimed, were wedded to an archaic empiricism and 'objectivism' while the rest of the scholarly world passed them by.[1] There was (and remains) some truth in this portrait; some researchers do still seem to believe that the discovery of new facts, rather than the interpretation of those facts, is the central task of the discipline. Nevertheless, Maier's portrait was a caricature then and would be an even greater one today. What has been demonstrated here is that the best historians of US Cold War foreign policy, from William Appleman Williams to David Campbell, have demonstrated a sensitivity to methodological and theoretical questions that makes a mockery of the notion of a crisis in diplomatic history. None of the historians discussed is a mere grubber of archives or a barefoot empiricist. The perspectives discussed in this book embrace a wide range of theoretical and methodological commitments and provide students and scholars of US foreign policy with a rich array of options from which to choose as they approach it for themselves.

In that regard, it is important to stress that, while I, and everyone else who examines these issues, will have preferences amongst the perspectives available, all provide valuable and significant insights as well as having more or less serious failings. Traditionalism provides us with a sense of the contemporary fear of the USSR and communism, though it otherwise gives us a thoroughly inadequate account of the underpinnings of US foreign policy. With revisionism, in contrast, we get the first serious attempt to look beyond the reasons offered by policy-makers for their actions to the underlying factors that shaped and constrained their decisions. Here, for the first time, we see a stress on the importance of the reconstruction of international capitalism to

US policy, and the linking of foreign policy to the domestic socio-economic and political process. In the work of William Appleman Williams there is an attempt to demonstrate the importance of ideology and American culture to an understanding of US foreign policy. Unfortunately, revisionism also demonstrates an almost complete neglect of geopolitics and the systemic in general as well as a tendency towards economic reductionism that has proved to be a recurring problem.

Post-revisionism represents the first declared attempt to provide a multi-causal 'synthesis' combining all relevant factors in a complete explanation. Driven in part by the availability of new archival material, its practitioners were able to create an empirically richer account than their predecessors. Theoretically, its key contribution is to stress the importance of geopolitics and the need to understand US actions as a response to stimuli and constraints operating at the level of the international system. Despite its claims to the contrary, however, it treats economics as a secondary, and even trivial, explanatory factor and fails to provide a sufficiently sophisticated conceptualisation of the domestic sources of US foreign policy. Corporatism, in contrast, presents one of the most complex, yet theoretically coherent, depictions of the domestic dimension of foreign policy available. Its stress on the divisions within American society and political-economy, plus the autonomy of the state, represents a major advance on crude forms of revisionism. Nevertheless, the self-proclaimed corporatists typically fail to deploy these insights to full advantage and completely neglect the geopolitical dimension of the Cold War.

World-systems theory, in the hands of Thomas McCormick, simply transfers the economic determinism of Gabriel Kolko from American capitalism to the world capitalist system as a whole. As a generator of hypotheses and potential insights, McCormick's perspective is as powerful as any discussed, but the theory as a whole is simply too reductionist and ahistorical to provide a basis for future studies. McCormick nevertheless makes the fundamental point that there is a world capitalist system, just as there is a state system, of which the US economy is a part and in response to which US policy has to be made. This insight is developed with much more subtlety and insight, however, by Bruce Cumings. Cumings, in my view, has made the most successful effort thus far towards the kind of synthesis or total explanation of US foreign policy in the early Cold War that is sought by many diplomatic historians. He has a well-developed conceptualisation of both the systemic and state-level sources of foreign policy and demonstrates an acute sensitivity to the difficulties of combining them in a single explanation. On the other hand, it is not clear that he fully succeeds in that effort at reconciliation, nor that it is not achieved, if it is, at the expense of abandoning the influence of his systemic level of explanation. He also, of course, gives too short a shrift to the importance of politics and geopolitics.

Post-structuralists and culturalists add a wholly new dimension to the debate over US foreign policy. On the one hand, they revive Williams's focus on the significance of culture and demonstrate how a wide range of cultural assumptions permeated the thoughts and language of US policy-makers. They also make the profoundly important point that language in some sense constructs 'reality' and that language has and is power. The use of particular tropes and meanings, and the unquestioning cultural assumptions that infuse our thinking, privilege certain interpretations of reality and exclude others. Taken to the extreme, however, this logic asserts that language is all there is; that all meaning is a product of language, that 'facts' are available only through language, and that truth exists, as a result, only within languages or perspectives. On this account, all perspectives are equally valid and there is no means of choosing between them. Culturalist accounts, however, demonstrate the impossibility of sustaining such a position. Not only is it seriously self-contradictory, but it is more honoured in the breach than in the observation, as culturalists repeatedly rely on truth claims about reality to sustain their arguments. Given this fact, and the non-explanatory, one-dimensional and reductionist nature of many culturalist accounts, there is a need for an engagement with the objective material world if this perspective is to move forward.

In sum, what these various perspectives show us is that US foreign policy during the Cold War had geopolitical, economic, social, cultural, linguistic and ideological dimensions. They all provide significant insights into US foreign policy and yet they are all also inadequate as complete explanations of that policy. Which fact inevitably raises the question of synthesis.

The first problem for any scholar who seeks to provide a successful synthesis incorporating multiple factors is how to steer a course between the twin perils of reductionism and 'mindless eclecticism'.[2] A successful synthesis must retain a theoretical framework that identifies key causal factors, prioritises certain factors over others and links them together in a coherent pattern. It cannot be a mere shopping list of variables. Yet a 'strong', complete theory of US foreign policy is not achievable. US foreign policy is too complex a phenomenon, too subject to contingency and change, to be captured in a simple formula or deterministic framework. What must be sought, therefore, as was argued in the introduction, is a 'weak' theory. The key characteristic of a weak theory is that it is non-deterministic. There will be a core set of ideas and assumptions about how a particular factor or system of factors operates and shapes policy – for example, the functioning of capitalism as a mode of production or the operation of the international system – and the research will be guided by these. But there is also an acknowledgement that, while these factors do operate in consistent and predictable ways, and do shape policy outcomes, there can be no a priori determination that they therefore explain the policies under examination. This is so because these factors are continually in interaction with others that, while perhaps not as important as the primary ones, are nevertheless capable of shaping, altering and even neutralising their effects. The historian can thus use theory to guide their research whilst accepting that the answers they seek will always be specific, empirical and historical in nature.

Looked at from this perspective, it can be argued, somewhat ironically, in view of the caricature, alluded to by Maier, of diplomatic historians as naive empiricists, that the historians discussed here have erred primarily by being overly theoretical and deterministic. That is to say, in the revisionist/corporatist/world-systems-theory accounts economics is given too consistent an explanatory role at the expense of other factors such as politics and geopolitics, while in post-revisionism the error is inverted. Post-structuralist and culturalist accounts, of course, also tend to be profoundly monocausal.

While the effort to formulate weak theoretical syntheses is certainly valid, it remains, nevertheless, profoundly unlikely that we will see a general intellectual convergence around a grand synthesis. Even if historians do seek to develop non-deterministic weak theories, if they are to avoid mindless eclecticism, they still have to have theories. And those theories will privilege certain factors over others, even if they do allow for contingency and the importance of other elements at certain times. There are, as we have seen, many explanatory variables for historians to choose from and, given the absence of testable hypotheses and decisive empirical evidence, no real possibility of ultimate agreement upon the appropriate priority to be accorded to those factors. Above all, perhaps, the overlapping, but not identical, economics/geopolitics and internal/external divides are likely to remain sources of continuing disagreement.

My personal preference, as the observant reader is probably aware by now, is for an explanatory framework that emphasises the internal and the economic, rather than the external and the geopolitical, as the dominant theoretical framework – hence my admiration for the work of Bruce Cumings. The reasons for my preferences should be clear from the analysis in the individual chapters and hence need no repetition here. Nevertheless, there are some general points that apply regardless of one's particular theoretical bent. In the first place, for example, it is vital that scholars pay attention to the need to incorporate factors operating at different levels. US foreign policy cannot be explained either by factors emanating purely from within the state or solely by factors operating at the level of the international system. A systemic level of analysis is vital, because the international system is the environment within which states operate and which they respond to. It is insufficient in itself, however, because it cannot explain either the origins of change within the system or the divergent policy responses of different states and groups within states to the constraints it exerts.

The necessity of combining different levels of analysis, however, is a simple issue compared to the problem of which perspective and which factors to emphasise at each level. Even if we take only the perspectives considered in this book (which hardly exhausts the possibilities), we can see that at the level of the system and at the level of state/society we have different and conflicting perspectives from which to choose – perspectives, moreover, that often contradict each other. That choice is a matter for the individual scholar in the light of his or her own purpose and interests. More to the point is that, whichever perspective or combination of perspectives is chosen, one must bear in mind the need to limit the explanatory factors emphasised and think about the compatibility of different factors. Bruce Cumings's synthesis, for example, is effective in large part because his systemic variable of the world capitalist system is compatible with an emphasis on the domestic socio-economic roots of foreign policy.

Nor should this discussion of the difficulties of producing analytically powerful synthetic explanations blind us to the extent of what has been achieved so far. The historians discussed herein have already done vast amounts of work towards this end. If none of the perspectives discussed succeeds totally, all retain useful core concepts upon which others can build. That building is likely to advance on two broad fronts: The externalists and geopoliticians of the post-revisionist school will doubtless continue to assert the primacy of factors emanating from the international system, yet their main goal must be to develop a more convincing conception of the domestic sources of US foreign policy than they have done so far. On the other side, the revisionist/corporatist/world-systems perspective has developed an increasingly sophisticated theory of the domestic and economic roots of US foreign policy. Scholars in this tradition, however, need to pay more attention to the thorny issues of the autonomy of the state from domestic socio-economic forces and how to accord geopolitics a more significant role in their explanations.

In summary, therefore, the grand synthesis that gives due weight to all the relevant variables while retaining an incisive explanatory edge is impossible. Coherent synthesis results only when a limited number of theoretically compatible factors are used to frame the analysis. Synthesis therefore requires the making of choices, at all levels of the analysis, of which explanatory factors should be privileged and which neglected. What this means is that, whatever perspective is used, it will only ever provide a partial and incomplete explanation of the events under scrutiny, even if the historian believes that it is the most compelling such partial explanation possible. This does not mean that the historian need abandon the ambition to capture complexity and totality. It means, however, recognising that that totality will not be wholly captured within whatever perspective one chooses to employ.

Historical events are a combination of structure and agency, shaping forces and individual choices, predictability and chance. A carefully developed and applied perspective can help the historian to explain important parts of those structures, forces and patterns but not all of them and certainly not the agency and chance. It should provide an explanatory framework that captures a key part of reality but to which the accidental, the ad hoc and the individual can be added. The best history is that which strives for a balance, however imperfect, between an explanatory framework that seeks to grasp the structures and determining forces that underlie events and the patterns and continuities that result, while also allowing space for individual agency and contingency and seeking to grasp the relationship between both dimensions.

There are certainly limits to the extent to which this ideal is achievable. Not only can a synthesis not incorporate every explanatory factor in a systematic fashion but there are other dilemmas – the relationship between the material and the ideal in ideology, that between structure and agency – that are not likely to be resolved soon. There is never going to be a perfect explanation. However, this does not mean there are not better or worse explanations. If a perfect synthesis is never going to be achieved, that is no reason not to pursue a partial synthesis. The objective, in the plainest terms possible, should be to combine complexity and simplicity in the same explanation. A clear theoretical framework that picks out the key structures and patterns should be combined with as many factors and as much richness of description and analysis as it can bear without the explanation becoming hopelessly muddled. There is no prescription for this, but the work of Bruce Cumings and Melvyn Leffler, with its combining of systemic and state/society levels of analysis plus its incorporation of multiple individual actions and events, seems to this author to be the closest approximation available.

Finally, it needs to be emphasised that synthesis is not the only valid goal of historians studying Cold War US foreign policy. Indeed, if you are a post-structuralist, then it is a perfectly iniquitous objective. If the point of history is to teach tolerance of diversity and doubt, then grand synthesis is a positive evil in its imposition of a single story on history. Indeed, even if you are not a post-structuralist, it is possible to have doubts about the wisdom and the consequences of constantly seeking to reduce history to a single true explanation given the way that this leads, more or less inevitably, to the privileging of certain explanations and the denigration of others.[3]

Rather than it not being possible, however, a better reason not to pursue synthesis is that you do not want to. The search for synthesis may detract from the pursuit of other, equally valid forms of analysis. Not everyone wants to pursue a complete explanation of US foreign policy. Many wish to study relationships with particular countries, or particular periods. Others want to study specific dimensions of US foreign policy and certain issues rather than others. There are many different questions and problems, some very broad and some incredibly narrow. There is no reason to assume that the broad ones are intrinsically more worthy of pursuit than the narrow ones. All have their own significance. And to each a different perspective or combination of perspectives will apply. Even if one believes that, at the broad level of explanation, certain explanatory factors are more important than others, therefore, there remains a place for all the perspectives discussed here and more besides. It simply depends on what question you want to answer.

NOTES

1. Maier, 'Marking time'.
2. Gaddis, 'New conceptual approaches', p. 409.
3. Hunt, 'The long crisis in diplomatic history: Coming to closure', p. 123.

Bibliography

Agh, A., 'The hundred years peace: Karl Polanyi on the dynamics of world systems', in K. Polanyi-Levitt (ed.), *The Life and Work of Karl Polanyi* (Montreal: Black Rose Books, 1990), pp. 93–7.

Allison, G. T., *Essence of Decision: Explaining the Cuban Missile Crisis* (Boston: Little, Brown, 1971).

Allison, G. T. and Halperin, M. H., 'Bureaucratic politics: A paradigm and some policy implications', in R. Tanter and R. H. Ullman (eds), *Theory and Policy in International Relations* (Princeton: Princeton University Press, 1972), pp. 40–79.

Anderson, P., *In the Tracks of Historical Materialism* (London: Verso, 1983).

Appy, C. G. (ed.), *Cold War Constructions: The Political Culture of United States Imperialism, 1945–1966* (Amherst, MA: University of Massachussetts Press, 2000).

Bailey, T. A., *America Faces Russia: Russian–American Relations from Early Times to Our Day* (New York: Cornell University Press, 1950).

Bailey, T. A., *A Diplomatic History of the American People* 5th edn (New York: Appleton Century Crofts, 1955).

Barratt Brown, M. (1972), 'A critique of Marxist theories of imperialism', in R. Owen and B. Sutcliffe (eds), *Studies in the Theory of Imperialism* (Harlow: Longman, 1972), pp. 35–70.

Barrow, C. W., *Critical Theories of the State: Marxist, Neo-Marxist, Post-Marxist* (Madison: University of Wisconsin Press, 1993).

Beard, C. A., *An Economic Interpretation of the Constitution of the United States* (New York: Macmillan Company, 1919).

Beard, C. A., *Economic Origins of Jeffersonian Diplomacy*, (New York: Macmillan Company, 1927).

Beard, C. A., *President Roosevelt and the Coming of War, 1941: A Study in Appearances* (New Haven: Yale University Press, 1948).

Beard, C. A., *The Idea of the National Interest: An Analytical Study in American Foreign Policy* (Chicago: Quadrangle, 1966).

Beard, C. A. and M. R. Beard, *The American Spirit: A Study of the Idea of Civilization in the United States* (New York: Macmillan, 1948).

Becker, W. H., 'Foreign markets for iron and steel 1893–1918: A new perspective on the Williams school of diplomatic history', *Pacific Historical Review*, 44 (1975), pp. 233–48.

Bemis, S. F., *A Diplomatic History of the United States* (New York: Holt, Rinehart and Winston Inc., 1936).

Bemis, S. F., 'American foreign policy and the blessings of liberty', *American Historical Review*, 67 (1961–2), pp. 291–305.

Bemis, S. F., *A Diplomatic History of the United States*, 5th edn (New York: Holt, Rinehart and Winston Inc., 1965).

Bernstein, B. J., 'Cold War orthodoxy restated', *Reviews in American History*, 1 (1973), pp. 453–62.

Berry, J. (1989), *The Interest Group Society*, 2nd edn (Glenview: Scott, Foresman/Little, Brown, 1989).

Best, S. and D. Kellner, *Postmodern Theory: Critical Interrogations* (London: Macmillan, 1991).

Block, F. and M. R. Somers, 'Beyond the economistic fallacy: The holistic social science of Karl Polanyi', in T. Skocpol (ed.), *Vision and Method in Historical Sociology*, (Cambridge: Cambridge University Press, 1984), pp. 47–84.

Borning, B. C., *The Political and Social Thought of Charles A. Beard* (Seattle: University of Washington Press, 1962).

Braeman, J., R. H. Bremmer, and D. Brady, (eds), *Twentieth Century American Foreign Policy* (Columbus, OH: Ohio University Press, 1971).

Brenner, R., 'The origins of capitalist development: A critique of neo-Smithian marxism', *New Left Review*, 104 (1977), pp. 25–93.

Buhle, P. M. and E. Rice-Maximin, *William Appleman Williams: The Tragedy of Empire* (London: Routledge, 1995).

Burman, S., *America in the Modern World: The Transcendence of United States Hegemony* (New York: Harvester Wheatsheaf, 1991).

Buzan, B., 'The level of analysis problem in international relations reconsidered', in K. Booth and S. Smith (eds), *International Relations Theory Today* (Cambridge: Polity, 1995), pp. 198–216.

Buzzanco, R., 'Whatever happened to the New Left?' *Diplomatic History*, 23 (1999), pp. 575–607.

Buzzanco, R., ' "Where's the beef?" Culture without power in the study of US foreign relations', *Diplomatic History*, 24 (2000), pp. 623–32.

Callinicos, A., *Against Postmodernism* (Cambridge: Polity, 1989).

Callinicos, A., *Theories and Narratives: Reflections on the Philosophy of History* (Cambridge: Polity, 1995).

Campbell, D., *Writing Security: United States Foreign Policy and the Politics of Identity* (Manchester: Manchester University Press, 1992).

Caplan, J., 'Postmodernism, poststructuralism and deconstruction: Notes for historians', *Central European History*, 22 (1989), pp. 260–78.

Cardoso, F. H. and E. Faletto, *Dependency and Development in Latin America* (Berkeley and Los Angeles: University of California Press, 1979).

Carlsnaes, W., 'The agency–structure problem in foreign policy analysis', *International Studies Quarterly*, 36 (1992), pp. 245–70.

Cawson, A., *Corporatism and Political Theory* (Oxford: Basil Blackwell, 1986).

Chandhoke, N., *State and Civil Society: Explorations in Political Theory* (New Delhi: Sage, 1995).

Cohen, I. J., 'Structuration theory and social praxis', in A. Giddens and J. Turner (eds), *Social Theory Today* (Cambridge: Polity, 1987), pp. 273–308.

Coolidge, A. C. *The United States as a World Power* (New York: Macmillan, 1908).

Costiglioga, F., 'The nuclear family: Tropes of gender and pathology in the Western Alliance', *Diplomatic History*, 21 (1997), pp. 163–84.

Costiglioga, F., 'Unceasing pressure for penetration: Gender, pathology and emotion in

George Kennan's formation of the Cold War', *Journal of American History*, 83 (1997), pp. 1309–39.

Crapol, E. P., 'Coming to terms with empire: The historiography of late nineteenth century foreign relations', *Diplomatic History*, 16 (1992), pp. 573–98.

Crockatt, R. and S. Smith (eds), *The Cold War: Past and Present* (London: Allen and Unwin, 1987).

Cumings, B., *The Origins of the Korean War: Liberation and the Emergence of Separate Regimes, 1945–1947* (Princeton: Princeton University Press, 1981).

Cumings, B., 'Power and plenty in Northeast Asia: The evolution of US policy', *World Policy Journal*, 5 (1987–8), pp. 79–104.

Cumings, B., *The Origins of the Korean War, Volume 2: The Roaring of the Cataract, 1947–1950* (Princeton: Princeton University Press, 1990).

Cumings, B., 'Archaeology, descent, emergence: Japan in British/American hegemony, 1900–1950', in M. Miyoshi and H. D. Harootunian (eds), *Japan in the World* (London: Duke University Press, 1993), pp. 79–111.

Cumings, B., ' "Revising postrevisionism": Or the poverty of theory in diplomatic history', *Diplomatic History*, 17 (1993), pp. 539–69.

Cumings, B., 'Japan and the Asian periphery', in M. P. Leffler and D. S. Painter (eds), *Origins of the Cold War: An International History* (London: Routledge, 1994), pp. 215–25.

Cunningham, V., *In the Reading Gaol: Postmodernism, Texts and History* (Oxford: Blackwell, 1994).

Curran, J. and M. Gurevitch, *Mass Media and Society*, 3rd edn (London: Arnold, 2000).

Davidson, D., *Inquiries into Truth and Interpretation* (New York: Oxford University Press, 1984).

Davidson, D., 'On the very idea of a conceptual scheme', in D. Davidson, *Inquiries into Truth and Interpretation* (New York: Oxford University Press, 1984, pp. 183–98.

Davis, L. E., *The Cold War Begins: Soviet–American Conflict over Eastern Europe* (Princeton: Princeton University Press, 1974).

Dean, R., 'Masculinity as ideology: John F. Kennedy and the domestic politics of foreign policy', *Diplomatic History*, 22 (1998), 29–63.

Dean, R., 'Tradition, cause and effect and the cultural history of international affairs', *Diplomatic History*, 24 (2000), 615–22.

Deighton, A., *The Impossible Peace: Britain, the Division of Germany and the Origins of the Cold War* (Oxford: Clarendon Press, 1993).

Dews, P., *Logics of Disintegration*: *Post-Structuralist Thought and the Claims of Critical Theory* (London: Verso, 1987).

Dye, T. R., *Who's Running America? The Clinton Years*, 6th edn (Englewood Cliffs, NJ: Prentice Hall, 1995).

Eagleton, T., *The Illusions of Postmodernism* (Oxford: Blackwell, 1996).

Eagleton, T., *Literary Theory: An Introduction*, 2nd edn (Oxford: Basil Blackwell, 1996).

Eckes, A. E., Jr, 'Open door expansionism reconsidered: The World War Two experience', *Journal of American History*, 59 (1972–3), pp. 909–24.

Elster, J., *Ulysses and the Sirens: Studies in Rationality and Irrationality* (Cambridge: Cambridge University Press, 1979).

Evans, P., *Dependent Development: The Alliance of Multinational, State and Local Capital in Brazil* (Princeton: Princeton University Press, 1979).

Evans, R., *In Defence of History* (London: Granta, 1997).

Fallows, J., *More Like Us: Making America Great Again* (Boston: Houghton Mifflin, 1990).

Fausold, M. L. and G. T. Mazuzan (eds), *The Hoover Presidency: A Reappraisal* (Albany, NY: State University of New York, 1974).

Feis, H., *Churchill, Roosevelt, Stalin: The War they Waged and the Peace they Sought* (Princeton: Princeton University Press, 1967).

Feis, H., *From Trust to Terror: The Onset of the Cold War, 1945–1950* (London: Anthony Blond, 1970).

Ferguson, T., 'From normalcy to New Deal: Industrial structure, party competition and American public policy in the Great Depression', *International Organization*, 38 (1984), pp. 41–94.

Ferguson, T., *Golden Rule: The Investment Theory of Party Competition and the Logic of Money-Driven Political Systems* (Chicago: University of Chicago Press, 1995).

Finlayson, A. and J. Valentine (eds), *Politics and Post-Structuralism: An Introduction* (Edinburgh: Edinburgh University Press, 2002).

Fish, C. R., *An Introduction to the History of American Diplomacy* (London: Society for Promoting Christian Knowledge, 1919).

Fordham, B. O., *Building the Cold War Consensus: The Political Economy of US National Security Policy* (Ann Arbor: University of Michigan Press, 1998).

Gaddis, J. L., *The United States and the Origins of the Cold War, 1941–1947* (New York: Columbia University Press, 1972).

Gaddis, J. L., 'The emerging post-revisionist synthesis on the origins of the Cold War', *Diplomatic History*, 7, (1983), pp. 171–90.

Gaddis, J. L., 'Comment', *American Historical Review*, 89 (1984), pp. 382–5.

Gaddis, J. L., 'The corporatist synthesis: A sceptical view', *Diplomatic History*, 10 (1986), pp. 357–62.

Gaddis, J. L., *The Long Peace: Inquiries into the History of the Cold War* (New York: Oxford University Press, 1987).

Gaddis, J. L., 'New conceptual approaches to the study of American foreign relations: Interdisciplinary approaches', *Diplomatic History*, 14 (1990), pp. 405–27.

Gaddis, J. L., 'On moral equivalency and Cold War history'. *Ethics and International Affairs*, 10, (1990), pp. 131–48.

Gaddis, J. L., *Russia, the Soviet Union and the United States: An Interpretive History*, 2nd edn (New York: McGraw-Hill, 1990).

Gaddis, J. L., 'The Cold War, the long peace, and the future', in M. J. Hogan (ed.), *The End of the Cold War: Its Meaning and Implications* (Cambridge: Cambridge University Press, 1992), pp. 21–38.

Gaddis, J. L., *The United States and the End of the Cold War: Implications, Reconsiderations, Provocations* (New York: Oxford University Press, 1992).

Gaddis, J. L., 'International relations theory and the end of the Cold War', *International Security*, 17 (1992–3), pp. 5–58.

Gaddis, J. L., 'The tragedy of Cold War history', *Diplomatic History*, 17, (1993), pp. 1–16.

Gaddis, J. L., 'History, science and the study of international relations', in N. Woods (ed.), *Explaining International Relations since 1945* (Oxford: Oxford University Press, 1996), pp. 32–48.

Gaddis, J. L., *We Now Know: Rethinking Cold War History* (Oxford: Clarendon Press, 1997).

Gardner, L. C., *Economic Aspects of New Deal Diplomacy* (Madison: University of Wisconsin Press, 1964).

Gardner, L. C., *Architects of Illusion: Men and Ideas in American Foreign Policy, 1941–1949* (Chicago: Quadrangle Books, 1970).

Gardner, L. C., *Imperial America: American Foreign Policy since 1898* (New York: HBJ Inc., 1976).

Gardner, L. C. (ed.), *Redefining the Past: Essays in Diplomatic History in Honor of William Appleman Williams* (Corvallis, OR: Oregon State University Press, 1986).

Gardner, L. C., *Spheres of Influence: The Partition of Europe, From Munich to Yalta* (London: John Murray, 1993).

Geertz, C., *The Interpretation of Cultures* (London: Hutchinson, 1975).

Geertz, C., 'Ideology as a cultural system', in C. Geertz, *The Interpretation of Cultures* (London: Hutchinson, 1975), pp. 193–233.

Giddens, A., *Central Problems in Social Theory: Action, Structure and Contradiction in Social Analysis* (London: Macmillan, 1979).

Giddens, A., *Studies in Social and Political Theory* (London: Hutchinson, 1979).

Gilbert, F., *History: Politics or Culture? Reflections on Ranke and Burckhardt* (Princeton: Princeton University Press, 1990).

Gilpin, R., *The Political Economy of International Relations* (Princeton: Princeton University Press, 1987).

Graebner, N., *Cold War Diplomacy: American Foreign Policy, 1945–1975*, 2nd edn (New York: D. Van Nostrand Company Inc., 1977).

Graemer, R. V., 'On poststructuralisms, revisionisms and cold wars', *Diplomatic History*, 19 (1995), pp. 515–24.

Halle, L. J., *The Cold War as History* (London: Chatto and Windus, 1967).

Halliday, F., *Rethinking International Relations* (London: Macmillan, 1994).

Halperin, M. H., *Bureaucratic Politics and Foreign Policy* (Washington: Brookings Institution, 1974).

Harbutt, F. J., *Iron Curtain: Churchill, America and the Origins of the Cold War* (New York: Oxford University Press, 1986).

Hart, A. B., *The American Nation: A History. Volume 26, National Ideals Historically Traced, 1607–1907* (New York: Harper and Brothers, 1907).

Hawley, E. W., 'Herbert Hoover and American corporatism', in M. L. Fausold and G. T. Mazuzan (eds), *The Hoover Presidency: A Reappraisal* (Albany, NY: State University of New York, 1974).

Hawley, E. W., 'Herbert Hoover, the Commerce Secretariat and the vision of an associative state', *Journal of American History*, 61 (1974), pp. 116–40.

Hawley, E. W., 'The discovery and study of a "corporate liberalism"', *Business History Review*, 52 (1978), pp. 309–20.

Hawley, E. W. (ed.), *Herbert Hoover as Secretary of Commerce: Studies in New Era Thought and Practice* (Iowa City: University of Iowa Press, 1981).

Hodges, H. A., *Wilhelm Dilthey* (London: Kegan Paul, Trench, Trubner and Co., 1944).

Hogan, M. J., *Informal Entente: The Private Structure of Cooperation in Anglo-American Diplomacy, 1918–1928* (Columbia, MO: University of Missouri Press, 1977).

Hogan, M. J., 'The search for a creative peace: The United States, European unity and the origins of the Marshall Plan', *Diplomatic History*, 6 (1982), pp. 267–85.

Hogan, M. J., 'Revival and reform: America's twentieth century search for a new economic order abroad', *Diplomatic History*, 8 (1984), pp. 287–310.

Hogan, M. J., 'American Marshall planners and the search for a European neocapitalism', *American Historical Review*, 90 (1985), pp. 44–72.

Hogan, M. J., 'Corporatism: A positive appraisal', *Diplomatic History*, 10 (1986), pp. 363–72.

Hogan, M. J., *The Marshall Plan: America, Britain and the Reconstruction of Western Europe, 1947–1952* (Cambridge: Cambridge University Press, 1987).

Hogan, M. J., 'The search for synthesis: Economic diplomacy in the Cold War', *Reviews in American History*, 15 (1987), pp. 493–8.

Hogan, M. J., 'Corporatism', in M. J. Hogan and T. G. Paterson (eds), *Explaining the History of American Foreign Relations* (Cambridge: Cambridge University Press, 1991), pp. 226–36.

Hogan, M. J. (ed.), *America in the World: A Historiography of American Foreign Relations since 1941* (Cambridge: Cambridge University Press, 1995).

Hogan, M. J., *A Cross of Iron: Harry S Truman and the Origins of the National Security State* (Cambridge: Cambridge University Press, 1998).

Hogan, M. J. and T. G. Paterson (eds), *Explaining the History of American Foreign Relations* (Cambridge: Cambridge University Press, 1991).

Hollis, M. amd S. Lukes (eds), *Rationality and Relativism* (Oxford: Blackwell, 1982).

Hollis, M. amd S. Smith, 'Beware of gurus: Structure and action in international relations', *Review of International Studies*, 17 (1991), pp. 393–410.

Hollis, M. and S. Smith, *Explaining and Understanding International Relations* (Oxford: Clarendon Press, 1991).

Hollis, M. and S. Smith, 'Structure and action: Further comment', *Review of International Studies*, 18 (1992), pp. 187–8.

Horowitz, D., *Corporations and the Cold War* (New York: Monthly Review Press, 1969).

Hunt, M., *Ideology and US Foreign Policy* (New Haven: Yale University Press, 1988).

Hunt, M., 'Ideology', in M. J. Hogan and T. G. Paterson (eds), *Explaining the History of American Foreign Relations* (Cambridge: Cambridge University Press, 1991).

Hunt, M., 'The long crisis in diplomatic history: Coming to closure', in M. J. Hogan (ed.), *America in the World: A Historiography of American Foreign Relations since 1941* (Cambridge: Cambridge University Press 1995), pp. 93–126.

Jeffords, S., 'Commentary: Culture and national identity in US foreign policy', *Diplomatic History*, 18 (1994), pp. 91–6

Jenkins, K., *Re-Thinking History* (London: Routledge, 1991).

Jessop, B., *State Theory: Putting Capitalist States in their Place* (Cambridge: Polity, 1990).

Jones, H. and R. B. Woods, 'Origins of the Cold War in the Near East: Recent historiography and the national security imperative', *Diplomatic History*, 17 (1993), pp. 251–76.

Julien, C., *The American Empire* (Boston: Beacon Press, 1971).

Kaldor, M., *The Imaginary War: Understanding the East–West Conflict* (Oxford: Basil Blackwell, 1990).

Kaplan, A., 'Commentary: Domesticating foreign policy', *Diplomatic History*, 18 (1994), pp. 97–105.

Kennan, G. F., *American Diplomacy, 1900–1950* (Chicago: Chicago University Press, 1950).

Kennedy, T. C., *Charles A Beard and American Foreign Policy* (Gainsville, FLA: University Press of Florida, 1975).

Keohane, R. O., *After Hegemony: Cooperation and Discord in the International Political Economy* (Princeton: Princeton University Press, 1984).

Keylor, W. R., 'Post-mortems for the American Century', *Diplomatic History*, 25 (2001), pp. 317–27.

Kimball, W. F., 'The Cold War warmed over', *American Historical Review*, 79 (1974), pp. 1119–36.

Kimball, W. F., 'The emerging postrevisionist thesis on the origins of the Cold War – response', *Diplomatic History*, 7 (1983), pp. 198–200.

Kindleberger, C. P., 'Dominance and leadership in the international political economy: Exploitation, public goods and free riders', *International Studies Quarterly*, 25 (1981), pp. 242–54.

Klein, C., 'Family ties and political obligation: The discourse of adoption and the Cold

War commitment to Asia', in C. G. Appy (ed.), *Cold War Constructions: The Political Culture of United States Imperialism* (Amherst, MA: University of Massachusetts Press, 2000), pp. 35–66.

Kolko, G., *The Roots of American Foreign Policy* (Boston: Beacon Press, 1969).

Kolko, G., *Main Currents in Modern American History* (New York: Harper and Row, 1976).

Kolko, G., *Vietnam: Anatomy of a War* (London: Allen and Unwin, 1986).

Kolko, G., *Confronting the Third World: United States Foreign Policy 1945–1980* (New York: Pantheon, 1988).

Kolko, G., *The Politics of War: The World and United States Foreign Policy, 1943–1945*, (2nd edn) (New York: Pantheon, 1990).

Kolko, G., *Century of War: Politics, Culture and Society since 1914* (New York: New Press, 1994).

Kolko, G. and J. Kolko, *The Limits of Power: The World and United States Foreign Policy, 1945–1954* (New York: Harper and Row, 1972).

Kristeva, J., *Strangers to Ourselves*, trans. Leon Radiez (Hemel Hempstead: Harvester Wheatsheaf, 1991).

Kucklick, B., 'Commentary: Confessions of an intransigent revisionist about cultural studies', *Diplomatic History*, 18 (1994), pp. 121–4.

Kuniholm, B. R., *The Origins of the Cold War in the Near East: Great Power Conflict and Diplomacy in Iran, Turkey and Greece* (Princeton: Princeton University Press, 1980).

Kuniholm, B. R., 'Comment', *American Historical Review*, 89 (1984), pp. 385–90.

Kuniholm, B. R., 'The origins of the first Cold War', in R. Crockatt and S. Smith (eds), *The Cold War: Past and Present* (London: Allen and Unwin, 1987), pp. 37–57.

Kurth, J. R., 'Testing theories of economic imperialism', in S. J. Rosen and J. R. Kurth, *Testing Theories of Economic Imperialism* (Lexington, MA: D. C. Heath and Co., 1974), pp. 3–14.

Kurth, J. R., 'The political consequences of the product cycle: Industrial history and political outcomes', *International Organization*, 33 (1979), pp. 1–34.

LaCapra, D., *History and Criticism* (Ithaca, NY: Cornell University Press, 1985).

Lafeber, W., *The New Empire: An Interpretation of American Expansion, 1860–1898* (Ithaca, NY: Cornell University Press, 1963).

Lafeber, W., *America, Russia and the Cold War, 1945–1996*, 8th edn (New York: McGraw-Hill, 1997).

Larrain, J., *The Concept of Ideology* (Aldershot: Gregg Revivals, 1992).

Leffler, M. P., *The Elusive Quest: America's Pursuit of European Stability and French Security, 1919–1933* (Chapel Hill, NC: University of North Carolina Press, 1979).

Leffler, M. P., 'The American conception of national security and the origins of the Cold War', *American Historical Review*, 89 (1984), pp. 346–81.

Leffler, M. P., 'Reply', *American Historical Review*, 89 (1984), pp. 391–400.

Leffler, M. P., 'National security', *Journal of American History*, 77 (1990), pp. 143–52.

Leffler, M. P., *A Preponderance of Power: National Security, the Truman Administration and the Cold War* (Stanford, CA: Stanford University Press, 1992).

Leffler, M. P., *The Spectre of Communism: The United States and the Origins of the Cold War, 1917–1953* (New York: Hill and Wang, 1994).

Leffler, M. P., 'New approaches, old interpretations, prospective reconfigurations', *Diplomatic History*, 19 (1995), pp. 173–96.

Leffler, M. P., 'Inside enemy archives', *Foreign Affairs*, 75 (1996), pp. 120–35.

Leffler, M. P., 'The Cold War: What do "We Now Know"'? *American Historical Review*, 104 (1999), pp. 501–24.

Leffler, M. P., and D. S. Painter, (eds), *Origins of the Cold War: An International History* (London: Routledge, 1994).

Lembruch, G. and P. C. Schmitter, (eds), *Patterns of Corporatist Policy-Making* (London: Sage, 1982).

Leopold, R. W., *The Growth of American Foreign Policy: A History* (New York: Alfred A. Knopf, 1964).

Lichtenberg, J., 'In defence of objectivity revisited', in J. Curran and M. Gurevitch (eds), *Mass Media and Society* 3rd edn (London: Arnold, 2000), pp. 238–54.

Lindblom, C. E., *Politics and Markets* (New York: Basic Books, 1977).

Lippman, W., *The Cold War: A Study in US Foreign Policy* (New York: Harper and Brothers, 1947).

Lundestad, G., *The American Non-Policy towards Eastern Europe, 1943–1947* (New York: Columbia University Press, 1978).

Lundestad, G., '*Empire by invitation? The United States and Western Europe, 1945–1952*', *Journal of Peace Research*, 23 (1986), pp. 263–77.

McCormick, T. J., *China Market: America's Quest for Informal Empire, 1893–1901* (Chicago: Quadrangle, 1967).

McCormick, T. J., '"Drift or mastery?" A corporatist synthesis for American diplomatic history', *Reviews in American History*, 10 (1982), pp. 318–30.

McCormick, T. J., 'Corporatism: A reply to Rossi', *Radical History Review*, 33 (1985), pp. 53–9.

McCormick, T. J., '"Every system needs a center sometimes": An essay on hegemony and modern American foreign policy', in L. C. Gardner (ed.), *Redefining the Past: Essays in Diplomatic History in Honor of William Appleman Williams* (Corvallis, OR: Oregon State University Press, 1986), pp. 195–200.

McCormick, T. J., 'World systems', in M. J. Hogan and T. G. Paterson (eds), *Explaining the History of American Foreign Relations* (Cambridge: Cambridge University Press, 1991), pp. 89–98.

McCormick, T. J., *America's Half Century: United States Foreign Policy in the Cold War and After* (Baltimore: Johns Hopkins University Press, 1995).

McClellan, D., *Ideology* (Milton Keynes: Open University Press, 1986).

McNeill, W. H., *America, Britain and Russia: Their Cooperation and Conflict, 1941–1946* (New York: Johnson Reprint Corporation, 1970).

McQuaid, K., 'Corporate liberalism in the American business community, 1920–1940', *Business History Review*, 52 (1978), pp. 342–68.

Maddox, R. J., *New Left Historians and the Origins of the Cold War* (Princeton: Princeton University Press, 1973).

Magdoff, H., *The Age of Imperialism* (New York: Monthly Review Press, 1969).

Maier, C. S., 'Revisionism and the interpretation of Cold War origins', *Perspectives in American History*, 4 (1970), pp. 313–47.

Maier, C. S., *Recasting Bourgeois Europe: Stabiliization in France, Germany and Italy in the Decade after World War One* (Princeton: Princeton University Press, 1975).

Maier, C. S., 'Marking time: The historiography of international relations', in M. G. Kammen (ed.), The Past before Us: Contemporary Historical Writing in the United States (Ithaca, NY: Cornell University Press, 1980), pp. 355–87.

Maier, C. S., 'The two postwar eras and the conditions for stability in twentieth century Western Europe', *American Historical Review*, 86 (1981), pp. 327–52.

Maier, C. S., 'The politics of productivity: Foundations of American international economic policy after World War Two', in C. S. Maier (ed.), *The Cold War in Europe:*

Era of a Divided Continent (New York: Markus Wiener Publishing Inc., 1991), pp. 169–201.

Maier, C. S. (ed.), *The Cold War in Europe: Era of a Divided Continent* (New York: Markus Wiener Publishing Inc., 1991).

Mark, E., 'American policy towards Eastern Europe and the origins of the Cold War: An alternative interpretation', *Journal of American History*, 68 (1981), pp. 313–36.

Mastny, V., *The Cold War and Soviet Insecurity: The Stalin Years* (New York: Oxford University Press, 1996).

Mastny, V., *Russia's Road to the Cold War: Diplomacy, Warfare and the Politics of Communism, 1941–1945* (New York: Columbia University Press, 1979).

May, E. R., *US Cold War Strategy: Interpreting NSC-68* (New York: St Martin's Press, 1993).

Melanson, R. A., 'The social and political thought of William Appleman Williams', *Western Political Quarterly*, 31 (1978), pp. 392–409.

Melanson, R. A., *Writing History and Making Policy: The Cold War, Vietnam and Revisionism* (London: University Press of America, 1983).

Michalak, S. J., Jr. (ed.), *Competing Conceptions of American Foreign Policy: Worldviews in Conflict* (New York: HarperCollins, 1992).

Miliband, R., *The State in Capitalist Society* (London: Quartet Books, 1982).

Miller, S. M., R. Bennett and C. Alapatt, 'Does the US economy require imperialism?', *Social Policy*, 1 (1970), pp. 12–19.

Miyoshi, M. and H. D. Harootunian (eds), *Japan in the World* (London: Duke University Press, 1993).

Moore, J. B., *American Diplomacy: Its Spirit and Achievements* (New York: Harper and Brothers, 1905).

Morgenthau, H. J., *Politics among Nations: The Struggle for Power and Peace*, New York: Knopf, 1949).

Morgenthau, H. J., *In Defense of the National Interest: A Critical Examination of American Foreign Policy* (New York: Knopf, 1951).

Mullins, W. A., 'On the concept of ideology in political science', *American Political Science Review*, 66 (1972), pp. 498–510.

Neu, C. E., 'The changing interpretive structure of American foreign policy', in J. Braeman, R. H. Bremmer and D. Brady (eds), *Twentieth Century American Foreign Policy* (Columbus, OH: Ohio University Press, 1971), pp. 1–57.

Ninkovich, F., *The Diplomacy of Ideas: US Foreign Policy and Cultural Relations, 1938–1950* (Cambridge: Cambridge University Press, 1981).

Ninkovich, F., 'Ideology, the open door and foreign policy', *Diplomatic History*, 6 (1982), pp. 185–208.

Ninkovich, F., 'Interests and discourses in diplomatic History', *Diplomatic History*, 13 (1989), pp. 135–62.

Ninkovich, F., 'The end of diplomatic history?' *Diplomatic History*, 15 (1991), pp. 439–48.

Ninkovich, F., *Modernity and Power: A History of the Domino Theory in the Twentieth Century* (Chicago: University of Chicago Press, 1994).

Ninkovich, F., 'No post-mortems for postmodernism please', *Diplomatic History*, 22 (1998), pp. 451–66.

Ninkovich, F., *The Wilsonian Century: US Foreign Policy since 1900* (Chicago: University of Chicago Press, 1999).

Norris, C., *Uncritical Theory: Postmodernism, Intellectuals and the Gulf War* (London: Lawrence and Wishart, 1992).

Norris, C., *Truth and the Ethics of Criticism* (Manchester: Manchester University Press, 1994).

Novick, P., *That Noble Dream: The 'Objectivity Question' and the American Historical Profession* (Cambridge: Cambridge University Press, 1988).

Ovendale, R. (ed.), *The Foreign Policy of the British Labour Governments, 1945–1951* (Leicester: Leicester University Press, 1984).

Owen, R. and B. Sutcliffe (eds), *Studies in the Theory of Imperialism* (Harlow: Longman, 1972).

Painter, D. S., *Private Power and Public Policy: Multinational Oil Companies and American Foreign Policy, 1941–1954* (London: I. B. Tauris and Co., 1986).

Paterson, T. G., *On Every Front: The Making of the Cold War* (New York: W. W. Norton and Company, 1979).

Perkins, B., 'The tragedy of American Diplomacy: Twenty-five years after', *Reviews in American History*, 12 (1984), pp. 1–18.

Perkins, D., *The American Approach to Foreign Policy* (Cambridge, MA: Harvard University Press, 1962).

Perry, M., *Marxism and History* (Basingstoke: Palgrave, 2002).

Pletcher, D. M., *The Diplomacy of Trade and Investment: American Economic Expansion in the Hemisphere, 1865–1900* (Columbia: University of Missouri Press, 1998).

Polanyi, K., *The Great Transformation: The Political and Economic Origins of our Times* (New York: Rinehart and Co. Inc., 1944).

Polanyi-Levitt, K. (ed.), *The Life and Work of Karl Polanyi* (Montreal: Black Rose Books, 1990).

Pollard, R. A., *Economic Security and the Origins of the Cold War, 1945–1950* (New York: Columbia University Press, 1985).

Pratt, J. W. (1955), *A History of United States Foreign Policy* (Englewood Cliffs, NJ: Prentice Hall, 1955).

Prestowitz, C., *Trading Places: How We Allowed Japan to Take the Lead* (New York: Basic Books, 1989).

Putnam, H., *Reason, Truth and History* (Cambridge: Cambridge University Press, 1981).

Quester, G. H., 'Origins of the Cold War: Some clues from public opinion', *Political Science Quarterly*, 93 (1978–9), pp. 647–63.

Reynolds, D. 'The origins of the Cold War: The European dimension, 1944–1951', *Historical Journal*, 28 (1985), pp. 497–515.

Reynolds, D. (ed.), *The Origins of the Cold War in Europe: International Perspectives* (New Haven: Yale University Press, 1994).

Richardson, J. L., 'Cold War revisionism: A critique', *World Politics*, 24 (1972), pp. 579–61.

Rigby, S. R., *Marxism and History: A Critical Introduction* (Manchester: Manchester University Press, 1987).

Roberts, G., 'Ideology, calculation and improvisation: Spheres of influence and Soviet foreign policy, 1939–1945', *Review of International Studies*, 25 (1999), pp. 655–74.

Rogin, C. and D. Chirot, 'The world system of Immanuel Wallerstein: Sociology and politics as history', in T. Skocpol (ed.), *Vision and Method in Historical Sociology* (Cambridge: Cambridge University Press, 1984), pp. 276–312.

Rosen, S. J. and J. R. Kurth, *Testing Theories of Economic Imperialism* (Lexington, MA: D. C. Heath and Co., 1974).

Rosenau, P. M., *Post-Modernism and the Social Sciences: Insights, Inroads and Intrusions* (Princeton: Princeton University Press, 1992).

Rosenberg, E. S., 'US cultural history', in E. R. May (ed.), *American Cold War Strategy: Interpreting NSC-68* (New York: St Martin's Press, 1993), pp. 160–4.

Rosenberg, E. S., 'Foreign affairs after World War Two: Connecting sexual and international affairs', *Diplomatic History*, 18 (1994), pp. 59–70.

Rosenberg, E. S., 'Revisiting dollar diplomacy: Narratives of money and manliness', *Diplomatic History*, 22 (1998), pp. 155–76.

Rossi, J. P., '"A silent partnership?" The US government, RCA and radio communications with East Asia, 1918–1928', *Radical History Review*, 33 (1985), pp. 35–52.

Rotter, A. J., 'Gender relations, foreign relations: The US and South Asia, 1947–1964', *Journal of American History*, 81 (1994), pp. 518–42.

Rotter, A. J., 'Christians, Muslims and Hindus: Religion and US–South Asian Relations', *Diplomatic History*, 24 (2000), pp. 593–613.

Rotter, A. J., *Comrades at Odds: Culture and Indo–US Relations, 1947–1964* (Ithaca, NY: Cornell University Press, 2000).

Ruggie, J., 'International regimes, transactions and change: Embedded liberalism in the post-war economic order', *International Organization*, 36 (1982), pp. 379–415.

Ruggie, J., 'Continuity and transformation in the world polity: Towards a neorealist synthesis', *World Politics*, 35 (1983), pp. 261–85.

Rupert, M. E., 'Producing hegemony: State/society relations and the politics of productivity in the United States', *International Studies Quarterly*, 34 (1990), pp. 427–56.

Salisbury, R. H., 'Why no corporatism in America', in Schmitter and Lembruch (eds), *Trends towards Corporatist Intermediation*, pp. 213–30.

Schattschneider, E. E., *The Semisovereign People: A Realist's View of Democracy in America* (New York: Holt, Rinehart and Winston, 1960).

Schlesinger, A. M., Jr, 'Origins of the Cold War', *Foreign Affairs*, 46 (1967), pp. 22–52.

Schlozman, K. and J. Tierney, *Organized Interests and American Democracy* (New York: Harper and Row, 1986).

Schmitter, P. C., 'Still the century of corporatism', *Review of Politics*, 36 (1974), pp. 85–131.

Schmitter, P. C. and G. Lembruch, *Trends towards Corporatist Intermediation* (London: Sage, 1979).

Schraeder, P., 'Historical reality vs Neo-Realist theory', *International Security*, 19 (1994), pp. 104–48.

Schurman, F., *The Logic of World Power: An Inquiry into the Origins, Currents and Contradictions of World Politics* (New York: Pantheon, 1974).

Singer, J. D., 'The level of analysis problem in international relations', in K. Knorr and S. Verba (eds), *The International System: Theoretical Essays* (Princeton: Princeton University Press, 1961), pp. 77–92.

Siracusa, J. M., *New Left Diplomatic Histories and Historians: The American Revisionists* (New York: Kennikat Press, 1973).

Sklar, M. J., *The United States as a Developing Country: Studies in US History in the Progressive Era and the 1920s* (Cambridge: Cambridge University Press, 1992).

Skocpol, T., 'Wallerstein's world capitalist system: A theoretical and historical critique', *American Journal of Sociology*, 82 (1976), pp. 1075–90.

Skocpol, T. (ed.), *Vision and Method in Historical Sociology* (Cambridge: Cambridge University Press, 1984).

Skocpol, T., 'Bringing the state back in: Strategies of analysis in current research', in P. B. Evans, D. Rueschmeyer and T. Skocpol (eds), *Bringing the State Back In* (Cambridge: Cambridge University Press, 1985), pp. 3–43.

Slater, J., 'Is United States foreign policy imperialist?', in S. J. Michalak Jr, *Competing Conceptions of American Foreign Policy: Worldviews in Conflict* (New York: HarperCollins, 1992), pp. 226–35.

Smith, G. S., 'National security and personal isolation: Sex, gender and disease in the Cold War United States', *International History Review*, 14 (1992), pp. 221–40.

Smith, G. S., 'Commentary: Security, gender and the historical process', *Diplomatic History*, 18 (1994), pp. 79–90.

Spanier, J. W., *American Foreign Policy since World War Two*, 2nd edn (New York: Praeger, 1965).

Stephanson, A., 'Commentary: Ideology and neo-realist mirrors', *Diplomatic History*, 17 (1993), pp. 285–95.

Stephanson, A., 'Commentary: Considerations on culture and theory', *Diplomatic History*, 18 (1994), pp. 107–19.

Stephanson, A., 'The United States', in D. Reynolds (ed.), *The Origins of the Cold War in Europe* (New Haven: Yale University Press, 1994), pp. 23–52.

Stern, P., *The Best Congress Money Can Buy* (New York: Pantheon Books, 1986).

Tallis, R., *In Defence of Realism* (London: Edward Arnold, 1988).

Tallis, R., *Not Saussure: A Critique of Post-Saussurean Literary Theory*, 2nd edn (Basingstoke: Macmillan, 1995).

Thomas, P., *Alien Politics: Marxist State Theory Revisited*, (London: Routledge, 1994).

Thompson, J. A., 'William Appleman Williams and the American empire', *Journal of American Studies*, 7 (1973), pp. 91–104.

Thompson, K. W., *Cold War Theories* (Baton Rouge, LA: Louisiana State Press, 1981).

Tilly, C., *Big Structures, Large Processes, Huge Comparisons* (New York: Russell Sage, 1984).

Tucker, R. W., *The Radical Left and American Foreign Policy* (Baltimore: Johns Hopkins Press, 1971).

US President, *Public Papers of the Presidents of the United States: Harry S Truman, 1947* (Washington: US Government Printing Office, 1963).

Van Wolferen, K., *The Enigma of Japanese Power: People and Politics in a Stateless Nation* (New York: Alfred A. Knopf, 1989).

Vernon, R., *Sovereignty at Bay: The Multinational Spread of US Enterprises* (New York; Basic Books, 1971).

Walker, W. O., 'Melvyn P. Leffler, ideology and American foreign policy', *Diplomatic History*, 20 (1996), pp. 663–73.

Wallerstein, I., *The Modern World System: Capitalist Agriculture and the Origins of the European World Economy in the Sixteenth Century* (New York: Academic Press, 1974).

Wallerstein, I., *The Capitalist World Economy* (Cambridge: Cambridge University Press, 1979).

Wallerstein, I., *The Modern World System II: Mercantilism and the Consolidation of the European World Economy* (New York; Academic Press, 1980).

Wallerstein, I., *The Politics of the World Economy: The States, the Movements and the Civilizations* (Cambridge: Cambridge University Press, 1984).

Wallerstein, I., *The Modern World System III: Second Great Era of Expansion of the Capitalist World Economy, 1730–1840* (New York: Academic Press, 1989).

Wallerstein, I., *Geopolitics and Geoculture: Essays on the Changing World System* (Cambridge: Cambridge University Press, 1991).

Waltz, K., *Theory of International Politics* (Reading, MA: Addison-Wesley, 1979).

Warren, B., *Imperialism: Pioneer of Capitalism* (London: New Left Books, 1980).

Watt, D. C., 'Rethinking the Cold War: A letter to British historians', *Political Quarterly*, 49 (1978), pp. 446–56.

Weisskopf, T., 'Theories of American imperialism: A critical evaluation', *Review of Radical Political Economics*, 6 (1974), pp. 41–60.

Wendt, A., 'Bridging the theory/meta-theory gap in international relations', *Review of International Studies*, 17 (1991), pp. 383–92.

Wendt, A., 'Levels of analysis vs agents and structures part III', *Review of International Studies*, 18 (1992), pp. 181–5.

Williams, W. A., 'The frontier thesis and American foreign policy', *Pacific Historical Review*, 24 (1955), pp. 379–95.

Williams, W. A., 'A note on Charles Austin Beard's search for a general theory of causation', *American Historical Review*, 62 (1957), pp. 159–80.

Williams, W. A., *The Contours of American History* (Chicago: Quadrangle, 1966).

Williams, W. A., 'The large corporation and American foreign policy', in D. Horowitz (ed.), *Corporations and the Cold War* (New York: Monthly Review Press, 1969), pp. 71–104.

Williams, W. A., *The Roots of the Modern American Empire: A Study of the Growth of Social Consciousness in a Marketplace Society* (London: Anthony Blond, 1970).

Williams, W. A., *The Tragedy of American Diplomacy*, 2nd rev. edn (New York: W. W. Norton and Co., 1972).

Williams, W. A. (ed.), *From Colony to Empire: Essays in the History of American Foreign Relations* (New York: John Wiley and Sons, 1972).

Williams, W. A., *America Confronts a Revolutionary World: 1776–1976* (New York: William Morrow and Co., 1976).

Williams, W. A., *Empire as a Way of Life: An Essay on the Causes and Character of America's Present Predicament along with a Few Thoughts about an Alternative* (Oxford: Oxford University Press, 1980).

Williams, W. A., 'Thoughts on rereading Henry Adams', *Journal of American History*, 68 (1981), pp. 12–13.

Williamson, P. J., *Corporatism in Perspective: An Introductory Guide to Corporatist Theory* (London: Sage, 1989).

Wilson, G., 'Why is there no corporatism in the United States?', in Lembruch and Schmitter (eds), *Patterns of Corporatist Policy-Making*, pp. 219–36.

Wilson, J. H., *American Business and Foreign Policy, 1920–1933* (Lexington, KY: Beacon Press, 1971).

Wilson, J. H., *Herbert Hoover: Forgotten Progressive* (Boston: Little, Brown, 1975).

Wolfe, A., *The Limits of Legitimacy: Political Contradictions of Contemporary Capitalism* (New York: Free Press, 1977).

Woods, N., 'The uses of theory in the study of international relations', in Woods (ed.), *Explaining International Relations*, pp. 9–31.

Woods, N. (ed.), *Explaining International Relations since 1945* (Oxford: Oxford University Press, 1996).

Woods, R. B. and H. Jones, *Dawning of the Cold War: The United States Quest for Order* (Athens, GA: University of Georgia Press, 1991).

Yergin, D., *Shattered Peace: The Origins of the Cold War and the National Security State* (London: Penguin, 1980).

Young, J. W., *France, the Cold War and the Western Alliance, 1944–1949* (Leicester: Leicester University Press, 1990).

Index